UNLEVEL PLAYING FIELDS

UNDERSTANDING WAGE INEQUALITY AND DISCRIMINATION

UNLEVEL PLAYING FIELDS

UNDERSTANDING WAGE INEQUALITY AND DISCRIMINATION

Randy Albelda
University of Massachusetts

Robert W. Drago
University of Wisconsin-Milwaukee

Steven Shulman
Colorado State University

THE McGRAW-HILL COMPANIES, INC.

New York   St. Louis   San Francisco   Auckland   Bogotá
Caracas   Lisbon   London   Madrid   Mexico City   Milan   Montreal
New Delhi   San Juan   Singapore   Sydney   Tokyo   Toronto

McGraw-Hill

A Division of The **McGraw·Hill** *Companies*

This book was set in Times Roman by ComCom, Inc.
The editors were Lucille H. Sutton, Adrienne D'Ambrosio, and Elaine
Rosenberg; the production supervisor was Annette Mayeski.
The cover was designed by Carla Bauer.
Project supervision was done by Hockett Editorial Service.
R. R. Donnelley & Sons Company was printer and binder.

UNLEVEL PLAYING FIELDS: UNDERSTANDING WAGE INEQUALITY AND DISCRIMINATION

This book was printed on acid-free paper.

Library of Congress Cataloging-in-Publication Data

Albelda, Randy Pearl.
    Unlevel playing fields : understanding wage inequality and
discrimination / Randy Albelda, Robert W. Drago, Steven Shulman,
      p. cm.
    Includes bibliographical references and index.
    ISBN 0-07-000968-6
    1. Pay equity. 2. Discrimination in employment.   I. Drago,
Robert W. (Robert William) II. Shulman, Steven. III. Title.
HD6061.A53   1997
331.2'163—dc20   96-36356

1 2 3 4 5 6 7 8 9 0 DOC DOC 9 0 9 8 7 6

ISBN 0-07-000968-6

For Rick Edwards

ABOUT
THE AUTHORS

RANDY ALBELDA is an associate professor of economics in the College of Arts and Sciences at the University of Massachusetts in Boston. Her research and teaching focus is on women's economic status, income inequality, family structure, labor markets, and state and local finance. Recent research includes an examination of the relationship of family structure to access to income with special attention to single-mother families, a statistical profile of women in Massachusetts, and a book on the impact of feminism on the economics discipline. Albelda was the former Research Director of the Massachusetts Legislative Special Commission on Tax Reform and of the Massachusetts Senate Taxation Committee. She is an editorial board member of *Dollars and Sense* magazine and coauthor of *The War on the Poor: A Defense Manual* (The New Press, 1996) and *Glass Ceilings and Bottomless Pits: Women, Poverty, and Welfare* (South End Press, 1997). Albelda received her Ph.D. in economics from the University of Massachusetts-Amherst in 1983.

ROBERT W. DRAGO is professor of economics and Director of Masters in Industrial and Labor Relations Program at the University of Wisconsin-Milwaukee. He holds a B.S. in business administration from the University of Tulsa, an M.A. in economics and a Ph.D. in economics from the University of Massachusetts-Amherst. In 1988 he was Senior Fulbright Research Scholar at the National Institute of Labour Studies in Australia. Professor Drago is a leading scholar on the topics of participatory management, work incentives, and industrial relations, with over 60 published articles on the topics. He is coauthor with Mark Wooden and Judith Sloan of *Productive Relations Workplace Performance and Industrial Relations in Australia* (Allen & Unwin, 1992). Currently he is conducting research on teachers and family life with Robert Caplan under a grant from the Alfred P. Sloan Foundation. He is a member of the American Economic Association, the Industrial Relations Research Association, and the Union for Radical Political Economics. He enjoys traveling to Australia, cooking, and outings with his family.

STEVEN SHULMAN is professor of economics at Colorado State University. He has published numerous articles on racial inequality and discrimination, and is the coeditor of *The Question of Discrimination: Racial Inequality in the US Labor Market* (Wesleyan University Press, 1989). Professor Shulman is a recipient of a Kellogg National Fellowship and the CSU Excellence in Teaching Award. Currently he is working on a book entitled *Does Discrimination Still Matter? Racial Inequality and Equal Opportunity in the Post-Civil Rights Period.* He and his family spend as much time as possible camping, skiing, biking, and running in the Rocky Mountains.

BRIEF TABLE OF CONTENTS

TABLE OF CONTENTS

LIST OF TABLES AND FIGURES

PREFACE

Labor markets in the United States have experienced dramatic shifts since the 1950s. One such shift has been the steady entrance of white women into the paid labor force. In 1954, 33.3% of all white women were in the labor force, a figure that rose to 58.9% by 1994. An equally dramatic change occurred for black workers (both men and women) but of a different nature: the type of work performed. Since the 1950s, the percentage of black men and women working outside of agriculture and private households has increased dramatically. In 1950, 41% of all black women were working in the homes of white Americans as domestics; today, only 2% are. In 1950, 25% of all black men worked in agriculture; today, less than 3% do.[1]

White men also have seen dramatic changes in their jobs and job prospects. In addition to the integration of women and blacks into the manufacturing and nondomestic service sector, white men have seen the disappearance of many blue-collar manufacturing jobs that traditionally were available to white men who had not attended college.

These changes have caused the experiences of working women and black men to look increasingly similar to those of white male workers. One might expect these similar experiences to bring about more equality among workers, and perhaps even a shared appreciation of race and gender differences. However, wage differences between white men and everyone else persist, unemployment rates of blacks are twice that of whites, women are still concentrated in low-paying "female" jobs, and minorities and women argue there is a "glass ceiling" at the upper rungs of the job ladder. This new competition in the face of declining economic opportunities has resulted in a backlash against labor market policies such as affirmative action, which attempt to integrate women and blacks into managerial positions.

What exactly is going on? Is the playing field for jobs and wages level or not? Do white men really have an advantage in the labor market: more easily getting jobs, better pay, and promotions? Are women and people of color not as well qualified or motivated

[1]Labor force participation data are from *Economic Report of the President,* Washington, DC: Government Printing Office, 1995. The figure on black women's employment in 1950 comes from Randy Albelda, " 'Nice Work If You Can Get It:' Segmentation of White and Black Women Workers in the Post WWII Period," *Review of Radical Political Economics* 17(3), 1985. The figure on black men's employment in 1950 is from Michael Reich, *Racial Economic Inequality: A Political Economic Analysis,* Princeton, NJ: Princeton University Press, 1981. Data on black men's and women's employment in 1993 are from U.S. Bureau of Labor Statistics, *Employment and Earnings* 41(1), 1995.

as their white male competitors? Should they stop "whining" and playing the race or gender card when they can't get ahead? In short, do women and blacks face labor market discrimination? If the answer is yes, what can be done about it? If the answer is no, what explains the large and persistent wage, unemployment, and job differences?

Answering these questions is not easy. Because most people define themselves either as men or women, discussions of gender issues involve most everyone. The same can be said about race. While most of the U.S. population is white, no one is untouched by the historic and contemporary "color lines" in this country. No one is a neutral spectator. To complicate matters further, social scientists offer conflicting answers to these questions depending on their view of the world. Answers to these questions, however, are crucially important. They shape government and corporate policies, and they shape the way that we think about people—in our homes, in our neighborhoods, in our workplaces, and in our country.

Recently, governmental, corporate, and university policies regarding race and gender have become a flashpoint in our society, and debates over these policies often are implicitly or explicitly shaped by the discipline of economics. While economists have produced some very good books on the topic for use by senior undergraduates both inside and outside the field of economics, economists have been surprisingly quiet in terms of books that work for the average undergraduate, who has no prior knowledge of economics or how economists treat discrimination. That's why we wrote this book.

This book fills a large gap, but it is incomplete. We have intentionally kept it narrowly defined to deal with women and blacks to provide students and their teachers a springboard from which to emphasize the areas of labor markets and differences in which they are most interested. The book is short enough to allow teachers to supplement it with additional texts, student presentations, articles, movies, guest speakers, and so forth. As the reader will quickly see, history in general and groups other than heterosexual black and white Americans largely are neglected. There is much wonderful work by scholars like Teresa Amott, Lee Badgett, Nancy Folbre, Eugene Genovese, Claudia Goldin, Alice Kessler-Harris, Patrick Mason, and Julie Matthaei (all of whom are cited later) that fills these gaps, and we hope that people will read further on the topic than this book.

This book is a collaborative effort, made possible almost entirely by the Internet (while the authors worked away at their computers in Boston, Milwaukee, and Ft. Collins) and our graduate school experiences (we attended the University of Massachusetts-Amherst together in the late 1970s and early 1980s). Bob Drago dragged Albelda and Shulman into the project with just a few e-mail messages arguing that we could use a book like this and that it would not take long to write. Four years later, the book is being published. We think it is more than three times better than if any one of us had worked on it alone!

No book is ever published without the help and support of friends, family, and colleagues. This book is no exception. We wish to thank our professors and fellow graduate students at the Economics Department, University of Massachusetts-Amherst, where we learned much of what we know about neoclassical economics and political economy. They can take a fair amount of the praise—or blame—for setting us on the road that ultimately led to *Unlevel Playing Fields*. Thanks also go to Lucille Sutton, our editor at McGraw-Hill. We deeply appreciate her support and commitment to this project. In addition, we are grateful to the hundreds of students at the University of Wisconsin-Milwaukee who struggled through early drafts of the book. Their insights and opinions improved the final product enormously, and we hope their education was not damaged too severely by our learning process. We appreciate the small grant for research support from the University of Massachusetts-Boston, and, finally, many thanks to the following people for their advice (although not always taken) at various stages: Jeanne Alexander, Margo Anderson, Lee Badgett, Bob Cherry, Eva Drago, Sophia Drago, Rick Edwards, Nancy Folbre, Herbert Gintis, Daniel Hamermesh, John Heywood, Mary King, June Lapidus, Meg Lewis, Tiffany Manuel, Elaine McCrate, Richard Perlman, Peter Philips, Charles Sackrey, Ronnie Steinberg, Mary Stevenson, Andres Torres, Frank Wilson, and Jan Yoder.

Randy Albelda
Robert W. Drago
Steven Shulman

UNLEVEL PLAYING FIELDS

UNDERSTANDING WAGE INEQUALITY AND DISCRIMINATION

PART ONE

INTRODUCTION TO
WAGE INEQUALITY

1

TWO VIEWS ON INEQUALITY AND DISCRIMINATION

A GLIMPSE AT DISCRIMINATION

Julie lives in a section of New York City called Harlem. She is 20 years old, shares a tiny apartment with her two young children, and completed high school with a "B" average. Like most residents of Harlem, Julie is black. She receives a monthly stipend from a federal government program called Aid to Families with Dependent Children (AFDC) that she uses for rent and bills; she buys milk and cereal for her children with coupons from the Women, Infants, and Children (WIC) program; and she uses Food Stamps to buy the rest of her groceries. Her family receives medical coverage through the Medicaid program. Still, putting it all together, Julie's family is officially below the U.S. government's poverty line.

A message comes from Washington, D.C., that Julie is glad to hear: the government wants her to get a job. Now maybe her high school diploma will pay off. Fortunately, her mother volunteers to care for her children while Julie is at work, and Julie decides to apply for a job at a burger joint around the corner called Burger Hut. Surely, they will give her a chance.

While this story is fictitious, we know the likely ending because of research undertaken by anthropologists Katherine Newman and Chauncy Lennon (1995) on job applicants for fast-food restaurants in Harlem. Julie will probably be turned down for the job.

Two things do work in Julie's favor, however. Unlike most AFDC recipients, Julie has a high school degree, as do most employees at the Burger Hut in Harlem. Julie also has an advantage in that she is older than many applicants. This factor alone doubles her chance of getting the job compared with an 18-year-old's.

So, why is Julie likely to be turned down? First, she lives in Harlem, and local

3

fast-food employers do not like to hire people from that area. Maybe their friends will come in to hang out or get free food. If Julie lived 3 miles from Burger Hut, her chances of getting the job would more than triple, but then she would have an expensive commute and couldn't get to her children immediately in an emergency. Second, because so many employees commute to the store from elsewhere, Julie doesn't know anyone working at the store, and her chances would almost triple if she knew a current Burger Hut employee. Third, while no whites will apply for the job, and although most of Burger Hut customers are black, Julie suffers because of her skin color. Indeed, a foreign-born applicant would be almost three times more likely to get the job, even though Julie undoubtedly would communicate more effectively with the customers. Fourth, Burger Hut tends not to hire AFDC recipients, and this cuts in half Julie's chance of getting the job. Finally, even if we ignore all the specifics regarding Julie, jobs at Burger Hut are hard to land; there are 14 applicants for every opening.

Having lost out at Burger Hut, Julie may be frustrated and confused. Part of her says that it was her own fault for not getting the job. If only she had prepared better for the questions they asked, applied at a different time of day, or been an "A" student, maybe it would have worked out. Even if Burger Hut doesn't want to hire a young black woman from Harlem, she'll show them. She'll find a job with someone else. Besides, with so many people applying for so many jobs, she is likely to get one eventually if she just keeps trying. Further, she *must* get a job, because the federal government will no longer support single mothers like herself for much longer.

Another part of Julie says that she is not alone in her frustration. She lost the job not because of anything she did but because of who she is, the color of her skin, and where she was born. This part of her is angry. Why should some white guy from the suburbs make money by owning Burger Hut, selling to a black clientele, and discriminating against people like her? And even if she had gotten the job, why should she need a high school degree to flip burgers or punch pictures of hamburgers on a cash register just to get the legal minimum wage?

Julie also is very worried. She loves her children and works hard to be a responsible mother, but the job she is likely to get won't pay much, probably won't have health insurance, and will keep her away from her children for long hours. She knows that she can't rely on her mother to take care of her children all the time but also that she won't make enough to afford child care. This part of Julie recalls Martin Luther King's "dream" of equality and tells her that to change things, she needs to be part of an organized movement telling employers, the government, and white male America that she and others like her will not put up with such inequalities, unfairness, and injustice anymore.

TWO VIEWS FROM ECONOMICS

Julie is caught between two different approaches to understanding her situation. For economists, these approaches are termed *neoclassical economics* and *political economy*. Both views admit that Julie's individual actions count and that Julie is operating on an unlevel playing field that works against her. Both approaches provide explanations for why women and blacks earn less than white men, and both explanations are consistent with their general approach to economic phenomena. Beyond these commonalities, however, the emphases of neoclassical economics and political economy diverge. The former views competitive markets, individual initiative, and government policies that leave the market alone as being sufficient to level the playing field. The latter views Julie as being caught in a web of oppressive class, race, and gender relations that can be changed only by fighting alongside others who are committed to her cause.

We can introduce these two views by casting our glance backward in time to two founders of economics: Adam Smith, an 18th-century Scottish scholar; and Karl Marx, the 19th-century German scholar and social activist. Smith argued that competitive markets caused people to serve the common good—increasing the wealth of the nation—by acting in their own self-interest. As he put it in what is probably the most famous single line of *The Wealth of Nations,* an individual functioning in a market economy is "led by an invisible hand to promote an end which was no part of his intention" (Smith, 1910; 400). If the market works, then there is no obvious role for the government except to print money and defend the country militarily. Those who followed in Smith's footsteps—called *neoclassical economists*—extended this argument to suggest that the market will take care of discrimination and will ultimately help to provide opportunities for Julie so long as she is willing to work hard and persist.

On the other end of the political spectrum, we find Karl Marx. Marx believed that capitalism—a profit-driven, market economy where some people own businesses while others work for them—serves the interests of the few at the expense of the many. Marx's most well-known line appears in the Communist Manifesto, which he coauthored with Frederick Engels. It concerned the need for collective action against capitalists: "working men of all countries, unite!" (Marx and Engels, 1972; 362). By extension, economists following in Marx's footsteps argued that the end of capitalism was required to alleviate the problems of discrimination. This is the origin of the voice calling Julie to band together with others against oppression.

Most economists fall somewhere in between these two extreme views (indeed, many economists would be offended if you called them by either label).[1] There are several reasons for relatively few economists fitting our "neoclassical" and "political economy" molds. As economics has developed, economists have discovered greater complexity in the world than is suggested by these two views. Some economists respond by using neoclassical tools but, after challenging key assumptions, and by arguing that people are concerned with fairness, that they cannot accurately forecast the future, or that markets usually are not competitive. Other economists believe that a detailed examination of history is more important than using the tools of either neoclassical or political economy. Nonetheless, we present these two views

---

[1]For example, only 11% of graduate students in economics disagree with the statement that "Neoclassical economics is relevant for the economic problems of today." Nonetheless, the laissez-faire policy conclusions that are associated with neoclassical economics do not necessarily follow, because most of these same students agree that "The income distribution in developed nations should be more equal." (*Source:* David Colander and Arjo Klamer, "The Making of an Economist," *Journal of Economic Perspectives* 1(2), 1987.)

alone, because they provide logical and compelling frameworks for gaining an initial understanding of economic approaches.

This book looks at how the two economic approaches understand wage discrimination. *Discrimination* is defined as adverse treatment based on some defining characteristic(s) of an individual, such as race, ethnicity, gender, sexuality, or religion. *Labor market discrimination* means adverse treatment in hiring, firing, and treatment in a job. Labor market discrimination could mean not being able to get a job, limited job opportunities, or being paid less than others based solely on characteristics that have nothing to do with a person's ability or effort.

Discrimination: Adverse treatment of people based on group identity

---

Neoclassical economists focus on how individuals discriminate and how that discrimination is translated into labor market outcomes. Political economists focus on how institutions in society (*eg,* firms, unions, schools, the government) have rules and regulations that are discriminatory, even if the individuals in those institutions do not personally discriminate.

Economists have noted that women and blacks face very different labor market situations than whites and men do. Typically, women and black writers have called attention to the role of gender and race discrimination as a cause of these differences, but their work has never been widely or well received.[2] Only recently have a substantial number of neoclassical and political economists extended their work to include a more thorough investigation of women's domestic work and blacks' exclusion in wage labor.

Discrimination entered the economic lexicon in reference to blacks, and particularly black men, during the 1940s and 1950s. In this area, economists were led by the pioneering works of neoclassical economist Gary Becker (1957) and political economist Gunnar Myrdal (1972), both of whom eventually won the Nobel prize. Their research forms the bedrock upon which the theories of discrimination presented here were built.

The neoclassical view looks at discrimination from the standpoint of supply and demand within markets, while the perspective of political economy emphasizes the interplay of economic, social, and political forces. To simplify, Becker argued that individuals of one type may object to associating with individuals of another type, which can result in discrimination by employers, employees, and/or customers. Neoclassical economists put an individual's likes and dislikes, loves and hates, and so forth under the heading "tastes." While you might think of taste as concerning goods—as in, "I have a taste for tofu"—the meaning is here broadened to include such things as having a "taste" for discrimination. Discrimination then is like tofu

---

[2]At the turn of the 20th century, W.E.B. DuBois, a black economist who received his PhD from Harvard, wrote extensively on the labor market conditions of black workers. Charlotte Perkins Gilman also wrote on women's unequal and unfair status, as did Karl Marx's colleague, Frederick Engels. See books by DuBois (1939), Gilman (1898), and Engels (1948), or Francis Edgeworth's 1922 paper in the list of suggested readings at the end of this chapter.

in that it is something you are willing to pay for—if you have the "taste." Becker was presenting an alternative to Myrdal's theory, in which prejudice creates discrimination and discrimination in turn reinforces prejudice. According to Myrdal, discrimination is a vicious cycle between white perceptions and black behaviors that results from economic exploitation, social hierarchy, and political repression.

When women made their initial entrance as a proper subject for economic study, the issue of discrimination was far from central to the debate. After all, if you work in the home, how could you experience discrimination? Becker's and Myrdal's theories of discrimination rest on the notion that whites do not "like" blacks. This idea might be right as far as it goes, but it simply doesn't wash when we ask about discrimination against women. How many men would admit to "disliking" their mother, wife, sisters, or daughters? In her trailblazing work on women's wages, economist Barbara Bergmann (1971) noted this problem and argued that a theory of social roles, socialization, or appropriate social behavior was needed to understand discrimination against women. Similar arguments have been extended to blacks. Instead of thinking about discrimination in terms of an irrational prejudice, many economists now emphasize the incentives that encourage discrimination both inside and outside of the marketplace.

Indeed, until the 1960s, women hardly appeared in economists' models. Part of the reason for this historical absence of research on the topic is hinted at in the fact that both the Smith and Marx quotations cited earlier refer only to "men." This was not a fluke of language; when Smith or Marx wrote about the economy, they pictured men going about the business of buying, selling, and working. When women make their rare appearances in these works, it often is as a homemaker or sexual object. So, it is not surprising that when women did begin to appear explicitly in much of the economics literature during the last few decades, it was largely in the role of homemaker.

Until recently, Julie's situation would have been ignored by most economists, but the fact that over half of all U.S. women of working age currently are employed means that theories based on women as homemakers and men as breadwinners are flawed. In response, research and writing on women in the workplace have grown explosively during the last decade, and you will see much of that new literature cited in later chapters.

While both neoclassical and political economists have made great strides toward understanding discrimination against black men and white women, there remains a kind of uncomfortable gap regarding black women. A large segment of black women have worked for wages since shortly after the end of the Civil War, suggesting this group might be thought of as similar to black men. On the other hand, the situation of black women in terms of occupations and wages is fairly close to that of white women, suggesting that we should analyze the group as women. Discrimination against black women is not a simple mix of the particular barriers that face black men and white women, and this implies that the story of "Julie" is one that we cannot fully explain even today.

The study of discrimination contains many such conundrums and complexities. Because we are not here to advance novel theories, we have taken what exists at present on the neoclassical and political economy sides of the fence and tried to present it as clearly and simply as possible. The references at the end of each chapter suggest further readings that explore some of the problems beyond the scope of this book.

It has proven to be difficult to incorporate the roles that race and gender play into traditional economic theories. Researchers like Claudia Goldin (1990) and Nancy Folbre (1994) have striven to do so and enriched our understanding about the dynamics of discrimination. In the process, they have laid the groundwork for a "common ground" perspective that incorporates aspects of both neoclassical economics and political economics. This book explains the debate about inequality and discrimination between the two dominant perspectives, and it returns to the common ground alternative in the concluding chapter.

WHAT'S AT STAKE HERE

This book explains why blacks[3] and women earn less than white men (or at least why economists think they do); however, our focus on blacks and women relative to white men clearly restricts our view and understanding of the world. Where are Native Americans and Asians, Mexicans, and Persians—or gays and lesbians? Haven't they experienced discrimination? For many members of these groups, the answer is "yes," but we ignore those groups here for two reasons. First, the economic literature on white–black relations and on gender is far more developed than for these other groups. Second, we believe that theories of discrimination built to explain white–black and female–male differences do not provide good explanations for discrimination in other contexts. For example, a gay male may experience little overt discrimination at work if he "pretends" to have a girlfriend or a wife, which is a situation with little relevance to the experience of heterosexuals, whether male or female, black or white. We have purposefully kept this book short so that in relevant courses it can be supplemented with material on other groups that have experienced discrimination. Stated differently, we hope to give readers a good idea of how economists view discrimination against women and blacks, but we urge readers to extend their horizons beyond these two groups.[4]

Turning to the two groups of interest, we believe there are sound political and moral reasons to examine discrimination against blacks and women. Blacks were brought to this country in chains and enslaved, segregated and disenfranchised by the system of U.S. apartheid called "Jim Crow," systematically terrorized by lynchings and mob violence, and isolated as sharecroppers in the south and in ghettos in the north. Arguably, the black poor of today are more segregated from society at large than any other minority group (Massey and Denton, 1993). Black Americans have not simply given up in the face of such violence, oppression, deprivation, and dis-

---

[3]We use the term *black* rather than *African-American* throughout the book. Both terms are commonly used in the literature (both by neoclassical and political economists), but "black" is simpler to write and speak. Our apologies to anyone who is offended by the term (as would be true, for example, in Australia, where "black" is considered to be a racial slur against Aboriginal people).

[4]To look at discrimination against other ethnic groups in the United States, a good place to start is Teresa Amott and Julie Matthaei (1991). On sexual orientation, see Lee Badgett (1995).

crimination, however. The civil rights struggle of blacks over the course of the 20th century made it impossible for the rest of the country to ignore the contradiction between racism and democracy that Myrdal emphasized.

Women also bring a crucial historical perspective to the question of inequality, although one that is quite different from that of blacks. Women also were disenfranchised and considered to be the property (although they could not be sold) of their owners (*ie,* their husbands) until the 20th century. Often, they were the victims of violence in the home and on the street—as they are today in shocking numbers. Their lives were limited by deeply rooted gender roles that created a sexual division of labor inside the home and the workplace. However, in contrast to the social segregation that is characteristic of race relations, gender relations are defined by the integration, and often the intimacy, of men and women within most households. This curious and combustible mixture of oppression and love makes it clear that discrimination and inequality are not a simple issue of "us-against-them." Instead, it has more to do with the systems in which all of us live and work—the market system, the production system, the reproduction system. These systems may work with us and allow us to express our individual preferences and abilities, or they may work against us and limit our opportunities.

Thus, the issues of race and gender inequality are at heart issues of morality, of democracy, of family, and of opportunity. They are deeply embedded in our social soul. They also are political issues, in part because slavery, Jim Crow, and disenfranchisement existed by governmental decree and in part because the political struggles of women and blacks changed that history. Debates over inequality and discrimination always also are debates over the proper role of government and its relation to the market. For this reason, the differing interpretations of inequality and discrimination offered by neoclassical economists and political economists are at the same time differing interpretations of the meaning of U.S. life, and that is the larger theme of this book.

PLAN OF THE BOOK

The introductory section (of which this is part) concludes in Chapter 2 with a look at the numbers that are relevant to discrimination. For each of the four groups that we address—black women, white women, black men, and white men—the chapter details historical trends in terms of differences in wages, unemployment, and occupations. The data in Chapter 2 urge us to look for reasons why blacks and women suffer economically.

The following section contains three chapters explaining the neoclassical view of discrimination. Chapter 3 outlines the basics of neoclassical economics—utility maximizing individuals, supply and demand, competition, efficiency, and a look behind the scenes at the division of labor. An appendix is provided for those who want to know the source of these ideas. Chapter 4 takes the neoclassical vision into the labor market, looking at the supply and demand for labor, reasons other than discrimination for wage differences, and unemployment. Chapter 5 goes to the heart of the matter, with the neoclassical view of discrimination. Becker's "taste for discrimination" as well as the "statistical" theory of discrimination are presented, and then we ask about the role of competitive markets in ending discrimination, measures of wage discrimination, why discrimination persists, and what the government might do to alleviate its ill effects.

The third section discusses the political economy approach. We begin as before with the basics, as captured in the "Four C's" of political economy—context, collective behavior, conflicting interests, and change—then apply these to relations of class, race, and gender. These in turn are connected to various forms of oppression—exploitation, exclusion, and domination—that keep some people in power at the expense of others. The role of the marketplace and why oppression might end are discussed at the end of Chapter 6; again, an appendix is provided for those who want a look back to the origins of this theory. Chapter 7 takes the political economy view into the labor market and the workplace; starting with the notion of wages reflecting a customary standard of living, it explores the roles of the labor theory of value, work in the home, and government services in explaining wage levels. The chapter then turns to the impact of the business cycle on wages and looks at how capitalists get people to work hard. The chapter concludes with political economy's model of why wages differ among workers. Chapter 8 presents the political economy view of discrimination, starting with the role of context and the notion of "institutional discrimination" (which often is unconscious). We then look at the economic incentives for firms and workers to discriminate, how the economy perpetuates discrimination through "positive feedback," and why firms abandon discriminatory practices only slowly—if at all. The chapter looks at how discriminatory outcomes and attitudes change both over the business cycle and in the long run. It concludes with a discussion of government policies to reduce wage discrimination.

Chapter 9 finishes the book with an attempt to put it all together. We begin by setting the neoclassical and political economy theories of discrimination side by side to highlight the strengths and weaknesses of each. Then, we turn to policies to combat discrimination. Rather than taking either the political economy or neoclassical approach, we have selected policies that many economists on both sides of the fence will find reasonable and practical. These policies concern education, full employment, and family-friendly measures. Those who believe that discrimination is no longer a problem as well as those who believe that every government policy will hurt the little people more than it helps will find much to disagree with here. However, we believe most economists, and hopefully you, the reader, will find much common ground.

For those who are wondering where the authors fall along the "neoclassical" and "political economy" divide, we consider ourselves to be political economists. The reasons for our position are explained best, we believe, in Chapters 6 through 8. We do not accept the neoclassical economics' emphasis on individual's tastes and preferences as a guiding principle for economic behavior and outcomes, nor do we have as much faith in the ability of markets to correct glaring inequalities. Nonetheless, we have worked hard to present a positive and clear exposition of the neoclassical view.

This book does not provide a critique of either neoclassical economics or political economy. We wrote this book because when we teach this material, there is an absence of texts that clearly and simply describe the general elements of *both* views, explaining how the economy in general, labor markets, and discrimination operate. This approach is not meant to downplay the importance of critical thinking. Rather, we encourage teachers and students to use what follows as a springboard for analyzing the shortcomings of each theory. We also encourage readers to supplement this book with other materials that focus on specific groups who face labor market discrimination.

DISCUSSION QUESTIONS

1 In the story of Julie, if you were in her shoes and got turned down for the job at Burger Hut, what would you do?
2 Referring to the same story, do you think the ending might have been different if the government abolished the minimum wage? Are there reasons why she might have found it easier to get a job if the minimum wage was *increased*?
3 Economic historians have found evidence of discriminatory wages for women and blacks dating back at least 100 years, and often earlier. Why do you think it took U.S. economists so long to begin studying this phenomenon seriously?
4 Myrdal called his famous book on racism *An American Dilemma* to highlight the conflict between U.S. ideals and the denial of civil and economic rights to blacks a half-century ago. Do you think that a similar dilemma exists today? What evidence can you cite to support your opinion?
5 Why do you think that neoclassical economists tend to run the political gamut from conservatism to liberalism, while political economists tend to run the political gamut from liberalism to radicalism?
6 Have you ever observed an incident of discrimination? Describe the incident, and explain why you think it occurred.
7 How do you respond to people when you hear them make racist or sexist remarks?

SUGGESTED READINGS

Amott, Teresa L. and Julie A. Matthaei. 1991. *Race, Gender & Work.* Boston: South End Press.
Badgett, M.V. Lee. 1995. "The Wage Effects of Sexual Orientation Discrimination." *Industrial and Labor Relations Review* 48(4).
Becker, Gary. 1957. *The Economics of Discrimination.* Chicago: University of Chicago Press.
Bergmann, Barbara. 1971. "The Effect on White Incomes of Discrimination in Employment." *Journal of Political Economy* 79 (March-April).
DuBois, W.E.B. 1939. *Black Folk, Then and Now: An Essay in the History and Sociology of the Negro Race.* New York: H. Holt & Co.
Edgeworth, F.Y. 1922. "Equal Pay to Men and Women for Equal Work." *Economic Journal* 32(128).
Engels, Frederick. 1948 (originally 1884). *The Origins of the Family, Private Property and the State.* Moscow: Progress Publishers.
Folbre, Nancy. 1994. *Who Pays for the Kids?* New York: Routledge.
Gilman, Charlotte Perkins. 1898. *Women and Economics.* Boston: Small, Maynard & Co.
Goldin, Claudia. 1990. *Understanding the Gender Gap.* Oxford: Oxford University Press.
Marx, Karl and Frederick Engels. 1972 (originally 1848). "Manifesto of the Communist Party." In *The Marx-Engels Readers.* Robert C. Tucker, ed. New York: W.W. Norton & Co.

Massey, Douglas and Nancy Denton. 1993. *American Apartheid: Segregation and the Making of the Underclass.* Cambridge, MA: Harvard University Press.

Myrdal, Gunnar. 1972 (originally 1944). *An American Dilemma: The Negro Problem and Modern Democracy.* Two volumes. New York: Harper and Row.

Newman, Katherine and Chauncy Lennon. 1995. "Finding Work in the Inner City: How Hard is it Now? How Hard will it be for AFDC Recipients?" Mimeo. Department of Anthropology, Columbia University.

Smith, Adam. 1910 (originally 1776). *The Wealth of Nations.* New York: E.P. Dutton.

2

LABOR MARKET INEQUALITY BY THE NUMBERS

INTRODUCTION: LIES, DAMN LIES, AND STATISTICS

Julie's predicament in Chapter 1 gave us a glimpse at a small slice of the problems that people face in U.S. labor markets. To broaden our view, we need to look at some numbers on overall inequality. For many economists, numbers are the central facts used to describe, think about, and explore a society. However, there are diverse ways to look at numbers describing inequality, so disagreements among economists about the extent and causes of, as well as cures for, labor market inequality abound. Economists continue to debate the best way to measure inequality and interpret its trends.

These debates are not merely academic. The issue of wage growth has made important appearances in recent U.S. presidential campaigns. One candidate typically argues that Americans are better off now because per-capita income (*ie*, the average amount of money that each person has) has risen steadily over the last 20 years. The other candidate often argues that most workers are worse off now than they were 20 years ago; the evidence given here is the fall in average inflation-adjusted wages since the early 1970s. Obviously, one candidate wants to emphasize people's continued prosperity as a reason for the electorate to stick with a current administration (or at least the party in power). The other candidate is trying to convince the American people that they need new leadership to move the country toward a path of high-wage growth.

Who's facts are right? Both are! Because more and more people are working in the 1990s than in the 1960s (as a percentage of the population) and the economy has grown, there is more income per person generated, which by definition means per-capita income rises. The increase in the percentage of the population working is almost all because of more women working outside the home and the coming of age of the post–World War II baby boomers. Over the same period, however, average real wages (*ie,* measured in terms of what you can buy with them) have been falling, so for every hour that a typical person in 1970 worked, he or she made more 20 years ago in terms of purchasing power.

This chapter looks more carefully at the extent of inequality in recent years by looking at three labor market areas: wages, unemployment, and the distribution of jobs by occupation and industry. You may ask, if social scientists cannot agree on the extent of inequality, does it make sense to argue there are a set of "facts" about wage inequality? The answer is yes—for two reasons. First, it is crucial to see what the numbers are as well as what they do and don't say when it comes to differences by race and gender so you can become a more critical consumer of these numbers. Second, believe it or not, there is almost universal agreement among economists that: 1) white men, on average, make more than anyone else;[1] 2) average real wages, especially for men, have been falling since the 1970s; 3) white unemployment rates (for men and women) are much lower than black unemployment rates; and 4) men and women typically work in different jobs. Familiarity with these facts brings you up to speed with what economists and policy makers already know and debate.

You may be wondering why we present data on unemployment and occupational and industry distribution of jobs in a book about wage inequality. The answer is simple. The inability to get a job (*ie,* unemployment) is a crucial factor in determining anyone's wage. Because lower wages for women and blacks can result from being in different kinds of jobs than white men are, the occupational and industry distribution of jobs is important. We present this data here because throughout the book we will refer to the definitions, trends, and differences in wages, unemployment, and job distributions provided in this chapter.

WAGES: THE "U's" OF WAGE INEQUALITY

Most adults have income because they have a job that provides a paycheck for the work they perform. The Census Bureau refers to this form of income as *earnings*. Technically, there are three forms of earnings: wages (usually an amount paid per hour worked), salaries (paid as lump sum regardless of hours worked), and self-employment income.[2] Earnings are not the only form of income most people have, although it usually is the most important. Other types of income include interest, dividends, rent, government assistance, lottery winnings, and alimony. Together, non-earnings income accounts for less than 20% of all income generated in the United States every year.

While wages are the primary source of income, not all people in the United States work for wages—nor does society necessarily expect them to. Our country and many others do not expect children to earn wages. We do, however, expect them to be sup-

---

[1]These differences persist even after adjusting for the age, education, and experience of individual workers. Studies that make those adjustments are explored in Chapter 5.

[2]In much of this book, we use the term *wage* to refer to both wages and salaries. Because self-employment income is a relatively small portion of earnings, the trends in earnings and wages are similar.

ported by their parents or other family members. Further, we typically expect people to retire from paid work when they are 65 years of age, and we typically do not expect severely disabled persons to work. However, society's expectations about who should work for wages and how to support those who do not have changed considerably over time. One-hundred years ago, it was not uncommon or unexpected to see children in poor families working. Until 1935 and the passage of the Social Security Act, every adult male was supposed to work until he died (or be supported by his adult children), and until recently, we as a society did not expect women with children to do paid work. Now, as debates around welfare reform make clear, we are a society that expects every nonelderly, able-bodied adult to earn a wage and not receive public assistance.

Earnings: Income from employment, including hourly wages, salaries, and money from self-employment

---

The Inverted U of Real Wages

Documenting wage inequality can be a tricky business. First, each researcher must decide which workers' wages to compare. Two of the thorniest choices are: 1) whether to compare wages of all workers, regardless of how many hours a week or weeks per year they work, or instead only to compare workers who work comparable hours; and 2) whether to compare wages received for the entire year or those received for an hour's worth of work. These choices matter because some workers are more likely to work fewer hours or fewer weeks per year (*eg*, teens, college students, mothers) than other workers. Because women, for example, are much more likely to work fewer hours than men, comparing all women workers with all men workers would show substantial wage differences; however, their hourly wages may not differ greatly.

A second difficulty that researchers face is the availability of data. Economists typically rely on nationally collected data from government-sponsored wage surveys, which provide extensive information on a random sample of all workers. We look at wage data from two surveys in this section. Each survey has certain data limitations and forces researchers to make decisions about which workers to compare. Still, the picture emerging from both is consistent on one front: workers (particularly men) have faced declining wages over the last several decades.

One of the two most widely used surveys is the Establishment Data Survey, which is undertaken by the U.S. Labor Department's Bureau of Labor Statistics (BLS). Employers are asked how much they pay nonsupervisory workers on an hourly and weekly basis.[3] Data from this survey have the advantage of comparing wages earned per hour worked, which avoids the problem of total hours worked per year. How-

---

[3]Each year, the annual results of the Establishment Data Survey are published in the January issue of the U.S. Labor Department, Bureau of Labor Statistics, *Employment and Earnings* (Washington, D.C.: U.S. Government Printing Office).

ever, these data exclude about 20% of all workers, mainly supervisors. Figure 2.1 depicts average weekly earnings from 1955 through 1993 for all workers using data from the Establishment Survey and adjusted for inflation. The phrase "adjustment for inflation" means that the real wages tell us about how much a worker can actually purchase. (Because wages and prices both rise over time, it is impossible without adjusting for inflation to tell if workers can purchase more or less with their increased wages.) Real wages, then, are adjusted by some measure of price changes from year to year. The most common index of price changes currently used is the Consumer Price Index (CPI) for urban dwellers.

The shape of the graph is clear—it is an inverted U. From 1955 until 1973, average real earnings for all nonsupervisory workers climbed steadily. Since then, however, average weekly earnings have been eroding. In 1993, at $373.64 a week, average weekly earnings were only slightly higher than they were in 1955, when they were $365.13 (and actually are lower than the 1956 amount of $375.81).

There are some specific benefits from looking at Establishment Survey data. First, they are not self-reported but rather come directly from payroll information. The advantage to employer-reported information is that it avoids the problem of people either overreporting or (as is more likely) underreporting their income. Both rich and poor people might have an incentive to underreport to a government agency collecting data (some rich people might fear the Internal Revenue Service [IRS], while some low-income people might fear losing government aid). Further, the data give a truer measure of all workers' wages when they actually do work, because the data are based on a weekly rather than an annual basis.

There are drawbacks to the Establishment Survey as well. First, the survey only col-

FIGURE 2.1
AVERAGE WEEKLY EARNINGS, 1955 TO 1993 (IN 1993 DOLLARS).

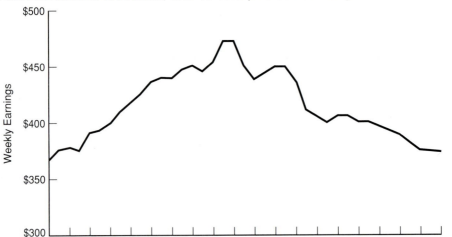

(*Source: Economic Report of the President,* 1995, Table B-15.)

lects information on nonsupervisory workers. This is a problem, because over the last 20 years, the number of supervisory workers has increased as a percentage of all workers and there are good reasons to believe that supervisors' wages also have increased over that time. Therefore, the trends depicted in Figure 2.1 might be overstated. Second, the wage data don't necessarily tell you how well off a certain worker might be, just how much he or she made on a weekly basis. For example, how much you get from earnings over the year depends on whether you had a job the week that the survey was taken, whether you worked full- or part-time, or whether you have more than one job. The Establishment Survey only provides a snapshot from the employer's view.

The second commonly used source of data on annual earnings comes from the U.S. Commerce Department's Census Bureau Household Data, collected in the Current Population Survey (CPS). Each March, the Department interviews about 0.1% (1 out of every 1000) of U.S. households at length about income sources and work experiences from the previous year. Income information from that survey is published by the Commerce Department.[4]

The advantage of the CPS data is they include annual income, including earnings from work. Further, CPS data include both supervisory and nonsupervisory workers. However, it too has its disadvantages. Because the data are self-reported, they likely suffer from underreporting by earners at both the low and the high ends of the wage scale. Further, the data are "top-coded" (*eg,* before 1993, the highest earnings reported was $299,999, so people earning millions appear like people earning $299,999 in the data). Hence, data from the CPS often are considered to be inaccurate at the two ends of the income scale. Second, because they are annual data based on each person's memory of the previous year, the data are not considered to be as reliable a source for hourly earnings information as the BLS data,[5] making comparisons of annual earnings less meaningful unless they first are adjusted for hours and weeks worked. Finally, income data are reported separately for men and women. While this is extremely useful for examining differences by gender, it makes getting the overall picture (*ie,* the "average" worker) unclear.

Figure 2.2 depicts the median annual earnings of male workers who worked year-round (*ie,* 50 or more weeks a year) and full-time (*ie,* 35 hours or more a week). The median income is the exact midpoint—meaning that half of year-round, full-time (YRFT) workers made more than that amount and half made less. While the inverted U shape is not as pronounced, the trend of rising and falling earnings is still apparent. For men who worked all year at full-time jobs, their earnings in 1993 are about the same, adjusted for inflation, as they were in 1969.

Regardless of the drawbacks, both the CPS Household Data and the BLS Establishment Data show a fundamental change in overall wage trends in the United States. Since the early 1970s, the average male worker is not bringing home as much in his paycheck.

---

[4]The income data collected from the March CPS are published in the Department of Commerce's P-60 Series. The 1993 income and earnings data (collected in March 1994) can be found in a single printed report: U.S. Department of Commerce, Census Bureau, 1995. *Income, Poverty, and Valuation of Noncash Benefits: 1993,* P60, No. 188, Washington, D.C.: U.S. Government Printing Office.

[5]A subset of people are asked about their weekly and hourly earnings, however.

FIGURE 2.2

MEDIAN EARNINGS OF YRFT MALE WORKERS, 1955 TO 1993 (IN 1993 DOLLARS).

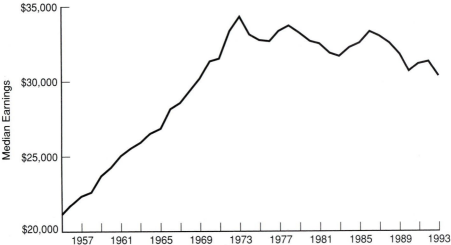

(*Source:* Current Population Reports, Series P-60, selected issues. The data for 1955 to 1991 have been compiled by the Women's Bureau in their *1993 Handbook on Women Workers: Trends and Issues,* Table 1.)

The Increase in Wage Inequality

Over the same period that real earnings have declined, the distribution of earnings has become more unequal. The gap between low- and high-wage workers has grown, and the gap between wages and profits also has grown. The old saw that "the rich get richer while the poor get poorer" has become ever more true. A large fraction of Americans have seen their economic fortunes fall faster than the trends in overall earnings would suggest.

Table 2.1 shows the earnings that wage workers at the 20th, 40th, median, 60th, and 80th percentile earn. The 20th percentile includes the lowest-earning fifth of all workers, the 40th percentile includes the lowest-earning 40% of all workers, and so on. The wages of workers at the low end of the distribution fell more rapidly than the wages of workers at the high end. For example, the highest-paid worker among the bottom 20% of wage earners in 1973 made $6.87 per hour (adjusting for 1993 dollars). In 1991, after adjusting for inflation, the highest-paid worker in that group made only $6.06. Overall, workers at the bottom 20% of all wage earners saw their real wages fall by 11.8%, while workers at the top 80% of wage earners saw their wages increase by 2.7%, between 1973 and 1991. The top-earning 80% of workers made $9.28 more per hour than the best-paid workers in the bottom 20% of earners in 1973; by 1993, this gap had grown to $10.53. In short, the workers who could afford to lose the least wound up losing the most.

In addition to growing inequality between executives and other workers, inequality also grew between wage workers and the owners of capital. From 1979 to 1993, the average real total labor income grew by 1.9% per year (primarily because of growth in the number of workers, not in wages per worker). Over that same pe-

TABLE 2.1.

HOURLY WAGES FOR WAGE WORKERS (ADJUSTED FOR INFLATION TO 1993 DOLLARS)

| Year | Percentile | | | | |
	20th	40th	Median (50th)	60th	80th
1973	$6.87	$9.33	$10.75	$12.28	$16.15
1979	$6.80	$9.21	$10.43	$12.27	$16.67
1989	$6.10	$8.70	$10.21	$11.77	$16.75
1991	$6.06	$8.49	$9.95	$11.68	$16.59
Change 1973–1991	−11.8%	−9.0%	−7.4%	−4.9%	2.7%

Source: Lawrence Mishel and Jared Bernstein, *The State of Working America 1994–95,* 1994, Table 3.6, using CPS data.

riod, real total income from ownership (*ie,* capital income) grew by an average of 4.2% annually (Mishel and Bernstein, 1994; Tables 1.14 and 3.52). The causes of this rise in inequality are debated, but the consequences are clear: low-wage workers were hurt the most, while the rich made out quite well.

The combination of falling wages for workers in the bottom 60% of all earners since the early 1970s and the increase in income from ownership in the 1980s has resulted in a dramatic redistribution of all income in the United States. In 1973, the poorest 40% of all U.S. families had 17.4% of all the income, compared with the 15.5% of all income received by the richest 5% of all families. By 1993, there was a distinct reversal of fortune: the poorest 40% held 14.3% of total income, while the richest 5% had garnered 19.1% (Mishel and Bernstein, 1994; Table 1.6).

Wage Inequality by Race and Ethnicity

It is common knowledge that blacks earn less than whites, but how much less? What changes have occurred? Unfortunately, we can only look back to 1967 for black/white comparisons, because before then, the Census Bureau lumped all nonwhite persons into a category called "black and others."

Figure 2.3 includes men's earnings, while Figure 2.4 includes women's. The bars depict the median earnings of YRFT white and black workers in selected years between 1969 and 1993 using CPS data. The most striking aspect of Figure 2.3 is the racial wage gap. On average, black men earned 67% of what white men did in 1969, and they earned 74% by 1993. In 1993, however, two-thirds of all white men worked YRFT, and 56% of black men did. If we compare the median earnings of *all* men with earnings, black men made 67% of white male earnings regardless of hours worked.

While racial differences in men's earnings have improved only slightly over the last 25 years, the pattern of black and white women is quite different. In contrast to men's median earnings, women's earnings have been rising over time. Further, the racial wage gap among women is much smaller than it is for men. Until the late 1970s, black and white women's earnings were converging, with black women's YRFT median earnings at 92% of white women's. Since the early 1980s, however, this earn-

FIGURE 2.3
MEDIAN ANNUAL EARNINGS FOR YRFT WHITE AND BLACK MALE WORKERS,
SELECTED YEARS, 1969 TO 1993 (IN 1993 DOLLARS).

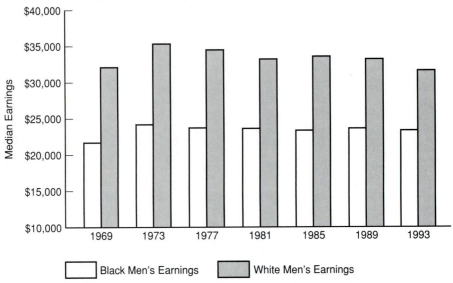

(*Source:* U.S. Commerce Department, Census Bureau, Current Population Reports, P-60 Series
1989, 1992, 1993.)

FIGURE 2.4
MEDIAN ANNUAL EARNINGS FOR YRFT WHITE AND BLACK FEMALE WORKERS,
SELECTED YEARS, 1969 TO 1993 (IN 1993 DOLLARS).

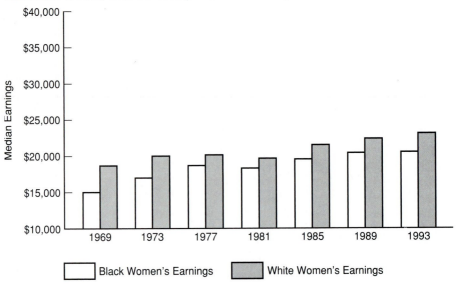

(*Source:* U.S. Commerce Department, Census Bureau, Current Population Reports P-60 Series,
1989, 1992, 1993.)

ings ratio has fallen somewhat. In contrast to men, black women are much more likely than white women to work YRFT.

The U of Male–Female Wages

In the late 1970s, the National Organization for Women (NOW) had a 59-cent button campaign to call attention to the fact that women made 59 cents to every man's dollar. The 59 cents referred to the median earnings ratio of women's and men's YRFT earnings. Figure 2.5 depicts men's and women's median earnings and their earnings ratio between 1953 and 1993. The bars depict earnings, and the line is the ratio of women's earnings to men's, with the scale on the right-hand side of the graph.

The female–male earnings ratio (depicted by the line in Fig. 2.5) has a definite U shape: it is high in the early 1950s, falls until the early 1970s, and then rises. However, as the bars in the graph indicate, women have gained relative to men, because male wages have performed poorly. Women's earnings have crept up slowly, while men's earnings have fallen. YRFT women workers earn about 70% of YRFT men workers. The ratio of median earnings for all women workers to all male workers

FIGURE 2.5
MEDIAN ANNUAL EARNINGS AND EARNINGS RATIO OF YRFT MALE AND FEMALE WORKERS FOR SELECTED YEARS, 1953 TO 1993 (IN 1993 DOLLARS).

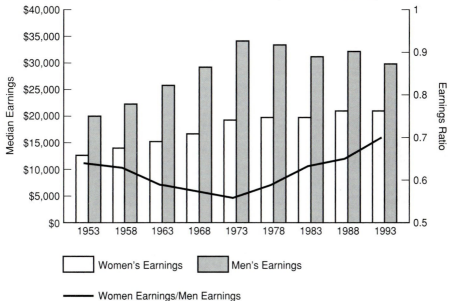

(*Source:* Current Population Reports, Series P-60, selected issues. The data for 1953 to 1993 appear compiled in the Women's Bureau's *1993 Handbook on Women Workers: Trends and Issues,* Table 1.)

was .59 in 1993. The ratio is so much lower than that of YRFT workers because women are much less likely than men to work YRFT.

Finally, Figure 2.6 depicts the median income of black and white men and women from 1967 through 1993. Note that this figure concerns income from *all* sources (not just earnings) and that it does not adjust for hours worked. White men lead the pack. Their incomes peaked in the early 1970s, and white men have lost some ground since then. However, white men's incomes are far and away higher than others. Black men fare less well than white men but better than women of any race (their median income hovers below $15,000 per year). Finally, while all women have seen income gains over the last 25 years, their income still lags far behind that of their male counterparts.

UNEMPLOYMENT TRENDS SINCE THE 1950s: PERSISTENT INEQUALITIES

If you don't work at a job, you won't have any earnings. It's about that simple. Therefore, the ability to get a job, if you want one, is going to be a pretty important factor behind your overall economic well being. In the United States, there are two important facts about unemployment. First, it gyrates wildly with the ups and downs of the economy. Second, whites (both men and women) face far less unemployment

FIGURE 2.6

MEDIAN INCOME FOR WHITE AND BLACK MEN AND WOMEN, 1967 TO 1993 (IN 1993 DOLLARS).

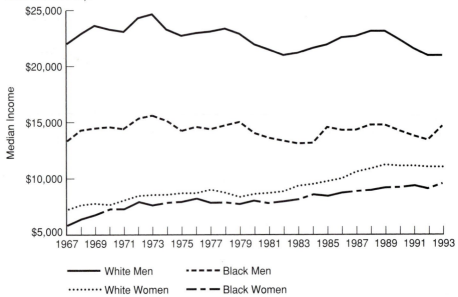

(*Source:* U.S. Commerce Department, Census Bureau, Current Population Report, P-60 Series, various years.)

than other racial and ethnic groups. We will discuss each of these phenomena, but first, it is useful to get a look at how unemployment is defined.

Measuring Unemployment and Employment

The Bureau of Labor Statistics (BLS) is the government agency that tracks unemployment. Every month, the BLS randomly selects 60,000 households to phone and ask questions on the employment status of household members over the age of 16. The BLS then decides whether household members are employed, unemployed, or out of the work force all together. The first Friday of every month, the Labor Department announces the results of the previous month's survey.

The BLS considers you employed if:

- You worked full- or part-time for pay.
- You worked 15 or more hours without pay in a family business.
- You are on unpaid leave because of a labor dispute, illness, or personal reasons.

Being employed is pretty easy to determine, but how does the BLS decide if you are unemployed? Being without a job is not necessarily being unemployed. The BLS classifies someone as unemployed only if the person was jobless during the interview week, available to work, and made some specific effort to find a job in the last month. Anyone who is not working for pay because of a long-term disability or who is home taking care of children, in school full-time, or just discouraged from looking for work is considered to be out of the labor force altogether, and he or she is not classified as unemployed. Box 2.1 defines some of the key terms economists use in discussions on employment and unemployment.

Before turning to more facts about unemployment, it is worthwhile to think about why unemployment rates are important and what they do and don't tell us about labor markets and the economy. Politicians and economists typically look to unemployment rates as a crucial indicator of how the economy is working. When unemployment rates are low, it indicates that the economy is generating a high demand for workers, which is assumed to be a sign of a healthy, or at least a growing, economy. Conversely, high unemployment rates are one indication of a sluggish economy. However, there are reasons to be cautious about looking at unemployment rates as an indicator of economic health.

The BLS is criticized for both over- and underestimating unemployment rates. People who work informally and in the underground economy usually are not counted as employed. If they were, unemployment rates would be smaller than they are. People working irregularly, "under the table," or who are engaged in illegal activities would be reluctant to give that information to the BLS (or the IRS!). Further, some of the unemployed may exaggerate their job search efforts. For these reasons, the official measures may overstate unemployment.

The BLS also underestimates unemployment rates for two reasons. First, there are people who would like to work and have been looking for a while but who can't find work. If they give up even temporarily and don't actively look for work that month, the BLS classifies them as being out of the labor force. Economists refer to

SOME LABOR MARKET TERMS

Measures of employment and unemployment not only provide a wealth of information for labor economists, they also provide the tools necessary to understand some common labor market terms:

The **labor force** is defined as the sum of the number of people employed and the number of people unemployed (16 years old and over) at any given point in time:

Labor Force (LF) = # of Employed + # of Unemployed   (2.1)

The **labor force participation rate** is the percentage of the entire noninstitutional population 16 years and older that are either employed or unemployed:

LF participation rate = $\dfrac{\text{\# in LF} \times 100}{\text{\# in Noninstitutional Population}}$ (2.2)

The **employment-to-population ratio** is given as the percentage of the noninstitutional population 16 years and older that is employed:

Employment/Population ratio = $\dfrac{\text{\# Employed} \times 100}{\text{\# in Noninstitutional Population}}$ (2.3)

Finally the **unemployment rate** is defined as the percentage of the labor force that is unemployed:

Unemployment rate = $\dfrac{\text{\# Unemployed} \times 100}{\text{\# in LF}}$ (2.4)

Table 2.2 gives labor force, employment, and unemployment statistics for all persons (men, women, whites, and blacks) for 1993. In that year, the United States had 119 million people in jobs and almost 9 million people "pounding the pavement"—wanting to work but unable to find a job. You can see from the table that there are large differences in labor force participation rates between men and women and in unemployment rates between blacks and whites.

TABLE 2.2.
LABOR FORCE, EMPLOYMENT, AND UNEMPLOYMENT STATISTICS FOR CIVILIAN POPULATION, 1993[a]

	Total	Men	Women	White	Black
Noninstitutional Population	193,550	92,596	100,876	163,957	22,343
Labor Force	128,040	69,632	58,407	109,359	13,942
Employed	119,306	64,700	54,606	102,812	12,146
Unemployed	8,734	4,932	3,801	6,547	1,796
Labor Force Participation Rate	66.2%	75.2%	57.9%	66.7%	62.4%
Employment-Population Ratio	61.6%	69.9%	54.1%	62.7%	54.4%
Unemployment Rate	6.8%	7.1%	6.5%	6.0%	12.9%

[a]Numbers in thousands.
Source: U.S. Department of Labor, Bureau of Labor Statistics. Reported in *Economic Report of the President,* 1995, Tables B-33 to B-41.

this as being a "discouraged worker." In 1994, there were half a million discouraged workers. Second, the BLS counts workers as being employed regardless of whether they are working part- or full-time. People who can only find part-time work but want full-time work and are working at a job in which they are overqualified probably consider themselves at the very least to be "underemployed." In 1994, there were 4.3 million workers who were working part-time involuntarily.

Unemployment and the Business Cycle

The periodic ups and downs of economic activity in market economies are referred to as *business cycles*. The downswings are called *recessions* (with the lowest point being the *trough*), and the upswings are called *expansions* (with the highest point being the *peak*). No one really knows exactly why a bust turns into a boom, or vice versa, although there are lots of theories. However, everyone knows that it will happen—like the sun rising and setting every day. Unlike the position of the sun in the sky, however, business cycle movements are virtually impossible to predict with accuracy. It is even hard to figure out exactly when the economy is—or was—in a recession. To deal with this problem, there is a group of economists who officially pronounce when a recession or expansion is over. The Commerce Department has charged the National Bureau of Economic Research (NBER), a private research organization, with calling the business cycle play-by-play. The NBER's Business Cycle Dating Committee consists of seven economists who judge the beginning, middle, and end of a business cycle. The committee looks at a variety of economic indicators—including unemployment rates—but really has no hard and fast rules to decide the precise dates of peaks and troughs. The NBER defines a recession as a recurring period of decline in total output, income, employment, and trade, usually lasting from 6 months to 1 year, and marked by widespread contractions in many sectors of the economy.

Business cycles: Periods of three or more years during which the economy busts or has a recession and then booms or has a recovery

---

Table 2.3 lists the nine business cycles the NBER has tracked from 1945 to 1995. Until the mid-1970s, the entire business cycle (from peak-to-peak or from trough-to-trough) lasted anywhere from 3 to 5 years. Since that time, however, the length of business cycles has been far less predictable. There have been some very short business cycles and one very long one, lasting most of the 1980s.

When the economy expands, there is increased demand for workers. As a result, unemployment falls. At this point, wages should rise, because as firms need new workers, they are willing to pay a little more for them if they are hard to find. Figure 2.7 gives unemployment rates from 1947 to 1994, and it shows that peak business cycle years are associated with lower unemployment rates.

Figure 2.7 also illustrates an important trend in unemployment rates. Besides unemployment rates moving with business cycles, there is a secular or long-run trend as well. Over the entire post–World War II period, unemployment rates have crept

TABLE 2.3.
BUSINESS CYCLE PEAKS AND TROUGHS, 1945–1995

Peak Month	Year	Trough Month	Year
November	1948	October	1949
July	1953	May	1954
August	1957	April	1958
April	1960	February	1961
December	1969	November	1970
November	1973	March	1975
January	1980	July	1980
July	1981	November	1982
July	1990	March	1991

Source: National Bureau of Economic Research. A complete list of Working Papers and Reprints can be accessed on the Internet at http://nber.harvard.edu or gopher://nber.harvard.edu.

FIGURE 2.7
UNEMPLOYMENT RATES, 1947 TO 1994.

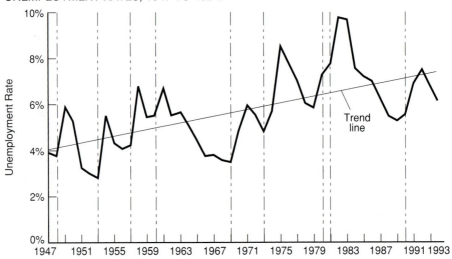

Dotted lines indicate the peak year of each business cycle.
(*Source: Economic Report of the President,* 1995, Table B-40.)

upward. The trend line in Figure 2.7 shows this upward creep, the unemployment rate having moved from a 4% average in the late 1940s to a 7% average in the 1990s.

The Race Gap

Unemployment is not spread evenly across the economy, and one striking and persistent difference is by race. Generally, black workers are twice as likely to be unemployed as white workers. Figure 2.8 depicts black and white unemployment rates

FIGURE 2.8
BLACK AND WHITE UNEMPLOYMENT RATES, 1954 TO 1994.

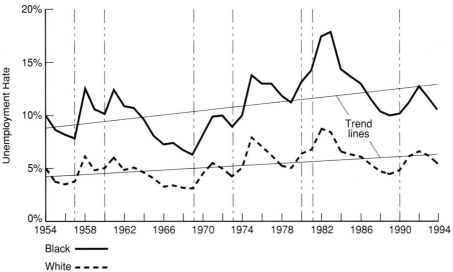

Black ———
White - - - -

Dotted lines indicate the peak year of each business cycle. "Black" includes blacks as well as other ethnic groups.
(*Source: Economic Report of the President,* 1995, Table B-40.)

from 1954 to 1994. Table 2.4 further breaks down unemployment rates by gender and age and includes the black (and other)/white unemployment ratio for men, women, and youth in peak and trough years of the business cycles between 1954 and 1994.

The race gap has important economic implications in the United States. First, it means that one of the harshest aspects of a market system—unemployment—is not shared equally among whites and blacks. Second, because of residential segregation, the impact of high black unemployment rates is felt deeply on a community-wide basis in black communities. To the degree that government policies can affect unemployment rates, there are political implications to the racial disparity in unemployment rates as well. If whites, with their large electoral majority, do not perceive unemployment as being a major problem in this country, they may vote in officials who are willing to accept high rates of unemployment.

Gender Differences

Women and men are equally susceptible to the business cycle in that unemployment rates move in the same direction for both; up in recessions, and down in recoveries. However, there has been an important, recent change in the relationship between men's and women's unemployment rates, as shown in Figure 2.9. Until the 1980s, women's unemployment rates always exceeded those of men's for both blacks and whites, but since that time, women's unemployment rates usually have been lower than men's, especially in economic downturns. One possible explanation for this is

TABLE 2.4.

UNEMPLOYMENT RATES AND RATIOS BY GENDER, RACE, AND AGE IN TROUGH AND PEAK YEARS OF THE BUSINESS CYCLE

Year	Males White	Males Black and Other	Males B/W Ratio	Females White	Females Black and Other	Females B/W Ratio	Ages 16–19 White	Ages 16–19 Black and Other	Ages 16–19 B/W Ratio
				Trough Years					
1954	5.0%	11.4%	2.3	5.9%	10.2%	1.7	13.7%	19.9%	1.5
1958	6.5%	15.9%	2.5	6.6%	12.1%	1.8	16.8%	37.8%	2.3
1961	5.7%	12.8%	2.2	6.5%	11.9%	1.8	15.3%	27.7%	1.8
1970	4.2%	7.9%	1.9	5.7%	10.3%	1.8	15.6%	40.9%	2.6
1975	7.8%	15.8%	2.0	9.4%	16.2%	1.7	21.6%	57.7%	2.7
1980	6.5%	15.2%	2.3	6.9%	15.0%	2.2	18.4%	54.7%	3.0
1982	9.6%	22.3%	2.3	9.0%	19.6%	2.2	25.6%	78.4%	3.1
1991	6.8%	13.0%	1.9	5.9%	12.0%	2.0	19.6%	49.0%	2.5
				Peak Years					
1957	3.8%	9.1%	2.4	4.5%	7.9%	1.8	11.9%	23.6%	2.0
1960	5.0%	12.0%	2.4	5.6%	10.4%	1.9	15.5%	32.1%	2.1
1969	2.6%	5.6%	2.2	4.4%	8.4%	1.9	12.0%	31.7%	2.6
1973	3.9%	8.4%	2.1	5.6%	11.8%	2.1	14.4%	43.3%	3.0
1980	6.5%	15.2%	2.3	6.9%	15.0%	2.2	18.4%	54.7%	3.0
1981	7.0%	16.4%	2.4	7.4%	16.6%	2.3	20.9%	60.9%	2.9
1990	5.1%	11.7%	2.3	4.9%	10.9%	2.2	15.5%	39.3%	2.5

Source: Economic Report of the President, 1995, Table B-36.

FIGURE 2.9

MALE AND FEMALE UNEMPLOYMENT RATES, 1947 TO 1993.

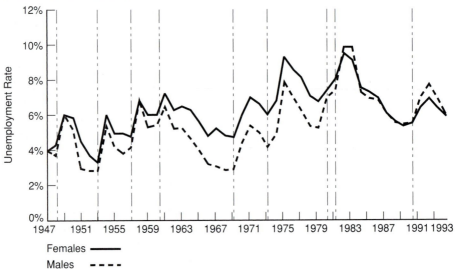

Females ——
Males - - - -

Dotted lines indicate the peak year of each business cycle.
(*Source: Economic Report of the President,* 1995, Table B-40.)

28

that women are more likely than men to fall back on their spouse's wages if they become unemployed. As a result, women are more likely than men to leave the labor force and become discouraged workers, so they "look" like they are out of the labor force when in fact they are unemployed in the everyday sense of the word. Another explanation has to do with the specific ways in which the economy has changed since the mid-1970s and the fact that many jobs are sex segregated. Jobs in industries that are more likely to hire women have experienced tremendous growth, while industries that tend to hire men have experienced steady declines in employment. Now, we turn to the distribution of jobs, because it also has important implications for wage differences.

THE DISTRIBUTION OF JOBS: NICE WORK IF YOU CAN GET IT

Everybody knows that some jobs pay better than others. For example, doctors make more money than orderlies in the same hospital. This makes sense, because doctors have to train for many years while you often don't even need a high school diploma to become an orderly. There are some jobs, however, that pay better than others in which it is hard to understand the reason. For example, median weekly earnings of YRFT truck drivers were $481 in 1993, while median weekly earnings for bookkeepers were $365. These jobs are very different and require very different skills, but in terms of the education and training needed to be good in either field, the jobs are comparable. A more vexing comparison is that between child-care workers and animal caretakers. Median weekly earnings for full-time child-care workers were $151, while median earnings for full-time animal caretakers were $273![6]

Industry Differences

Social scientists who are interested in understanding wage differences and trends watch both the occupation and the industry in which workers are employed. Industrial employment figures tell us the total number of people who are employed, categorized by the type of good or service they produce. There are several broad industrial sectors. One that receives a lot of attention because it is shrinking and has traditionally paid high wages is the manufacturing sector, which includes the automobile and steel industries. A particularly fast-growing sector is the service industry, which includes health care, education, personal services, and entertainment. Table 2.5 provides employment by industry for 1970, 1980, and 1993.

The data in Table 2.5 reveal an important trend: a smaller and smaller percentage of the workforce is employed in manufacturing. This shift often is referred to as *deindustrialization,* which is a phrase made popular by economists Bennett Harrison and Barry Bluestone in their book *The Deindustrialization of America* (1982). In 1970, 26.4% of employed persons worked in the manufacturing sector, but by 1993, only 16.4% did so. Note that deindustrialization between 1970 and 1980 took place even though the absolute number of people employed in that sector increased. The rela-

---

[6]*Source:* CPS, March 1994 (by authors) and *Employment and Earnings, op cit.,* pp. 245–246.

TABLE 2.5
EMPLOYMENT BY INDUSTRY, 1970, 1980, 1993[a]

	1970		1980		1993	
	Number	Percentage	Number	Percentage	Number	Percentage
Agriculture	3,463	4.4	3,364	3.4	3,074	2.6
Mining	516	0.7	979	1.0	669	0.6
Construction	4,818	6.1	6,215	6.3	7,220	6.1
Manufacturing	20,746	26.4	21,942	22.1	19,557	16.4
Transportation and Communications	5,320	6.8	6,525	6.6	8,481	7.1
Wholesale Trade	2,672	3.4	3,920	3.9	4,606	3.9
Retail Trade	12,336	15.7	16,270	16.4	20,113	16.9
Finance, Insurance, Real Estate	3,945	5.0	5,993	6.0	7,962	6.7
Services	20,385	25.	28,752	29.0	41,817	35.1
Public Administration	4,476	5.7	5,342	5.4	5,756	4.8
TOTAL	78,677	100.0	99,303	100.0	119,305	100.0

[a]Numbers in thousands.
Source: U.S. Department of Commerce, Census Bureau, *Statistical Abstract of the United States,* Washington, D.C.: U.S. Government Printing Office, 1994, Table 641.

tive decline in manufacturing occurred because employment in other industries increased faster. However, between 1980 and 1993, there was both a relative and an absolute decline in the manufacturing sector, with fewer people being employed in that sector in 1993 than in 1980.

Deindustrialization: The long-term decline in employment in blue-collar jobs in manufacturing industries

---

Table 2.6 depicts the composition of industrial employment for women and blacks in 1993 and gives the average weekly earnings of all workers in each industry. In 1993, women represented 45.8% of all persons employed. If they were equally distributed across all industry sectors, we would expect to see 45.8% of those employed in the craft industry or the service industry to be female. This is not the case. Instead, we find that women were only 8.6% of all persons employed in the construction industry but almost 62% of those in services. Women are overrepresented in low-paying industries like retail trade; finance, insurance, and real estate; and services.

In a similar fashion, 1 out of every 10 workers in 1993 was black, and they also are not evenly distributed among industry sectors. Blacks were overrepresented in transportation and communications, service, and public administration industries. They were underrepresented in agriculture, mining, construction, and retail and wholesale trade.

The industrial distribution of jobs seems to matter in terms of wages paid. Those

TABLE 2.6.
COMPOSITION OF INDUSTRIAL EMPLOYMENT BY GENDER AND RACE AND
AVERAGE WEEKLY EARNINGS, 1993

	Percentage of Each Industry		
	Female	Black	Average Weekly Earnings (All Workers)
Agriculture	20.7	4.6	—
Mining	16.2	3.7	$645
Construction	8.6	6.4	$551
Manufacturing	32.3	10.1	$487
Transportation and Communications	28.5	13.8	$542
Wholesale Trade	28.9	6.0	$447
Retail Trade	50.8	8.9	$210
Finance, Insurance, and Real Estate	58.6	8.4	$404
Services	61.7	11.4	$351
Public Administration	42.9	15.0	—
TOTAL	45.8	10.2	$374

Source: Statistical Abstract of the United States, [op cit.], Tables 641 and 654. Data from BLS.

who work in the retail trade and service industries make considerably less than those in other industries. Because wages depend in part on the level of technology, certain industries with high levels of technology will probably have higher wages than labor-intensive, low-technology industries. Further, if workers in some industries are more likely to be represented by unions than others, it might help them to bargain successfully for higher wages.

Occupational Differences

We tend to have an image of the kinds of jobs that people do in different industries. For example, in the mining industry, we think of people actually extracting minerals from the ground, and the retail trade industry conjures up a sales clerk. However, the industrial distribution of jobs includes everyone who works in that industry, regardless of the work they do there. For example, a clerical worker or nurse at General Motors will be included in the manufacturing sector, while the machine repair technician and plumber who is employed by a hospital complex will be included in the service industry.

Occupational distributions classify jobs by the type of work performed, regardless of the industry. So, for example, managers are listed in the managerial occupation category whether they manage a McDonald's, supervise a farm equipment factory, or work as a Chief Executive Officer (CEO) in a hospital. Table 2.7 lists the occupational distribution of jobs in 1983 and 1993. Table 2.8 depicts the percentage

TABLE 2.7.
EMPLOYMENT BY OCCUPATIONS, 1983 AND 1993[a]

	1983		1993	
	Number	Percentage	Number	Percentage
Managerial	10,772	10.7	15,376	12.9
Professional	12,820	12.7	16,904	14.2
Technical	3,053	3.0	4,014	3.4
Sales	11,818	11.7	14,245	11.9
Administrative Support	16,395	16.3	18,555	15.6
Service	13,857	13.7	16,522	13.8
Precision Production, Craft and Repair	12,328	12.2	13,326	11.2
Operators, Fabricators and Laborers	16,091	16.0	17,038	14.3
Farming, Forestry, and Fishing	3,700	3.7	3,326	2.8
TOTAL	100,834	100.0	119,306	100.0

[a]Numbers in thousands.
Source: Statistical Abstract of the United States, [op cit.], Table 637. Based on CPS data.

TABLE 2.8.
OCCUPATIONAL COMPOSITION OF EMPLOYMENT BY GENDER AND RACE AND MEDIAN WEEKLY EARNINGS OF FULL-TIME EMPLOYEES

	Percentage of Each Occupation				Median Weekly Earnings for Full-Time Workers, 1993
	Female		Black		
	1983	1993	1983	1993	
Managerial	32.4	42.0	4.7	6.2	$528
Professional	48.1	53.2	6.4	7.0	$457
Technical	48.2	50.5	8.2	9.6	$392
Sales	47.5	48.1	4.7	6.7	$293
Administrative Support	79.9	78.8	9.6	11.2	$501
Service	60.1	59.5	16.6	17.3	$365
Precision Production, Craft, and Repair	8.1	8.6	6.8	7.4	$269
Operators, Fabricators, and Laborers	26.6	24.5	14.0	14.9	$664
Farming, Forestry, and Fishing	16.0	15.4	7.5	6.3	$668
TOTAL	43.7	45.8	9.3	10.2	$463

Source: Percentage distribution from *Statistical Abstract of the United States, [op cit.]*, Table 637. Median weekly earnings from *Employment and Earnings,* January 1994, Table 56. Based on CPS data.

of each occupation that is female and black and also includes the median weekly earnings for full-time workers.

Table 2.8 reveals an uneven distribution of occupations by gender and race. Close to four out of every five administrative support (*ie*, clerical) workers were female in 1993, while 9 out of every 10 precision production (*ie*, skilled machinists), craft, and repair persons were male. The shifts in occupational distribution are nowhere near as dramatic as those found when we looked at industrial data. For women, there was very little change in their representation across these broad occupational categories, with two exceptions: an increase in the percentage of professional and managerial jobs they held. Black workers saw relatively large increases in the managerial category as well as in sales and administrative support.

Figure 2.10 provides a different way of looking at occupational distribution; it shows how employed men and women are distributed across occupational categories in 1993. The figure indicates that about the same percentage of men and women work in managerial and professional, technical, and sales categories, but the distribution among other occupations is very different. For example, 26.8% of all employed women were clerical workers (in the administrative support category) versus 6.1% of all employed males. Women are much more likely to be in service occupations than men, but they are less likely to be machine operators, craftspersons, or skilled machinists.

Similarly, Figure 2.11 looks at the occupational distribution of white and black women and men. In some occupational categories, racial differences prevail, such as in managerial and sales occupations. In other occupations, such as administrative support, precision production, craft and repair, and farming, forestry, and fishing, gender seems to be the distinguishing factor. In still other occupations, both race and gender seem to matter. For example, black men's representation in the operators, fabricators, and laborers category far surpasses that of all women and white men, while black women are most likely to be in service occupations. These are complicated patterns that defy any simple explanation.

Occupational Segregation

Both the CPS and the BLS collect data on occupational and industrial categories that are much more detailed than those presented in the previous tables and figures. For example, there are close to 480 detailed occupations included in the CPS data, and Tables 2.9 and 2.10 present a closer look at the 10 detailed occupations that account for the greatest share of women's and men's employment, respectively. For women, the top 10 occupations employ one-third of all women. There is a distinct bunching of women into a small number of occupations. In three of those occupations, over 90% of persons who work in them are women, and another four have over 80% women in them. Social scientists refer to the crowding of a large number of women or men into a small number of occupations as *occupational segregation.*

Occupational segregation: When groups are disproportionately overrepresented in some types of jobs and underrepresented in others

---

FIGURE 2.10
OCCUPATIONAL DISTRIBUTION OF MEN AND WOMEN, 1993.

WOMEN

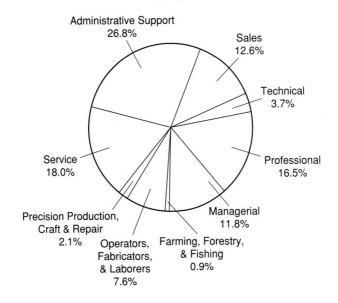

MEN

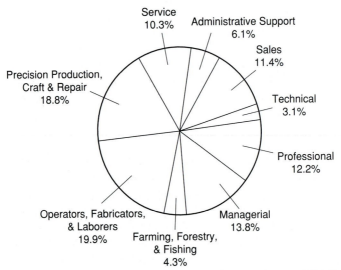

(*Source:* U.S. Bureau of Labor Statistics, *Employment and Earnings,* January 1994, Table 21.)

FIGURE 2.11
OCCUPATIONAL DISTRIBUTION OF BLACK AND WHITE WOMEN AND MEN, 1993.

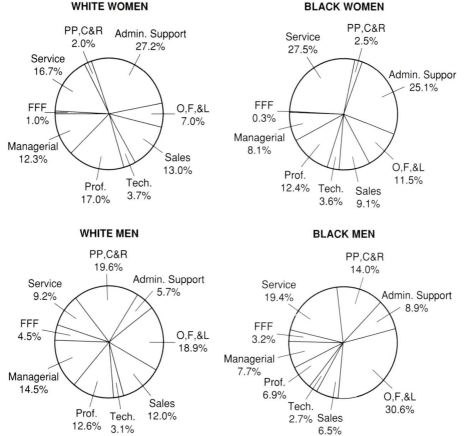

(FFF—Farming, Fishing, and Forestry; PP, C & R—Precision Production, Craft, and Repair; O, F, & L—Operators, Fabricators, and Laborers.)
(*Source:* U.S. Bureau of Labor Statistics, *Employment and Earnings,* January 1994, Table 21.)

    By looking at more detailed occupations, a different view of occupational segregation emerges than if we just look at broad occupational categories.[7] For example, men and women are equally represented overall in professional, technical, and sales occupations, yet a closer look reveals distinct women's and men's jobs within these categories. Consider nurses and teachers, which together account for one out of every three women employed in the professional occupational category; as Table 2.9 indicates, these two occupations are highly segregated by sex.

---

[7]Similar, although not as pronounced, differences are found by looking at detailed industrial breakdowns. For example, while women are 32% of all workers in manufacturing, 72% of those employed in textile manufacturing are female, while only 11% of those who work in steel and iron foundries are women. (*Source:* U.S. Department of Labor, *Employment and Earnings,* 41(1), 1994.)

TABLE 2.9.
TOP 10 DETAILED OCCUPATIONS FOR ALL EMPLOYED WOMEN, 1993

Detailed Occupational Category	Women in Occupation		Median Weekly Earnings of YRFT Female Workers[a]
	Number	Percentage Female	
Secretaries	3,569,723	99.0	$393
Cashiers	2,934,725	82.3	$204
Bookkeepers, Accounting, and Audit Clerks	1,921,525	91.8	$365
Managers, n.e.c.[b]	1,854,241	30.1	$596
Nurses Aides, Orderlies, and Attendants	1,767,611	87.1	$280
Supervisors, Sales	1,762,332	38.0	$404
Registered Nurses	1,681,391	93.8	$731
Teachers, Elementary School	1,578,688	86.2	$577
Waitresses	1,451,536	80.2	$199
Administrative Support, n.e.c.[c]	1,233,673	73.9	$423
Top 10	19,755,445	67.7	$413
Total Women Employed	/61,726,065	46.1	$423
Top 10 as a % of All Employed Women		32.0	

[a]For YRFT workers (those who worked at least 35 hours a week for 50 or more weeks in 1993).
[b]These are managers not elsewhere classified in finance, marketing, food service, real estate, medicine and health, personnel and labor relations, purchasing, post office, or service organizations.
[c]These are miscellaneous administrative assistant occupations not elsewhere classified among the other 52 detailed occupational administrative support occupational categories.
Source: CPS, March 1994, by authors.

Occupational segregation is important because of the striking differences in pay that are associated with men's and women's jobs. As Tables 2.9 and 2.10 show, average weekly earnings for YRFT workers in the top 10 occupations for men are significantly higher than for the top 10 occupations for women. This is not the only source of pay differentials, however. Large pay gaps also exist *within* many detailed occupational categories. Consider the figures on "management-related occupations" shown in Table 2.11.

Management-related occupations are narrowly defined occupational categories, a sub-subset of all managerial occupations. The people in these positions are likely to have similar amounts of education, and these jobs do not require any attributes that are linked to sex differences or physical strength. Nonetheless, female underwriters make two-thirds the weekly wage of male underwriters. Female accountants and auditors make 77% of their male counterparts' weekly wage. Overall, women in management-related occupations (of which we list only a subset) make 73 cents for each dollar made by a man in a management-related occupation.

The Possibility of Discrimination

Differences in job distributions and wage disparities between men and women in similar occupations open up the possibility that discrimination is occurring. Stated

TABLE 2.10.

TOP 10 DETAILED OCCUPATIONS FOR ALL EMPLOYED MEN, 1993

| Detailed Occupational Category | Men in Occupation | | Median Weekly Earnings of YRFT Male Workers[a] |
	Number	Percentage Male	
Managers, n.e.c.[b]	4,307,541	69.9	$885
Supervisors, Sales	2,872,846	62.0	$577
Truck Drivers	2,850,712	94.7	$481
Janitors and Cleaners	1,672,819	67.4	$346
Cooks	1,545,143	59.0	$262
Carpenters	1,312,906	99.3	$385
Laborers	1,181,460	80.5	$346
Sales Representative, Mining, Manufacturing, & Wholesale	1,122,247	73.6	$769
Groundskeepers and Gardeners	1,092,288	93.9	$288
Stock Handlers and Baggers	1,046,295	76.4	$288
Top 10	19,004,257	73.8	$558
Total Men Employed	72,032,236	53.9	$577
Top 10 as a % of All Employed Men		26.4	

[a]For YRFT employees (those who worked at least 35 hours a week for 50 or more weeks in 1993).
[b]These are managers not elsewhere classified in finance, marketing, food service, real estate, medicine and health, personnel and labor relations, purchasing, post office, or service organizations.
Source: CPS, March 1994, by authors.

backward, if women's and men's wages were equal, there would be little reason to believe that discrimination was at work. However, as we will see in the remaining chapters, social scientists offer many possible explanations for such differences, and discrimination is only one.

Before we discuss these and other possibilities in subsequent chapters, let's take one more look at pay gaps within detailed occupational categories by using data from the 1990 census. This time, we adjust for age, hours worked, and educational attainment. Table 2.12 shows hourly earnings for selected detailed occupations in the professional category among YRFT workers between 35 and 44 years of age holding a graduate or professional degree.

TABLE 2.11.

MEDIAN WEEKLY EARNINGS OF FULL-TIME WORKERS BY SEX IN MANAGEMENT-RELATED OCCUPATIONS, 1993

	Male	Female	Female/Male
Accountants and Auditors	$710	$544	0.77
Underwriters and Other Financial Officers	$800	$550	0.67
Personnel, Training & Labor Relations Specialists	$749	$534	0.71
Buyers, Wholesale and Retail Trade (Except Farm)	$528	$445	0.84
All Management-Related Occupations	$713	$517	0.73

Source: Employment and Earnings, [op cit.], Table 56.

TABLE 2.12.
MEAN HOURLY EARNINGS AMONG YRFT WORKERS 35–44 YEARS OLD WITH A GRADUATE
OR PROFESSIONAL DEGREE, 1989[a]

Occupation	White Men	Black Men	White Women	Black Women
Counselors, Educational & Vocational	$16.19	$14.55	$14.53	$14.63
Librarians, Archivists & Curators	$16.18	$13.84	$14.10	$14.35
Social Scientists & Urban Planners	$22.81	$19.24	$18.03	$16.72
Social, Recreational & Religious Workers	$11.17	$12.72	$12.78	$13.98
Lawyers & Judges	$38.43	$28.05	$27.37	$22.99
Registered Nurses	$23.85	$22.26	$15.94	$17.04
Natural Scientists	$21.38	$16.69	$17.27	$20.45
Engineers, Architects & Surveyors	$24.45	$21.34	$19.55	$21.66

[a]Data here excludes Hispanics, regardless of race.
Source: Earnings by Occupation and Education, 1990 Census of Population and Housing, U.S. Department of Commerce.

These figures compare the hourly earnings in detailed occupational categories for white and black men and women of similar ages, educational attainment, and labor force commitments. Nonetheless, white men earn substantially more than any other group in all occupations except one. The earnings of black men, white women, and black women show no obvious pattern when compared with each other. Given their very different circumstances, the closeness of these hourly wage figures—and their common distance from white male wages—is striking. Black women, the only group "doubly oppressed" by race and gender, earn more than black men and white women in five of the eight occupations. We should be careful about generalizing from such a small sample of occupations. If we look at all occupations and continue to restrict our attention to all 35 to 44 year olds with a graduate or professional degree working YRFT, average annual earnings in 1989 were $70,127 for white men, $40,617 for white women, $48,655 for black men, and $36,358 for black women. Thus, wage ratios are as follows: white women/white men = 0.58, black men/white men = 0.69, black women/white women = 0.89, black women/black men = 0.74.

These numbers suggest that one straightforward statement of fact can be made about race and gender inequality: white men consistently earn more than blacks and women. Therefore, we need to explain why women and blacks are more likely to be found in lower-paying jobs, and why they are paid less even while working the same jobs as white men.

SUMMARY AND CONCLUSIONS

A lot of facts and statistics have been presented in this chapter, but concluding that discrimination exists from the data presented here would be hasty. Even so, the evidence does point to large and persistent labor market inequities based on race and gender. The rest of this book examines two very different approaches to why white men fare better in labor markets than women and blacks. As you begin to consider the explanations for inequality, here are several main points to keep in mind:

• Real wages rose steadily from World War II until the early 1970s. Since then, they have stagnated or fallen, especially for men.

• Over the same period that average wages have ceased to grow, inequality has increased. Low-wage workers have lost the most.

• Black men still only earn about three-fourths the wages of white males.

• The wage gap between black and white women fell over the 1960s and 1970s to less than 10%. Since then, it has risen slightly.

• The male–female wage gap has fallen steadily since the early 1970s; however, female earnings are still less than three-fourths of male earnings.

• There has been an upward trend in overall unemployment rates in the post–World War II period. Black unemployment rates have consistently been over twice as high as white unemployment rates. In contrast, female unemployment rates have been lower than male rates since the early 1980s.

• Blacks and women are much more likely than white men to work in low-wage industries and occupations. Nonetheless, race and gender wage gaps result from differences within as well as between occupations.

• Race and gender wage gaps persist even when age, education, and labor force commitment are comparable.

As you consider these trends, it is important to bear in mind that some inequality is not necessarily bad for the economy. If working harder or smarter pays off, inequality will result in economic growth with widely dispersed benefits. Further, some degree of inequality is inevitable in a world where individuals have distinct tastes and talents, nor would one expect groups to be automatically equal: cultural, social, and even biological differences can have economic effects. In other words, it is quite possible to look at the numbers in this chapter without getting upset.

On the other hand, it is possible to look at these same numbers and get very upset. As Robert Frank and Philip Cook argue in their book *The Winner-Take-All Society* (1995), too much inequality can reduce opportunity and hope—and we certainly have a lot of inequality. While groups will never be automatically equal, it is disturbing that today's losers are the same groups that lost yesterday, yesteryear, well into the last century, and often beyond. It is hard to believe that the racism and sexism that have run through U.S. history have disappeared without a trace. If inequality results from past or present discrimination, then our society is unjust. That would be a bitter pill to swallow.

Each of these interpretations is backed up by a substantial body of theory and evidence. We will explore both interpretations and related debates in detail in the chapters that follow.

DISCUSSION QUESTIONS

1 If discrimination is not responsible for inequality, how might differences in wages, unemployment rates, and occupational distributions by race and gender be explained?

2 If we were to equalize wages between blacks and whites and men and women, does this mean that white men's wages must fall further?

3 If discrimination has declined, why has the black–white unemployment gap widened?

4 If discrimination has not declined, why did the black–white wage gap among women decline until the 1980s?

5 If discrimination exists now but is reduced in the future, would inequality necessarily remain?

6 Using Figures 2.3 and 2.4, what has happened to the wage ratios between black and white men and women over the last several decades? Given what you already know about the labor force history of women and blacks, what might explain the wage ratio trends?

7 What reasons might explain the high unemployment rates for persons 16 to 19 years of age (see Table 2.4)?

8 Why do you think unemployment rates for blacks are so high?

9 Explain why unemployment rates rise during economic contractions and fall during expansions.

10 Between 1983 and 1993, the number of persons who were employed rose by close to 20%. Which occupations experienced relative, but not absolute, declines in employment?

SUGGESTED READINGS

Council of Economic Advisors. 1995. *Economic Report of the President,* Washington D.C.: Government Printing Office.

Frank, Robert H. and Philip J. Cook. 1995. *The Winner-Take-All Society.* New York: Free Press.

Harrison, Bennett and Barry Bluestone. 1982. *The Deindustrialization of America.* New York: Basic Books.

Mishel, Lawrence and Jared Bernstein. 1994. *The State of Working America 1994–95.* Armonk NY: M.E. Sharpe.

PART TWO

THE NEOCLASSICAL
APPROACH

3

THE BASICS OF NEOCLASSICAL ECONOMICS

CENTRAL IDEAS: MARKETS AND COMPETITION

Most economists share a core set of ideas—the *neoclassical approach.* This chapter provides a broad look at the neoclassical approach, its central concepts, how the model works, what it implies for government policies, and finally, a look behind the scenes to understand why markets exist. We start with this general overview as it helps to explain how most economists approach, explain, and make government policy recommendations on virtually any issue, including discrimination.

When political economists think about the economy, they focus first on work and production. When neoclassical economists approach the economy, they focus on how goods and services are exchanged. This latter approach takes us to the question of *markets.*

For example, suppose an economist is wandering the streets of downtown New York City, and someone asks her how the city ended up with so many skyscrapers. If she is a political economist, she would attribute the skyscrapers to the millions of hours of work that went into the structures, but if she is a neoclassical economist, she would argue that the skyscrapers result from the workings of supply and demand.

When you purchase a car, lemon, or artichoke, you engage in a market exchange. In each case, we can identify the price paid, the quantity of the good purchased, and the two sides of the market—those who supply the good and receive money, and those who demand the good and spend money. The goods and services that are exchanged in markets are called *commodities.* To be a commodity, a thing or activity must be owned and be exchanged in the market. After all, if something were sold and it were not owned, who would get the money?

Markets themselves may be beneficial for society if there is *competition.* The version of competition used in neoclassical economics is unlike that found in sports or scholarships, where there always are winners and losers. Instead, it centers on the notion that competition prevents individuals from exercising control over the market. Competition means that no one has power in the sense that no one can influence the price.

Market competition: Where no single buyer or seller controls the market price

---

How can we tell if a market is competitive? One check is whether there are many buyers and sellers. If you can only buy electricity from one company, there is not competition in the electricity market. Another check is whether the goods or services sold in the market are similar. The beer market may have lots of buyers and sellers, but if many consumers are convinced that "Bud is King," then competition is imperfect. A final check is whether buyers and sellers know about all the happenings in the market. There are lots of car dealerships in the world, but if people only check out the prices at one before buying, competition will again be imperfect.

While it is harder to see in practice, the surest sign of a competitive market is that neither buyers nor sellers control the price; a market-dictated price emerges instead. Consumers may try to reduce prices and producers to raise prices, but competition stops them cold. Producers charging higher prices will be unable to sell anything, and consumers looking for discounts will be unable to find any. The idea that the market, rather than individuals or corporations, controls what happens in an economy explains the quip that it doesn't take any neoclassical economists to change a lightbulb, because if it needed changing, the market would have done it already. This is an example of what neoclassical economists call the "invisible hand," by which markets create harmony among individuals with conflicting interests. This idea was developed by the father of neoclassical economics, Adam Smith, in *The Wealth of Nations* (1976), originally published in 1776.

This chapter begins with the concepts of markets and competition, because competitive markets are viewed favorably by neoclassical economists, and this view strongly flavors the neoclassical approach to economic phenomena, including discrimination. Why is competition viewed as desirable? You have seen one part of the answer already: no individual or company can control a competitive market. Another part is the belief that prices in competitive markets reflect the value that society places on each good or service. For example, if consumers desire more bread, they will

---

Conditions for Perfect Competition:
✔ *Many buyers*
✔ *Many sellers*
✔ *Homogeneous products*
✔ *Perfect information*

switch their purchases from some other product, and the new, and usually higher, price will reflect both the greater cost to society for producing more bread and the consumers' greater desire for the good. Related to this, competition also is an incentive mechanism: if people come to value horseshoes more than penknives, they will translate those preferences into new buying patterns, and producers will have an incentive to produce more horseshoes. A final part of the argument is that competitive markets are efficient, but this is getting ahead of our story.

By highlighting the role of markets and competition, neoclassical economics provides a strong vision of how market economies function and a powerful rationale for endorsing competitive markets over other mechanisms to govern the economy. When we come to the question of discrimination, neoclassical economists argue that market competition can even help to solve this problem (Box 3.1). To understand how we get there, we start by gathering up the neoclassical tools that will be needed in later chapters to analyze labor markets and discrimination.

BOX 3.1

DISCRIMINATION AND BARRIERS TO COMPETITION

In the neoclassical view, competition ensures that equally productive workers receive the same wages. If black or female workers are paid less than equivalent whites or males, this might result from discrimination (see Chapter 5). Such unfair (and inefficient) wage differences may emerge because competition is blocked by racist or sexist governmental policies or labor unions.

Robert Higgs shows that black economic progress after slavery was hindered by racist behavior (including the use of extreme violence) by government, unions, and communities in the southern United States. Blacks who were able to acquire skills and migrate north, however, escaped these barriers and often improved their circumstances. While blacks still faced much discrimination in the north United States, discriminatory laws and practices were less severe, so markets operated more freely. As a result of greater competition, Higgs concludes that blacks who moved north were better off.

Similarly, Herbert Hill argues that trade unions prevent competition from occurring (ie, an employer only has one source of labor) and often have been a major source of employment discrimination and job segregation. Dur-

ing the early part of the 20th century, the American Federation of Labor (AFL) consistently excluded blacks and organized strikes against employers who attempted to hire them. The Congress of Industrial Organizations (CIO, founded in 1935) improved matters, because it had a policy of solidarity among black and white workers. Nonetheless, after the 1955 merger that created the AFL-CIO, the trade union movement was largely absent from the civil rights struggles of the 1950s and 1960s, and since then often has opposed policies such as affirmative action.

Organizations such as unions or government can become means by which the white majority insulates itself from competition by blacks. In the neoclassical view, if competition had been allowed to operate freely, historical patterns of race and gender inequality might have been reduced dramatically.

Sources: Robert Higgs, "Black Progress and the Persistence of Racial Economic Inequalities, 1865–1940," and Herbert Hill, "Black Labor and Affirmative Action: An Historical Perspective," both in Steven Shulman and William Darity, Jr., eds., *The Question of Discrimination: Racial Inequality in the US Labor Market.* Middletown, CT: Wesleyan University Press, 1989.

HOW PEOPLE ACT: RATIONALITY, SCARCITY, AND OPPORTUNITY COST

The neoclassical vision of markets outlined earlier stems from assumptions about how people act. The key assumption is that economic behavior is undertaken by a *rational individual*. This individual has a set of likes and dislikes, which the theory takes as given. These likes and dislikes are called *exogenous preferences,* implying that people know what they want (*ie,* the preferences part) and that those wants come from outside the economy (*ie,* the exogenous part). The individual tries his or her best to fulfill those preferences using all available information and searching out all possible courses of action to maximize utility.

Rationality: Using all available information to make decisions which maximize individual utility

---

Rational individuals need not be hedonistic. Some might place a relatively high value on maintaining a healthy lifestyle, others on making money, and still others on the enjoyment of music, sleep, work, or fine foods. Individuals are not, however, permitted to feel positively or negatively about the utility of others.

The utility-maximizing individual must make consumption decisions because resources are scarce. *Scarcity* means that society cannot provide each individual with all the goods, services, or time that they desire. On the one hand, scarcity implies a finite quantity of resources and, on the other, that we desire more resources than are available.

Utility: A unit used by an individual to measure the pains, pleasures, costs, and benefits of some action

---

Scarcity is a truism. If you take $20 to the grocery store, then buying more bread means buying less ice cream. If you are reading this book, then you cannot be performing yoga at the same time (go ahead and try it). For neoclassical economists, the fact that you probably would like more money than you currently have, that there are other things you would *also* like to be doing while reading this, implies the problem of scarcity.

Scarcity: The clash of limited human and physical resources with unlimited individual wants

---

Assuming that we always desire more than we have, any activity we select necessarily implies giving up something else. The utility given up when selecting a particular activity (*eg,* through buying one good instead of another) is called the *opportunity cost* of that activity. This utility may be represented by the dollars that could have been spent on an alternative purchase. For example, consider the opportunity cost of attending college. Look at the direct costs of tuition and books and the psychological costs of going to class and taking tests (we assume you can put a monetary value on these), then compare this to the opportunity cost—the indirect costs of college in foregone wages from a job you would have held and the enjoyment or pain that would have gone along with that job (you also have to account for the fact that as a college graduate, you would earn more later in life, but that is a story for the next chapter). If you translate all this into monetary terms, or think of it in terms of utility, then you go to college only if the opportunity cost is sufficiently low.

Opportunity cost: The next most valued alternative to what you do or choose, what is "foregone" when you make a choice

---

The notion of rational individuals confronting scarcity by using the notion of opportunity costs is important for several reasons. First, because individuals make decisions based on their own desires, opportunity costs *diverge* across individuals. Faced with the same dollar costs of going to college, some people choose to attend and others to avoid college. In the neoclassical view, we all are distinct, so it is not surprising if we make different decisions.

Second, although we are individuals, the use of opportunity cost by rational individuals to make decisions implies that many economic actions are *predictable*. If wages for jobs held by high school graduates rise, then the opportunity cost of attending college also rises, so at least some people should drop out of college or never enroll. The notion of rational individuals applying the concept of opportunity cost means that neoclassical economists can make predictions about the behavior of individuals who may have very different wants and desires.

Third, if rational individuals use opportunity costs to make decisions, we can view people as *utility maximizers*. In other words, we each calculate how to make ourselves better off. You might ask why neoclassical economists do not just assume that money is the yardstick we use to calculate opportunity costs. The problem is that money would not allow each of us to differ in what we like, and it would imply that economists can compare how well-off various individuals are according to income. Neoclassical economists reject this possibility, because they assume we each have our own preferences. Even for identical twins, one might prefer blue clothing over green, while the other enjoys green clothing and detests blue. More directly, if two people purchase the same make of automobile, does this mean that they enjoy it equally? Such an occurrence would be entirely accidental, so neoclassical economists assume that each of us has our own measuring stick for pains and pleasure. We are unique.

The notion of opportunity costs may be applied to almost any decision, but it usually is applied to decisions about buying and selling. We now turn to these matters.

WELCOME TO THE MARKET: DEMAND AND SUPPLY

This section examines a specific market, looking first at demand, then at supply, and finally at equilibrium. Throughout, we assume there is competition, so that no one controls the price of the good.

Demand

Suppose you are thinking about purchasing a package of chewing gum. As a rational individual, you say, "Aha, I'll calculate the opportunity cost, then decide." Your alternatives may include purchasing candy instead, putting the money in a savings account, or perhaps working a few minutes less each day instead of earning money for gum. It does not matter which alternative is relevant, only that you think about the most-valued one. If the relevant alternative is purchasing candy, you compare the costs and resulting enjoyment from consuming gum and candy.

If the price of gum or candy is 30 cents, you decide to buy candy, but what if the price of gum were only 15 cents? Then, you would be more likely to buy the gum. If the price of gum drops to 5 cents, you would be even more likely to purchase gum and forget the candy.

This inverse relation between change in price and change in the quantity demanded is called the *law of demand*. This law helps to explain why markets are predictable. Also, notice that differences in people's preferences have not disappeared here, because the price you pay to buy a product does not signal its utility for you. Certainly, if you paid 5 cents for the gum, it is worth at least 5 cents, but maybe it is worth more to you, maybe even 30 cents a pack.

Law of demand: As the price of a good rises, desired purchases decline

---

Demand can, and does, change for a variety of reasons. In the gum market, if incomes rise as more people quit smoking or it is discovered that chewing gum leads to healthy teeth, demand would increase. In these cases, the law of demand is not involved: at any price, people want to buy more. It is only when the price of the good in question changes and people respond that we see the law of demand at work.

For our purposes, the most important reason for changes in demand is the availability of substitute goods. In the case of candy and gum, these are substitutes, and what we did not point out earlier is obvious: when the price of gum fell, consumers bought less candy. When two goods are substitutes, a fall in the price of one leads consumers to switch to that good and away from the other.

Why do we care about the notion of substitutes? Because in a crucial market—that for labor—employees of different races and genders may be viewed as substitutes by employers. To get somewhat ahead of our story, if equivalent black workers are much cheaper than white workers, then it would seem that rational employers would have a strong incentive to substitute blacks for whites.

Determinants of Demand:
✔ *Consumer preferences*
✔ *Income of consumers*
✔ *Population*
✔ *Availability of substitutes*

Substitute goods: Where buying more of one good usually means buying less of the other

---

Supply

Go back to the gum example, and consider the supply side. Unlike consumers, producers of gum do not worry about whether they enjoy chewing it, whether it is healthy, or whether used gum damages the environment or is a social nuisance. All the producers worry about is *profits.* Firms try to maximize profits, which is parallel to consumers who try to maximize utility. Consumers can deal with all the messy calculations involved in figuring out how much enjoyment they get out of gum or candy; firms keep their eye on the bottom line.

Profits: The difference between sales revenues and costs for a firm

---

When firms make a determination to supply some good or service to the market, they typically will obey the *law of supply,* which means that firms will produce more at higher prices and less at lower prices, all in an effort to maximize profits. Why would firms wish to sell more at higher prices? The short answer is that the more money a firm receives for producing a particular good, the higher the opportunity cost for producing something else (or for going out of business). Firms simply weigh these opportunity costs and move their efforts where profits are the highest. For example, suppose you are producing bagels and bags. If the market price (*ie,* the selling price) of bagels rises, then your profits go up if you switch at least some of your efforts away from bags and to bagels. Investors do much the same thing. As the price at which a good can be sold goes up, investment funds move toward producing more of that good.

Law of supply: As the price of a good rises, desired sales also rise

---

Alternatively, the law of supply may hold because average costs increase as production increases. For example, suppose that an automobile factory runs a single shift during the day and can produce 450 cars at an average cost of $10,000 per car. The only way to produce more cars is to pay workers overtime or hire another shift at higher wages (because people usually receive higher wages for working evenings or nights). Either way, the average cost of producing a car is bound to rise, perhaps to $11,000 per car. Once the plant is producing all the cars that its capacity will allow, efforts to produce even more cars will increase the average cost of a car even more dramatically. The bottom line here is that because car producers find average costs going up as they produce more, they will only be willing to sell more cars if the market price rises. The law of supply holds in this case.

There also are other reasons for average costs to rise along with production. Plant and equipment may be overworked as production increases, employees may need to be hired from increasingly distant locations, or inappropriate resources may have to be used to increase production (*eg,* using rain forests to produce wheat). For all of these reasons, average costs may rise with production, and the law of supply follows.

Like demand, supply can change such that firms will wish to sell more (or less) at any given price. As technology improves, this reduces a firm's costs and directly increases its profits. At the same time, new, lower-cost technologies give firms an incentive to produce and sell more goods. If wages or the price of other inputs fall, the firm similarly will wish to sell more at the going price. For a variety of reasons, some industries may have a large number of potential producers, where firms would find it easy to shift from one product to another. When this is the case, such as with producers of pants and blouses, supply is affected, because small changes in price can draw in or out a large number of producers. By extension, many firms keep an eye on a wide variety of potential markets, looking for the most profitable one.

The supply of goods to the market is based on profit maximization by firms. As the earlier examples suggest, firms have strong incentives to seek low-cost production methods and to provide goods that consumers will purchase. These incentives later turn out to help make competitive markets efficient.

Equilibrium

We now arrive at the combination of supply and demand in the market. Supply and demand are connected by the concept of market *equilibrium.* Equilibrium in a market is the price at which supply and demand are equal, subject to constraints such as scarce resources. At this price, everything that is produced is purchased, so no goods are left unsold and no desired purchases unmade. At all other prices, the amount supplied and the amount demanded will be unequal.

Equilibrium: A situation with no tendency to change

The notion of market equilibrium has long fascinated economists, because it implies that under competition, everyone is doing exactly what they wish to do. No one is forced to sell or buy, and no one who is willing and able to buy or sell is left out. Most remarkably, all this interaction occurs in a setting where individuals neither know nor care about who they are dealing with. If you want to buy Peruvian perfume, you don't need to know who produced it or whether they enjoy or detest the product. You only know they are willing to provide the product at the price you pay,

---

Determinants of Supply:
✔ *Technology*
✔ *Income of consumers*
✔ *Costs of capital, labor, or other inputs*
✔ *Alternative market opportunities*

so they must be better off producing perfume as opposed to doing something else. Similarly, the producer neither knows nor cares who you are.

Rarely do we see equilibrium in the real world, because the conditions that determine supply and demand frequently change. Consumer desires, incomes, population, technology and prices of inputs all are subject to change, so why is equilibrium important if it is a moving target? It is important because it tells us where the economy is going and something about what the economy will look like in the future.

BOX 3.2

GETTING TO EQUILIBRIUM: THE CASE OF ARTICHOKES

If we rarely see a situation in which equilibrium occurs, then where are we? We are heading toward equilibrium.

The artichoke market is described by Figure 3.1. Consumers purchase artichokes to eat and will purchase other vegetables when the price of artichokes rises, so it makes sense that the law of demand holds in this market. As the price of artichokes rises, consumers purchase fewer artichokes. As the price of artichokes falls, such as when they are in season, consumers purchase more. Figure 3.1 shows the law of demand with the quantity demanded increasing from 1000 to 2000 artichokes as the price of artichokes falls from $2.00 to $1.50. The quantity demanded continues rising to 3000 artichokes as the price falls to $1.00.

The law of supply also is likely to hold in the artichoke market, because as the price rises, farmers growing other foodstuffs will find artichokes increasingly attractive. The opportunity cost of growing tomatoes instead of artichokes goes up. Figure 3.1 shows a demonstration of the law of supply with the quantity falling from 3000 to 2000 artichokes as the price falls from $2.00 to $1.50, and falling again to 1000 artichokes as the price falls to $1.00.

The equilibrium price and quantity can be found where supply and demand cross—at $1.50 per artichoke. However, how do we get there if we are not there already? If the price is too high, such as $2.00, there will be excess supply. Farmers will grow and send

FIGURE 3.1
EQUILIBRIUM IN THE ARTICHOKE MARKET.

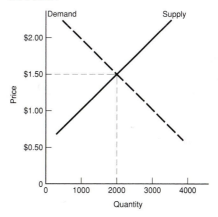

3000 artichokes to market, but consumers will only wish to purchase 1000 artichokes. Indeed, the only way to dump all 3000 artichokes is to sell them at $1.00 each, but farmers won't get caught napping again. Next season, they will produce less, until the equilibrium price of $1.50 is achieved.

Similarly, if the price is too low, such as $1.00, then consumers will want to buy 3000 artichokes but only find 1000 in the stores. Now the price goes up until it hits $1.50, where the amount that farmers wish to produce equals the amount that consumers will purchase.

Suppose we are in disequilibrium, with sellers' inventories of chewing gum stacking up on the shelves. Supply and demand theory tells us this is a situation of excess supply. Further, we can predict that price will fall and more gum will be sold as we move toward equilibrium (Box 3.2). In parallel fashion, if stands cannot keep gum in stock, there is excess demand, and we would expect the price to rise and less gum to be sold as we move toward equilibrium.

The speed at which a market approaches equilibrium depends on the specific market. In the market for chewing gum, it would be relatively easy for the quantity supplied to fall or rise to meet demand in a short period of time. Firms producing gum would put on or remove an extra shift. In a market such as that for nurses, however, disequilibrium could exist for a long period, because if there is an excess demand, it takes years to train more nurses. If there is an excess supply, nurses may find precious few comparable jobs available (given their skills), so many will stay on for decades, even if wages fall. Regardless of the speed at which equilibrium is approached, the point remains that the market will tend to balance supply and demand.

The main reason that we frequently are out of equilibrium is located in changes in demand and supply (Box 3.3). A change in any of the "givens," such as technology or tastes, will alter the relationship between supply and demand. Suppose consumers change their preferences and desire less of the product. This change will disrupt equilibrium, because sellers cannot sell all that they have produced. Then, we return to our story of disequilibrium (starting here with excess supply).

A drop in supply does the opposite. Suppose that an opportunity for especially high profits opens up in the chocolate market. Some chewing gum producers will close up shop or switch to chocolate production as investors move their capital out of the old market and into the new. In the gum market, we will find excess demand as fewer firms are willing to produce gum at the old equilibrium price. Now we are back at disequilibrium, although here with excess demand, so the price should rise as gum chewers entice producers back into the chewing gum market.

We have just argued that the forces of supply and demand drive a market toward equilibrium. Stepping back for a moment, however, we see that the real forces at work are those behind supply and demand—rational consumers and profit-maximizing firms. Rational consumers constantly seek out cheaper and higher-quality products. They place dollars behind that search, and they reward firms for reducing costs, improving quality, and generally giving consumers what they want. The firm, on the other hand, does not care what consumers want, but it does care about profits, which are a reward for keeping down costs and satisfying consumers. This reward system keeps firms and consumers moving toward equilibrium regardless of changes in the economy.

A variety of conclusions follow from these neoclassical stories. First, although we may have different wants and needs, may look and act differently from each other, and cannot pretend to even know how each other feels, competitive markets can generate an equilibrium where each of us does precisely what we wish to do. Second, although we are so diverse, our behavior in the market is largely predictable. While equilibrium does not often occur *per se,* economists can predict what will happen to prices and quantities sold in particular markets in the future by looking at changes in supply and demand or at disequilibrium situations. Third, competitive markets tend

BOX 3.3

CHANGING EQUILIBRIUM: ARTICHOKES AGAIN?

Much of the reason we rarely see equilibrium occurring is that supply or demand, or both, frequently change. The laws of supply and demand help us to predict how prices and quantities will respond to such changes.

Return to the artichoke market example. Suppose that the latest craze in cooking is braised artichokes, as shown around the country on the television series, "The Baltimore Chef" (name changed to protect the innocent). Soon, everyone is trying braised artichokes, or stated differently, demand for artichokes increases. Figure 3.2 shows such an increase in demand. Consumers who purchase artichokes wish to buy more than 2000, sold at $1.50 each. This results in excess demand (4000 artichokes is the quantity demanded, 2000 the quantity supplied, and 2000 the excess demand). The price will be bid up until the excess demand disappears and equilibrium is achieved—here, at a price of $2.00 per artichoke, with 3000 being bought and sold. Therefore, supply and demand allow us to predict that after "The Baltimore Chef" makes braised artichokes popular, more artichokes will be sold and at a higher price.

FIGURE 3.2
CHANGE IN DEMAND FOR ARTICHOKES.

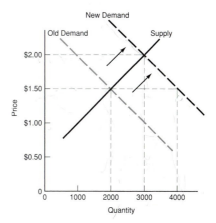

On the supply side, suppose that researchers develop a "super-artichoke seed" that doubles the yield of artichokes per acre of land employed and at a lower cost per artichoke. Supply and demand allow us to predict what will happen.

to eliminate overproduction and underproduction automatically. When consumers wanted "pet rocks," the rocks were produced in abundance, but thanks to competition, they are no longer produced now that the rocks are no longer desired. Finally, the movements of consumers and investors in and out of different markets make the market system work. Competition depends on mobility, and anything that obstructs mobility—such as legal restrictions or trade unions (Box 3.1)—will mean that some people are not being allowed to do as they wish. As a result, we all suffer. To see why, we turn to the neoclassical understanding of efficiency.

EFFICIENCY, EQUITY, AND THE GOVERNMENT

The neoclassical economic view favoring markets over government intervention stems from the claim that competitive markets are efficient and, at least in a weak sense, equitable. Here, we look at the ideas of efficiency and equity to reach the government policy conclusions.

Efficiency

Neoclassical economists use the concept of *efficiency* as defined by the turn-of-the-century Italian sociologist, Vilfredo Pareto. According to Pareto, a situation or event is efficient if no one can be made better off unless someone else is made worse off. This implies, for example, that it may be inefficient to use outdated technology. If we know how to produce automobiles on an assembly line using one-quarter of the labor it would take to assemble cars in someone's garage, it would be inefficient to build in the garage. Theoretically, the worker who builds in his garage could make more money producing on an assembly line (after paying for capital), and consumers would pay less for cars. Everyone would be better off, so efficiency can be improved. More directly, if you trade a popsicle for an ice-cream cone held by a friend, this must be an efficient outcome: if you were not *both* better off, the trade would not have occurred.

Efficiency: Situations where one person cannot be made better off without harming someone else

---

The last example explains why competitive markets are viewed so favorably by neoclassical economists. No rational individual would engage in a trade that would not leave him or her at least as well off as before the trade. You would not work for someone, buy a product from someone, or rent out a house or apartment unless you gained in the process. The person or corporation on the other side of the market must similarly gain. This is the sense in which there is no power held by anyone in a competitive market.

This neoclassical understanding of efficiency fits neatly with the notion that we cannot know the preferences and pains of others. All we know is that—because of scarcity—more is better, and that—because of rationality—people will strive to increase their utility. A market trade therefore is efficient even though we do not know why each participant engaged in the transaction.

In actual economies, it is difficult to think of changes that are efficient in the sense used here. If an automobile manufacturer introduces a new technology that uses fewer workers, the economy may be able to produce the same amount of cars using fewer resources. The laid-off workers will produce something else, but they may experience a pay cut in the process and so be worse off. Or, consider a government policy such as increasing taxes to fund an improved educational system. We might end up able to produce more as a result, but in the meantime, someone is paying higher taxes and so may be worse off.

Economists respond to these problems in various ways, but largely, they look at potential, rather than actual, efficiency improvements. In theory, the new automobile technology allows us to produce more, so the laid-off automobile workers could still receive their old wages and everyone would benefit. Similarly, the government could ask those who receive education to pay back the previous generation for their earlier funding of education, and everyone would gain. Stated differently, if some change in the economy results in our producing more goods and services with fewer resources, then this change represents an improvement in "potential efficiency." Often, improvements in potential efficiency are the most that we can hope for in the real world.[1]

Equity

When economists think of fairness or equality, they use the term *equity*. Historically, economists have thought of equity as meaning equal outcomes (Blaug, 1985). If you want to achieve an equitable distribution of a pie between two people, you divide it in half (you can ensure that the division is fair if one person cuts and the other chooses first). In the entire economy, equity may mean that everyone has an equal amount of wealth and receives the same income. The lower incomes and poorer housing that are experienced by the average black as opposed to white American are then "inequitable."

Equity: Either equal opportunities or equal outcomes

No one claims that competitive markets provide equity in this sense. To see why, try a "thought experiment" in which we assume that everyone starts out with the same amount of money when they are born and that we allow competition to rule the marketplace. Soon, some people will discover they are better at mathematics, some excel in literature, and others do not seem to do well at anything. When these people enter the job market, the laws of supply and demand will take hold. Those who produce more of the goods that people desire and will pay for in turn will receive higher incomes; those who produce less will receive less.

Just as you are ready to give up on the idea of having equity in a market economy, an idea dawns on you: tax the rich, and give the money to the poor. That way, the market still works, and we can have equity. Not so fast, however. You've accidentally stepped on the law of supply here, and the market will no longer be efficient. For example, someone who would have become a doctor now may deduce that they can earn the same money holding down an easier job requiring less education and having better hours.

This is just one example of what Arthur Okun (1975) called the "trade-off" between equity and efficiency. The trade-off emerges from the fact that as money, wealth, education, or any other economic resource is shifted from the rich to the poor, *everyone* has less reason to work hard and try to get ahead. This is particularly troubling for entrepreneurs and innovators. Such individuals take big risks, knowing that they likely will come out losers but hoping for the big score, to develop the next Microsoft, a cleaner fuel source, a better microwave popcorn, or a cure for AIDS. If they know that winning just means the government will take more from them, the incentive to innovate will be reduced, and we may all suffer as a result (*ie,* efficiency falls).

---

[1]For further discussion, see Charles Schultze, *The Private Use of Public Purpose*. Washington, D.C.: The Brookings Institution, 1977.

There is a more limited sense in which the notion of equity fits into a competitive economy: equity as equal opportunity. The market may not make each of us rich, but in the neoclassical view, it provides each and every one of us with the opportunity to try to start the next Apple Computers, to become a doctor, or to become a seamstress. Theoretically, the market is blind to who we are, what we like, and who we know, so each of us has an equal chance to contribute to the economy and be rewarded accordingly.

Laissez-faire

The major government policy conclusion for many neoclassical economists is that the government should "leave it alone," or as the French saying puts it, to engage in *laissez-faire* economic policies.

Laissez-faire: Government policies which do not interfere with markets

---

The chief reason for supporting laissez-faire policies follows from our discussion of the trade-off between equity and efficiency: government interference to create equity usually distorts the market and causes inefficiency. From the definition of efficiency, it follows that we could make at least one person better off without making anyone else worse off if the government stopped interfering. Neoclassical economists agree that certain types of markets warrant government intervention, but before turning to those cases, let's look at the rationale for laissez-faire policies.

A classic example of inefficient government interference is the imposition of *tariffs* or *quotas* on foreign goods. Tariffs are taxes on imports that make the products of domestic firms relatively cheaper. Quotas limit the amount of foreign imports and so also make domestic firms' products more attractive (or at least more available). Such policies are inefficient and may even be inequitable, so neoclassical economists argue that tariffs and quotas should be avoided.

In the early 1980s, the big three U.S. auto producers (GM, Ford, and Chrysler) were losing sales to Japanese producers, so they lobbied for—and got—a quota on the Japanese imports. The result? Consumers paid more for cars. How much more? The equivalent of $160,000 per year per U.S. worker whose job was "saved" by the quota.[2] Undoubtedly, the affected U.S. auto workers would have preferred a one-time cash payment of $160,000 as a bribe to leave the industry, and U.S. consumers would have saved the money in remaining years. A laissez-faire policy of no quotas, even with such a bribe, would have made many people better off without harming anyone; such a policy would be efficient without damaging our sense of equity.

You might wonder why, if an efficient policy was available, the U.S. government did not use it. Nobel prize winner in economics James Buchanan (1975) offers insight into this question. Buchanan argues that government officials should themselves

---

[2]See Robert Crandall, "Import Quotas and the Automobile Industry," *Brookings Review,* Summer 1984.

be viewed as rational utility maximizers. This means they act just like everyone else in the economy but with one crucial difference: there is no market-dictated, competitive price for government actions. Government officials therefore are able to improve their position regardless of whether their actions harm others. Periodic elections place a limit on the scope for officials to act in their own interests, but in Buchanan's view, elections do not provide anywhere near the strict discipline of the market. In fact, they may even lead directly to inefficient outcomes. Under Buchanan's approach, it is not surprising that the government acted inefficiently and imposed quotas on Japanese automobiles; campaign donations from the big three U.S. auto producers and votes from United Auto Workers union members ensured that a more efficient policy—free trade—simply was not in the cards.

For some neoclassical economists like Buchanan or another famous Nobel prize winner, Milton Friedman (1962), the cry for laissez-faire economic policies often is the first and last word, whether the topic is foreign competition, poverty, discrimination, or even illicit drug use. Many neoclassical economists, however, are more liberal (in the modern sense), so they tend to make four exceptions to this rule. The first concerns Okun's trade-off between equity and efficiency. If we value both equity and efficiency, then we would defend limited government intervention in the market, such as a graduated income tax (*ie,* increasing tax rates for higher incomes) or food programs for the poorest members of society in the name of equity, while mainly permitting markets to function in the name of efficiency. The second exception is *imperfect competition,* markets where there is power on either the supply or the demand side. In these cases, markets are inefficient, and government regulation might help. For example, if one type of computer software dominates 90% of the market, then prices will be high (*ie,* above the competitive price), so the government might regulate and reduce prices to improve efficiency. The third is *externalities,* or aspects of goods and services that affect people who do not buy the product. Cigarette smoke in a crowded elevator, a boombox on a neighbor's front porch, or the smell of flowers in an office are examples of products with externalities. Government regulations such as restrictions on permissible sound levels may improve efficiency in the presence of externalities.[3] The fourth exception concerns *public goods,* which are goods that everyone can enjoy regardless of who purchased them.[4] For example, if you plant a tree in your yard (assuming you have a yard), everyone can enjoy the greenery. By related logic, child care and education may have public-goods aspects insofar as we all benefit from having a well-educated and healthy populace.

Public goods: Goods or services the free market underproduces because everyone benefits regardless of who pays

---

[3]Bad externalities such as smoke or noise mean the government should restrict the production or use of the product. By the same token, good externalities such as the smell of flowers mean the government should subsidize and promote production of the product. Education may be an example of a product with good externalities.

[4]Intuitively, public goods can be thought of as having "superexternalities" of the good kind.

If there is a rule for neoclassical economists who step away from laissez-faire, it is that government policies should strive to create "market-like" conditions. If we cannot have a competitive market, at least we can come close. This approach, which is recommended by notable economists such as Alan Blinder (1987) and Nobel prize winner Robert Solow (1994), explains why economists believe that the problem of pollution can be solved by selling "rights to pollute," which firms could trade. Firms who find it very costly to reduce pollution would purchase the rights, while companies who can easily or cheaply cut back on pollution would sell those rights. Therefore, we would end up with pollution being reduced by the lowest-cost avenue, and by making this process like a market, efficiency is improved. Similarly, if education is underprovided by the market because it is a public good, neoclassical economists might recommend voucher systems to maintain competition between schools for students while providing public funding.

You may already guess the neoclassical response to discrimination at this point. Many neoclassical economists argue that the government should not respond at all, acting in a laissez-faire fashion and allowing the market to resolve the issue. Other neoclassical economists believe we should be willing to suffer some inefficiency to make life more fair for women and minorities (*ie,* trading off efficiency for equity). Still other neoclassical economists conclude that markets cannot eradicate the problems that are created by discrimination, or at least cannot do so quickly, so again, government intervention is warranted.

BEHIND THE MARKET: THE DIVISION OF LABOR AND COMPARATIVE ADVANTAGE

Why do markets exist? This seemingly innocuous question is not easy to answer. We know that competitive markets may be efficient and that government intervention may be harmful, but where do markets come from in the first place? The answer lies in the division of labor, whereby people specialize in various tasks. The reason for specialization and the division of labor in turn can be found in the concept of *comparative advantage.* We introduce these concepts here as they underpin the neoclassical explanation for why women typically earn less than men and bear the brunt of child-rearing tasks. To understand discrimination, you need to understand these concepts.

Adam Smith begins *The Wealth of Nations* by arguing that a major distinction between a rich and a poor society lies in the *division of labor.* In the rich society, everyone is doing something different, while in the poor society, most people struggle to grow or catch enough food to survive. The division of labor allows people to learn particular tasks, hone their skills, and develop improvements in how jobs are performed. In modern terminology, Smith was arguing that the division of labor is efficient.

Division of labor: Jobs are attached to particular products, and for a single product, there are various specialized jobs

---

Smith used the process of pin-making to describe how productivity improves with the division of labor, but we can see the process in any workplace. Some people learn how to handle paperwork, others to handle and develop relationships with customers, others to transport the product or supplies, and still others to work on producing the firm's good or service. Without this division of labor, no one person could know all the relevant jobs well enough to perform them efficiently.

The division of labor results in specialization. As jobs and tasks are divided, each of us becomes a specialist in his or her own area of expertise. We become more proficient and more knowledgeable. If you are thinking this may lead to drudgery, tedium, and repetitive work, you are right, and Smith agreed that specialization was not always pleasurable. Nonetheless, if we abandoned the division of labor, it would mean that the next time you are sick, your doctor would know as much about treating you as about building a car or farming. The actors that you see in the movies would have the expertise of your local community theater, and your lawyer would know as much about the law as you do.

There is another reason why the division of labor is efficient. It allows an economy to use the *law of comparative advantage*. This notion was developed by David Ricardo (1973) to account for the fact that nations often produce different commodities, which then are exchanged. The United States may produce wheat while Mexico produces tomatoes, and wheat flows south while tomatoes flow north. Ricardo asked himself why this occurred. One answer is that Mexico receives more sunshine and tomatoes grow well in high sunlight, so we have an efficient division of labor across national borders. Comparative advantage becomes an issue if we go slightly further and ask why wheat is not grown in Mexico as well.

Comparative advantage: When a person, community, or nation can produce a good or service for exchange *relatively* more cheaply than another

---

The law of comparative advantage implies that relatively poor resources should be applied to tasks where the relative cost of using superior resources is higher. If wheat can be grown just about anywhere but tomatoes only with high levels of sunlight, then even if Mexico can produce wheat more cheaply, it is efficient for them to specialize in tomatoes while the United States specializes in wheat.

Consider an example closer to home. Suppose that on average, men are taller than women. This gives men an advantage in cleaning windows, which often stretch above head level. If we found a married couple with a man avoiding windows and a woman cleaning them, the law of comparative advantage may help to explain why. Ask what the man and woman would have to give up to clean the windows (*ie,* the opportunity cost). If the man would have to give up $100 from paid employment to clean while the woman would only lose $50 for the same time, then it may be efficient for the woman to clean the windows. Implicitly, the couple has contracted for the man to bring in money in exchange for work by the woman at home; in that contract, the couple is using the law of comparative advantage.

Like the couple deciding about who cleans windows, competitive markets also should follow the law of comparative advantage. Your doctor might have become a very productive trolley operator, but the market rewards her more for going into the field where her comparative advantage is found. Many people can operate trolleys, but few have the aptitude to be a good doctor.

SUMMING UP

The neoclassical approach focuses on markets and competition. To understand how these phenomena operate, we consider how individuals make decisions. Rational individuals face the problem of scarcity and respond by weighing the costs and benefits of alternative actions; they measure the opportunity cost of actions. Stated differently, by making decisions based on opportunity costs and preferences, individuals maximize their individual utility. We cannot touch, taste, or measure the utility that others receive, but rationality and scarcity imply that we can think of people as maximizing utility.

We all may have different utility and different opportunity costs, but we also are predictable. As the costs of performing some activity rise, fewer people will want to engage in it. This predictability leads to the laws of supply and demand, so we know, for example, that when the price of gasoline rises, people will drive less and service stations will want to sell more.

Competitive markets head us toward equilibrium, a situation where everyone who is willing and able to sell or buy can do so at the going price. While we may not see equilibrium, there are powerful market forces pushing us in that direction, because only at that point is everyone who would benefit from trade able to do so. Equilibrium in competitive markets therefore is efficient: no one can be made better off unless someone else suffers.

Many neoclassical economists favor laissez-faire government policies, letting the market work efficiently to the benefit of all participants. Nonetheless, markets sometimes are imperfect, and even where competition rules, markets may lead to severe income inequality. For these reasons, other neoclassical economists believe there may be a positive role for government intervention.

Why are markets needed at all? The initial answer—that efficiency improves as the division of labor increases—helps to explain why we might find individuals doing very different jobs. More important, when people specialize in different jobs or tasks, the market will reward them for using their comparative advantage. It is what you are relatively good at, not just what you are absolutely good at, that you should focus on.

The next chapter takes these arguments into the workplace in search of an explanation for why some people earn more than others.

DISCUSSION QUESTIONS

1 What market for a good or service best fits the idea of competition and why? Are there numerous substitute goods or services in this market?

2 Could you use supply and demand to explain why as incomes rise, people typically have fewer

children? Could you also use supply and demand as an explanation if instead people had more children as incomes rise?

3 Do the notions of opportunity cost and utility maximization make sense of decisions you made on a recent shopping trip? If so, can you identify decisions that would have been "irrational"?

4 Do the notions of opportunity cost and utility maximization help to explain people's religious beliefs, choice of marriage partners, or choice of friends?

5 What is the opportunity cost of having a child? Is it the same for men as for women? Why, or why not? How can the notion of opportunity cost help to explain the steady decline in fertility of women over the last 150 years?

6 If a market was competitive but not in equilibrium, would it be efficient? If the market was not competitive but was in equilibrium, would it be efficient?

7 Can you explain why a neoclassical economist might or might not support a government program such as WIC (Women, Infants, and Children), which improves average nutrition by providing free milk, bread, and other necessities for poor children?

8 What's different about the market for child care as opposed to others (*eg*, the chewing gum market)? Is child care a public good?

SUGGESTED READINGS

Blaug, Mark. 1985. *Economic Theory in Retrospect,* 4th ed. New York, Cambridge University Press.

Blinder, Alan. 1987. *Hard Heads, Soft Hearts: Tough-Minded Economics for a Just Society.* Reading, MA: Addison-Wesley.

Buchanan, James. 1975. *The Limits of Liberty.* Chicago: University of Chicago Press.

Friedman, Milton. 1962. *Capitalism and Freedom.* Chicago: University of Chicago Press.

Okun, Arthur. 1975. *Equity vs. Efficiency: The Big Tradeoff.* Washington, D.C.: Brookings Institution.

Ricardo, David. 1973 [originally 1817]. *The Principles of Political Economy and Taxation.* London: J.M. Dent.

Smith, Adam. 1976 [originally 1776]. *An Inquiry into the Nature and Causes of the Wealth of Nations.* Oxford: Clarendon Press.

Solow, Robert. 1994. "How Race and Gender Issues Arise in Economics." In *Race and Gender in the American Economy.* Susan F. Feiner, ed. Englewood Cliffs, NJ: Prentice-Hall.

APPENDIX: A Closer Look: The Roots of Neoclassical Economics

Adam Smith and the *Wealth of Nations*

The founder of neoclassical economics, Adam Smith, was born in 1723 in the Scottish town of Kirkcaldy. While Smith was growing up, the town was a booming seaport, with local mining for export, manufacturing of nails and other products, and markets for both locally produced agricultural products and goods from abroad. The 18th century yielded the advent of large-scale industry and the emergence of democratic political theories. While most researchers attribute little to Smith's thinking that is particularly novel, his penultimate achievement in the *Wealth of Nations* (1976) was to integrate these events and phenomena into a coherent vision for understanding the economy.

Smith's exposure to markets and manufacturing led him to believe that the division of labor was a crucial step toward improving standards of living. Production could be increased if firms specialized in the creation of particular goods and the labor within firms were divided into specialized tasks. The market stimulated this development, because specialization would increase productivity and the lowest-cost producers wind up in the strongest market positions. Markets were able to expand the variety of goods available to consumers and have those goods produced in the most efficient manner possible.

Smith argued that competition benefitted society, because it stimulated economic growth. As improvements in technology increased productivity, more goods would be produced, and the economy would grow. More growth meant higher standards of living. As workers and owners produced more, wages and profits would rise, because competition would ensure that additional output was rewarded with additional income. Owners would raise wages in an attempt to hire more workers and produce more goods. Profits also would rise as markets expanded and more goods were sold. On the other hand, if economic growth slowed, then the reverse process would occur: prices, profits, and wages would fall. Competition thus regulated prices, production, and incomes without any need for conscious direction over the economic system as a whole. For this reason, Smith characterized competition as an "invisible hand" that guides the economy toward a better world.

David Ricardo and Comparative Advantage

Smith's defense of competition was elaborated in the early 1800s by David Ricardo (1973), an English financier. Ricardo tried to persuade the English government to shed its practice of restricting trade in foreign-grown corn through tariffs. His defense of free trade rested largely on the concept of *comparative advantage,* the notion that some countries find it relatively cheaper to produce a particular good while others must be relatively better at producing other goods. "Relatively cheaper" in this context means that less is given up in terms of the alternative uses of productive resources (*ie,* land, labor, capital). For example, assume that both the United States and France produce wheat and wine and that France is better at making wine while both are equally good at making wheat. To produce more wheat, the United States must give up less wine in comparison to France (because it cannot produce as much wine with the additional resources it has diverted from wheat production). To produce more wine, France must give up less wheat in comparison to the United States (because it needs to divert fewer resources from wheat production to wine production as a result of its greater productivity in wine production). The United States has a comparative advantage in wheat and France a comparative advantage in wine. Instead of both countries producing both goods, it would be better for each to specialize and trade. It is cheaper for France to produce only wine and trade for wheat and for the United States to produce only wheat and trade for wine than for each to produce both goods. In other words, specialization benefits both trading parties.

The Marginalists

Comparative advantage is a story about production. To be complete, a theory of market exchange also must explain purchasing or demand. This task was accomplished by the so-called *marginalist revolution* of the mid-19th century (Blaug, 1985). Marginalists such as Stanley Jevons, John Bates Clark, and Leon Walras believed that economic decisions could best be understood in terms of small, step-by-step changes (at the margin), which allowed the impact on costs to be compared with the impact on benefits. For example, if we want to understand the level of employment that is decided on by a firm, we can compare each additional worker's impact on production and revenues with their impact on costs. The firm will only choose to hire the worker if the former exceeds the latter (see Chapter 4). Total employment then can be analyzed in terms of the firm's decision to hire workers one at a time. This same logic can be applied to any economic decision.

The marginalists argued that the demand for commodities was determined by the *utility* or pleasure that the purchase would bring to the buyer. Although utility could not be seen or measured (and therefore could not be compared between individuals), the marginalists assumed that it existed for each person in discrete units called *utils*. Just as supply was governed by profit maximization, demand was governed by utility maximization. As more and more of a particular good was purchased, additional utils created for the consumer must fall. This is called the *law of diminishing marginal utility*. For example, if you decide to buy an ice-cream cone on a hot day, the first cone gives you a great deal of pleasure (*eg,* 10 utils). However, the second cone gives you some but not as much pleasure (*eg,* 6 utils), because your need for ice cream has already been slackened by the first cone. The third gives you almost no pleasure (*eg,* 1 util), the fourth cone makes you sick (*eg,* -3 utils), and so on. Because the additional pleasure created by additional purchases falls, the price that the consumer is willing to pay also must fall.

The marginalists made an analogous argument with respect to supply. They believed that costs would rise as production increased, because labor and materials would become more scarce and, hence, more expensive. Higher costs of production would force suppliers to raise their prices to maintain their profits. Prices and the quantity of supply therefore must rise together. Based on this type of reasoning, it is possible to show that price changes cause corresponding changes in the quantity of supply and the quantity of demand in a manner that results in systematic prices and levels of output in various markets.

Pareto and Efficiency

The argument that the interplay of supply and demand drives economic outcomes achieved its clearest expression in the early 20th century work of Italian sociologist Vilfredo Pareto, who sought to establish that competitive markets were *efficient* in the sense that neoclassical economists now use the term. By efficiency, Pareto meant a condition where, without comparing the utility of any individuals, we can show that no individual can be made better off without making someone else worse off. Because the utils of different persons could not be compared, the utility of one person was assumed to be independent of the utility of other people. Also, because competitive markets allow individuals to choose the jobs and consumer goods they as individuals value most highly (assuming that the jobs are available and the goods affordable), there can be no superior situation to competitive markets.

As an implication, if we believe a market is reasonably competitive and find inequality in the distribution of income or jobs, then any governmental action to alleviate that inequality will necessarily be inefficient and make some individuals worse off. Given the presumption that we cannot compare the utility levels achieved by different individuals, we cannot even say that the poor are worse off than the rich!

Thus, Pareto used the logic of those preceding him to provide a powerful and persuasive defense of Smith's predilection for competition in the market.

4

WORK AND WAGES IN THE NEOCLASSICAL MODEL

INTRODUCTION: THE MARKET FOR WORK

Most neoclassical research on discrimination looks at labor markets and, particularly, wages. If the labor market was similar to the chewing gum market, we could skip this chapter and move directly to the question of labor market discrimination. Using the tools of supply and demand from Chapter 3, we would analyze differences between blacks and whites or men and women as if they simply were different "flavors" or brands of gum.

Work, however, is not the same as chewing gum. When a pack of gum is sold, the producer no longer cares whether it is chewed, resold, or thrown away; when a worker sells his labor, he might not be happy about being chewed, resold, or thrown away. When people buy gum, they usually do so because they like chewing; employers buy labor to turn a profit.

These facts imply that we need to look specifically at supply, demand, and equilibrium in the labor market. Then, having done so, we ask whether wages would be unequal even if discrimination was absent. The answer is "yes," which in turn means that some—or all—of gender and race wage differences may have nothing to do with discrimination. To get to the neoclassical understanding of wage discrimination requires that we first understand why differences would exist without it; this chapter serves that purpose. Then, this chapter examines unemployment; after all, it does not matter whether you would earn a high or a low wage if you are out of a job. We conclude by looking at wage differences among groups that may have nothing to do with discrimination.

THE DEMAND FOR LABOR: WHY FIRMS EMPLOY PEOPLE

In contrast to demand in the chewing gum market, the demand for labor is called a *derived demand*. Firms do not hire employees because they like them, prefer them, or maximize some unknown utility through hiring. Firms hire to produce something that is sold to make a profit. Firms maximize profits by hiring people for the indirect gain. Stated differently, a firm's demand for labor is related to its supply on the output market.

Derived demand for labor: Firms hire people to produce goods and services that can then be sold

---

The road to maximum profits seems to be straight enough. Profit is the difference between the revenues from selling and the costs from producing. This implies that managers should strive to increase revenues and reduce costs, but what if you are deciding whether to hire another employee? This should result in more revenues but could not possibly reduce costs. How should the decision be made?

The answer in neoclassical theory is that the firm hires up to the point where the *marginal revenue product* for the last worker equals the wage (both in per-hour or per-day terms). The marginal revenue product tells the firm how much money in sales (*ie,* revenue) the last (*ie,* marginal) worker will generate (*ie,* produce) by working. The wage tells us how much the worker costs, so the trick to maximizing profits is to hire every worker who brings in more money than she or he costs and not to hire any worker who costs more than the money brought in.

Marginal revenue product: Extra sales resulting from the efforts of the last employee hired

---

The law of demand holds in the labor market for several reasons. First, if the last person hired was producing just enough marginal revenue to cover his or her wage and the wage goes up, the firm will no longer find that employee profitable. If higher wages translate into fewer workers, then the law of demand holds. Second, if the wage rises, the firm will find its costs going up. Provided there is competition, the only way that the output price will rise is if the market supply falls. Remember, consumers are only willing to pay more if less is available in the market (by their law of demand), so the only way to cover higher wages is to reduce production. Third, if the wage goes up, the firm has an incentive to find technology that replaces workers, again leading to fewer employees.

Law of demand for labor: As wages rise, the number of workers hired falls

---

Consider a hypothetical example to see how the law of demand works in the labor market. Workers at ABC, Inc., produce newspapers. They neither write nor sell the papers, just print them. ABC is doing well in the business, and this becomes known to a field representative of the typographers' union. She spots an opportunity and organizes the workers at ABC into a local of the typographers' union, promising them grievance procedures to protect them against arbitrary managers and seniority rules so that as workers age, their jobs will be more secure. And, yes, she promises higher wages. Later, a collective bargaining agreement is signed between the union local and ABC management, and sure enough, ABC employees receive higher wages. Is management likely to take this lying down? The law of demand says "no." First, ABC managers may find some marginally profitable production runs—for example, for community newspapers—and shut those down. The marginal revenue product on these jobs is lower than the wage, so some workers lose their jobs. Second, ABC managers may be able to crank up the price that they charge to produce some newspapers. This sounds great, but ABC likely will end up producing fewer newspapers as consumers balk at paying more for the same old paper (the law of demand again). Employment falls once more. Third, ABC managers may start looking for high-tech equipment to replace many of their typographers. A year earlier, such equipment didn't make sense, but with higher wages, it does—and again, employment falls.

This story of the law of demand should sound familiar. It echoes the argument of Chapter 3 that competition reduces the ability of anyone, either on the supply or the demand side, to influence price. Here, we see employees trying to raise the "price" of their labor (*ie*, the wage) through a union and running afoul of the law of demand. Even if workers can raise the wage, the cost will be steep: fewer jobs.

We have painted a picture of the demand for labor that makes it sound very impersonal. There is no room for loyalty or friendship in a firm whose sole purpose is to maximize profits. While this sounds harsh, it also implies there is no room for treachery or prejudice. The bottom line of profit is the only yardstick when it comes to hiring workers, and as Chapter 5 will show, there is little room for discrimination either in competitive labor markets.

THE SUPPLY OF LABOR: WHO WANTS TO WORK, AND HOW PRODUCTIVE ARE THEY?

The Work Decision

When a firm supplies a product to the market, the profit motive rules. When a worker supplies labor, however, we are back to utility, preferences, and opportunity costs.

If you are thinking about taking a paid job, you face a *labor–leisure choice*. As you mull over the decision, the major factors are that you will have more money if you work but less time to relax and enjoy life. In a word, you face a problem of "scarcity." From Chapter 3, we know that the neoclassical answer to scarcity is to be rational, to weigh the utility of leisure against the utility from being able to buy more and perhaps even to save a little.

Labor–leisure choice: For many people, the opportunity cost of work is more time off

---

Individuals weigh the opportunity cost of paid employment against leisure in several ways. First is the question of whether to take any job. Second is the issue of whether to work full- or only part-time. Third is whether to show up for work each day. And, finally, in some cases the decision of whether to work overtime emerges. These decisions are not made on a simple basis like profit maximization; instead, they involve feelings or preferences. You wake up some mornings and think, "Maybe I won't go to work today." You ponder "how do I feel" and then decide whether the money is worth more than the pleasure of sleeping in, going out, or whatever else you might do (less the aggravation from the boss for missing work).

The question of labor supply often is simplified from the four issues just discussed to the simpler question of how many hours people want to work. Focusing on the question of labor hours supplied, it turns out that the law of supply may *not* apply in the labor market. People might even want to work less for a higher wage. This argument may strike you as nonsense; after all, if someone offered you a job earning truly astounding wages, such as $1000 per hour, you would surely accept the job. Even if it meant quitting college, most people would have a hard time saying no. Those people fit the law of supply, but in other circumstances, the law of supply makes less sense. For example, once you have the $1000-per-hour job, this provides you with enough income to vacation abroad, take up deep-sea fishing, or follow your favorite performers on tour. Now, suppose you get a raise to $1100 per hour. Are you likely to work more or fewer hours? If you said, "Fewer hours, I'll take the deep sea fishing," you just broke the law of supply.

Law of supply for labor?: The law of supply—that more people seek jobs at higher wages—may not be true for labor

---

As this example suggests, the law of supply may not hold in the real world. One of the most well-studied cases of labor supply is that of white men and women in the United States. In general, these studies show that women obey the law of supply but that men are not always so obedient (Box 4.1).

The working-hours decision turns on many aspects of life. Family and community commitments, wealth, social background, and one's like or dislike of work, all are relevant, but neoclassical economists consider an individual's *rate of time preference* to be one of the most important determinants of working hours. This is an interest rate that each of us carries in our head, and it will be different for different people. Individuals with a low rate of time preference save for their retirement; individuals with a high rate spend their money when they are young.

Rate of time preference: Low for people who value the future and high for those who value the present

---

What do the terms *high* and *low* mean in this context? Basically, we can calculate rates of time preference by asking, for example, what interest rate on a savings

BOX 4.1

THE MALE AND FEMALE SUPPLY OF LABOR

Does the law of supply hold for labor? The short answer is "yes" for women and "sort of" for men. This finding from empirical studies means that as the wage rises, a large number of women enter the labor force, but only a few more men will. Conversely, as the wage falls, only a few men quit their jobs, but many women do. The supply of women is more sensitive than the supply of men to the wage.

Many studies have been performed to check the effect of wages on the labor supply. In a summary of this research undertaken by Mark Killingsworth, he concludes that the quantity of labor supplied by men is largely unaffected by the wage, while for women, a 1% increase in the wage draws in 0.6% more women into the labor market. Stated differently, a 1% drop in the wage would have no effect on how many men wanted to enter paid employment, but it would drive out 0.6% of women.[1]

The difference in female and male labor supply can be looked at graphically, and Figures 4.1 and 4.2 show labor supply for women and men. Start with a wage of $5 per hour. Coming across to the labor supply curves and down to the labor quantity axes, we discover that 2000 women and 2000 men wish to work at this wage.

What happens if the wage rises to $10 an hour? Here is where the greater sensitivity of women comes in. The female supply curve is relatively flat compared with that for men. Coming across from the $10 wage to the labor supply curves and down to the labor quantity axes, we find that the $5 wage increase draws 1200 more women into the labor force but no more men. In fact, the numbers fit those suggested by Kilingsworth because men are unresponsive to wages,

FIGURE 4.1
FEMALE LABOR SUPPLY.

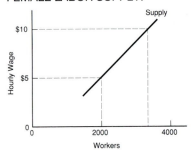

FIGURE 4.2
MALE LABOR SUPPLY.

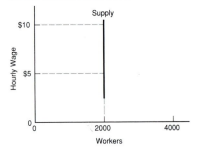

but a 100% increase in the wage leads to a 60% increase in the number of women entering the labor market.

[1]This literature largely ignores the potential effects of discrimination on the female labor supply.
Source: Mark Killingsworth, *Labor Supply,* Cambridge, England: Cambridge University Press, 1983; 185. (Note that most of the studies covered concern white men and white women.)

account would coax you into saving one-fifth of your income. Some people will save one-fifth of their income no matter what—they have a zero rate of time preference. Others will require an interest rate of 5%—they have a 5% rate of time preference.

Still others will require a 10% interest rate, while a few might require a 100% return before they would hand over one-fifth of their money to a bank.

What does the rate of time preference have to do with labor? It influences how much we work, how hard we work, and how much we save when we are young. Someone with a very low rate doesn't much care about the present, so he or she will take a very tough job with long hours and high wages to ensure a comfortable retirement in the future. Someone with a very high rate of time preference takes easy jobs with short hours and then spends the income from week to week, because the present is more important to them.

One of the most crucial roles that time preference plays is in the education decision. We focus on this issue next.

Human Capital

The neoclassical view of education was developed in large part by Gary Becker (1975). Becker won the Nobel Prize in economics in 1992 in part because of his work on education, but his research also is at the core of the neoclassical understanding of home production (examined in the next section) and discrimination (examined in the next chapter).

Before Becker's work, formal education was viewed by economists as consumption. The rich went off to elite colleges, where they learned about the finer things in life. Becker transformed this view by arguing that education is an investment.

Becker posited that if capitalists spend or invest money to receive a return, why not view education as a process with an investment that also yields a return. College is not free, and the opportunity cost often is quite high given that students could instead be earning money. The only reasonable neoclassical explanation for college is that it somehow enhances our ability to produce once we enter paid employment. We invest in *human capital* through schooling and later receive a return in higher wages.

Human capital: Improved productive capabilities due to investments in education

---

The notion of education as human capital, which largely was alien to students 20 or 30 years ago, now seems common. Just ask yourself whether you would be in college today if you did not expect to raise your earning power as a result. Or, looked at differently, ask whether you would be willing to take out a loan to pay for tuition if you did not expect to earn more than individuals who did not attend college.

Estimates suggest that human capital is critically important to our economy. Comparing the costs and returns of formal education in terms of higher wages to investments in physical capital, such as workplaces, tools, and machinery, suggests that human capital may account for more than half of all "capital" existing in the U.S. economy.[2]

---

[2]Figures in this paragraph and the next are from Ronald G. Ehrenberg and Robert S. Smith, *Modern Labor Economics,* 4th ed. New York: HarperCollins, 1991, Chapter 9.

Here is where the rate of time preference comes into play. The decision to "invest" in human capital is similar to the decision to save. Those with a low rate of time preference invest in education, and those with a high rate do not. Estimates of the returns from a college education (and there are many) suggest that the effective rate of return is between 5% and 15%. People with lower rates of time preference view college as a bargain; people with a higher rate prefer to go directly into the workforce.

Human capital is critical to the neoclassical understanding of discrimination. Suppose that some group chooses college attendance less frequently than others and earns less in the labor market. This outcome may simply be the product of a high rate of time preference rather than of discrimination. On the other hand, if the market for student loans is imperfect because banks worry about students defaulting, then college education will be constrained by parental income and wealth, which could allow past racial discrimination to affect present opportunities.

Human capital also feeds back into the question of labor supply. Individuals with high levels of education expect to earn a return, but they cannot if they do not work. Therefore, we can predict that individuals who acquire education plan to supply their labor later to the market.

Both the decision to supply labor and the education decision are complicated by the existence of another form of work—unpaid and at home.

Household Production

Following much debate in the late 1800s, the U.S. Bureau of the Census reached a decision that affects us to this day: women working at home are neither counted as employed nor as contributing to the economy.[3] While it is difficult to put a dollar figure on work done in the home, it is odd that two women working in their own homes would neither be counted as being employed nor as productive. By hiring each other to do the same work in each other's homes, both would suddenly be counted as employed and productive. What's the difference? According to Gary Becker's (1965) theory of household production, there is no meaningful difference. Parallel to his argument that college students might be engaged in a valuable activity, he argued that if women stay at home, there also must be an economic rationale. That rationale is that *household production* is as important as work done for a firm.

Household production: Unpaid work, as opposed to leisure, in the home

---

Becker's model starts with the observation that both work and leisure occur in the home, adding Adam Smith's assertion that the division of labor can improve economic efficiency. If one spouse cooks and the other cleans, each will become expert at that particular task. Additionally, a clear division of labor reduces the costs of coordinating work in the home; we need not begin each day by deciding who cooks

[3]See Nancy Folbre, "The Unproductive Housewife," *Signs,* Spring 1991.

and who cleans. These claims imply that families not only confront a choice between market work and leisure time but also one between using money or our own time at home to produce goods for consumption. If both spouses are employed, more money may be spent on child care, but if only one works for wages, the other can "produce" child care directly.

Looked at differently, Becker suggests that time and money are substitutes in the home. We can wash dishes by hand or save time at home by working for pay to buy an automatic dishwasher. Similarly, if you are at home a lot, you might learn to cook from scratch, but if you are working full-time, you might buy a microwave oven and stick to frozen dinners.

Few, if any, economists would quibble with the notion that a division of labor in the home can improve family welfare. Such a division, however, need not imply that either spouse will specialize in housework. To conclude that individuals will specialize, we must further posit that there exist economic advantages to working "full-time" in either paid employment or the home. Some evidence suggests that employers favor such specialization, on average paying 40% lower hourly wages for part-time as opposed to full-time workers.[4] Part of the reason for the large wage advantage accruing to full-timers may lie in the fixed costs of employing workers. Firms providing health, pension, or insurance benefits, or with expensive machinery and equipment, may find that these costs are the same regardless of how many hours a particular employee works. These costs can be spread over more hours as the employee's working time increases, thus giving a cost advantage to full-time employment.[5]

If someone is going to specialize in home production, who will it be? Most of us have a pretty good idea that the answer is "wives," but this begs the question of why it is women who are wives and specialize. While we consider discrimination later, there are other neoclassical explanations for why women tend to specialize in home production.

First, it may be that women have a greater preference than men for tasks that are performed at home. Victor Fuchs (1988) suggests as much by arguing that women in our society care more about children than men do.

Second, it may be that women have a comparative advantage over men in home production. Recall that comparative advantage means one party is relatively more productive at some task compared with another. Regarding work in the home, comparative advantage could imply that because of biology or socialization, women are better at most household production tasks, such as child care. Instead, or in addition, men may have a comparative advantage in paid employment.

It does not matter much in the labor market whether women simply prefer or exhibit a comparative advantage in home production, nor does it matter whether preferences or comparative advantage result from socialization or biology. What matters is that by the time people enter the labor market, it may be efficient for women

---

[4]Precise figures are $4.42 per hour for part-time compared with $7.43 for full-time. See Chris Tilly, "Short Hours, Short Shrift," in *New Policies for the Part-time and Contingent Workforce*. Virginia L. duRivage, ed. Armonk, NY: M.E. Sharpe, 1992.

[5]This argument implies that in gay or lesbian households, we would find a similar degree of specialization, with one person staying at home and the other going to work.

to specialize in home production and for men to take paid employment. Historical evidence suggests that a division very much like this has existed across many societies (Box 4.2).

To see why this pattern of specialization is efficient, imagine if we reversed traditional gender roles so that most men stayed at home and most women took paid employment. Each partner may receive lower utility in his or her new role, or total productivity may fall. In either case, the family would be worse off as a result. Of course, some couples may have different preferences or comparative advantages, but competitive markets do not stop them from choosing what is best for them (assuming there is no discrimination).

The sexual division of labor and Becker's theory of home production help to explain two important phenomena. First, a wave of women entered the U.S. labor force starting in the 1960s. Becker predicted this phenomenon by noting that as the price fell for purchased goods such as dishwashers, electric stoves, vacuum cleaners, and so on, people would increasingly move away from work at home toward work in the market. Purchased goods would be substituted for work in the home as the opportunity cost of taking paid employment fell.

Second, as noted earlier (Box 4.1), the law of supply seems to hold more for women than for men. This makes sense given that the opportunity cost of taking paid employment may be home production for many women but not for most men. In other words, women often may have a productive option outside of the labor market—

BOX 4.2

THE SEXUAL DIVISION OF LABOR ACROSS CULTURES

Have men and women everywhere always exhibited the same division of labor we see today? The answer is that for many tasks, the division of labor is remarkably stable across a host of societies historically.

Roy D'Andrade summarized a series of early studies on the matter and found that with some exceptions, many of the same jobs are dominated by either women or men in most societies. For example, in a study of subsistence activities in 224 societies, men performed the following tasks, either always or usually, in at least 90% of the societies: pursuit of sea mammals, hunting, trapping small animals, herding, metalworking, weapon-making, boat-building, manufacture of musical instruments, work in wood and bark, work in stone, and work in bone, horn, or shell. Women dominated activities to a similar extent in the cases of: grinding grain, carrying water, cooking, preserving meat or fish, and gathering herbs, roots, or seeds.

Whether because of physical differences, preferences, comparative advantage, or discrimination, men and women have historically performed different tasks. However, this historical division does not necessarily imply that it will continue forever. For example, if subsistence societies differentiate in terms of physical attributes, we might expect this division to break down as we move toward less physically strenuous white-collar occupations in the workplace.

Source: Roy G. D'Andrade, "Sex Differences and Cultural Institutions," in *The Development of Sex Differences.* Eleanor E. Maccoby, ed. Stanford, CA: Stanford University Press, 1966.

home production—that may not be readily available to men and so be readier to enter or exit the labor force as wages rise and fall.

This last argument can help to explain why women entered the labor force in the post–World War II period. Women's wages rose (see Chapter 2), thereby driving up the opportunity cost of home production and motivating women to seek paid employment. Note also that this argument has nothing to do with discrimination. Indeed, the argument suggests that like the consumer who is better off because of a wide range of substitutes in the market, women may be *better off* than men because women can substitute home production for work through the labor market.

EXPLAINING WAGE DIFFERENCES

Having looked at supply and demand, human capital, and home production, we now can think about wage differences that are generated by competitive markets.

Firm-specific and General Human Capital

Earlier, we discussed education as a human capital investment. Gary Becker (1975) labelled this *general human capital.* By "general," Becker meant that it was transportable, so it could be taken from one job to another or one firm to another. A college education fits the notion of general human capital and is closely related to earnings differences in the United States.

General human capital: Investments that make a person more productive at many jobs or firms

---

Becker argued that human capital can take on another form, that of *firm-specific human capital.* These are skills that usually are acquired during the early stages of employment. Such skills also are specific to the firm—knowing who to contact in case of foul-ups or emergencies, how particular machines work, how to operate within a particular bureaucracy, and where the lunch room and restrooms are located. For example, if you take a job managing a factory, you would have to get to know everyone, learn something about the machines, the accounting system, how wages and personnel decisions are made, who can decide on new investments, what to do with customer complaints, and so on. Much of this knowledge could be used in another factory owned by another firm, but much also could not. Other companies are likely to have different people, machines, accounting systems, and so on. So, as you acquire human capital as a manager, much of it is firm-specific.

Why should we care about general as opposed to firm-specific human capital? Because their implications for training and wages are quite different. General human capital typically is paid for by the employee. If you want a college degree, you apply to a college, do the work, and pay the tuition. In turn, you receive higher wages as a reward for your investment. This is not true with firm-specific human capital. If you pay for it, the firm knows that it is worthless elsewhere and so need not reward your higher productivity with higher wages. It may represent a coup to get a major proposal through a firm's bureaucratic red tape, but you may not be able to take that skill elsewhere.

Firm-specific human capital: Investments that make a person more productive at one particular firm only

---

Becker resolved these issues by arguing that *workers* choose to invest in general human capital and are rewarded by the market, but that *firms and workers* split the costs of firm-specific human capital. The reason for the split is that the only way firm-specific capital pays off is when the worker remains with the firm for a long period of time. If both the worker and the firm pay for and benefit from the initial investment, both have a strong incentive to maintain the relationship.

An implication of this argument is that the firm can simply take the most qualified applicant if general human capital is important. With firm-specific human capital, however, managers need someone who is qualified and likely to stay with the firm for many years.

Who is likely to stay with the firm over the long haul? One conclusion from the theory of home production is that women may have more productive opportunities than men outside the labor market and be more ready to leave the firm if wages fall. Therefore, employers may not provide as much firm-specific human capital to women as to men. Women then will earn less, because they are less productive. This is an example of "statistical discrimination," which we explain in the following chapter. Note also that as women's commitment to paid employment has increased in recent decades, we would expect employers to respond by providing greater amounts of firm-specific training to women.

As with general human capital, we may find differences across groups in terms of firm-specific human capital. The example here suggests that women may receive lesser investments because of a lesser commitment to paid employment. This same argument could be extended to different cultures or races if they too diverge in their commitment to the firm, which is a point that we take up later in this chapter.

Compensating Differences and Hedonic Wages

Neoclassical economists believe that hard work and sacrifice generally will be rewarded through the mechanism of *compensating differences*. If the firm sets wages equal to the marginal revenue product, then people who work harder should receive higher wages. The difference that is attributable to hard work is called a compensating difference.

Compensating differences: Higher wages for jobs that are difficult, dirty, disgusting, or dangerous

---

Compensating differences may apply to many characteristics beyond whether an employee works hard. If there are jobs that most people find repulsive, such as being a coroner or working in a meat-packing factory, the supply of labor will be low for those jobs and a compensating difference paid to attract people into the workplace. Similarly, jobs requiring trust, attention to detail, or that are boring should pay a compensating difference. This same argument applies to dangerous jobs as well. Indeed, estimates suggest that at a dangerous workplace with 1000 employees, the wage bill could be reduced by between $35,000 and $500,000 per year by a safety program that saved (on average) one life every 10 years.[6] A firm tolerating such dangerous conditions may pay a compensating difference to do so.

There is a problem with compensating differences. Many occupations where we would expect to find compensating differences are associated with low pay. Few of us can imagine employment more stressful than working the counter of a fast-food restaurant at rush hour, yet these jobs pay close to the legal minimum. Nor are there many jobs dirtier than picking up garbage, yet these jobs also are not known for high wages. Do these cases imply that the theory is wrong? Neoclassical economists have responded to this problem by modifying the theory of compensating differences with the concept of *hedonic wages* (Rosen, 1974).[7]

Hedonic wages: Wages that reflect the preferences of a particular worker in a job and not those of the general public

---

The idea of compensating differences starts from the notion that some jobs are simply bad or good. Hedonic wage theory suggests that we should look at the preferences of workers in the actual occupation. If some people do not mind picking up garbage (perhaps their sense of smell is poor), then a compensating difference will not be required to coax enough workers into this job. Similarly, some people might find that the stress of rush hour at a fast-food restaurant alleviates boredom. Therefore, as long as enough people can be located who have a relatively low distaste for such characteristics, compensating differences also will be relatively low.

At heart, hedonic wage theory is about the advantages of the division of labor. Part of the magic of the market is dividing tasks to improve productivity, but another part is that markets improve efficiency by matching individuals to the particular jobs they find most inviting or least onerous. Not surprisingly, when it is suggested that some jobs are underpaid because of discrimination, some neoclassical economists respond that because of hedonic wages, jobs cannot be compared; wages reflect the preferences of people who hold those jobs and not the likes and dislikes of the general populace.

---

[6]Figures from Ronald G. Ehrenberg and Robert S. Smith [1991, op. cit.], p. 276.
[7]*Hedonic* is defined as "pertaining to pleasure," or "of or related to hedonism or hedonists" [*Webster's New Twentieth Century Dictionary,* Unabridged 2nd ed. New York: Simon & Schuster, 1979].

Inheritance

Some people are born with a silver spoon in their mouth. If you were a daughter of the Sultan of Brunei, your labor market opportunities likely will be improved by your father's holdings of $25 billion.[8] You could afford the best schools, the most extensive job search, and if all else failed, simply start your own business. Few neoclassical economists believe that such differences are fair, but many believe they are efficient. If Michael Jordan became one of the most successful basketball players of all time because of biology or social inheritance, we might say this is unfair, but most of us would not respond by watching less talented players or by calling for Michael Jordan to take a pay cut. As Thomas Sowell argues,

> there is no more individual merit in having received a windfall gain in the form of brain cells rather than in the form of encyclopedias or private schooling. Each individual is born into a world he never made, with a brain he never made . . . [H]is value to society is the same, whether that value originated inside his head, or inside his home or school, or among his companions. [Sowell, 1983; 145]

While inherited wealth, culture, and ability make a great deal of difference regarding earnings potential, it is the market that motivates people to use those advantages in a productive fashion. The magic of the market prevents us from having a society that produces shoddy goods. That magic may result in wage differences that relate to either biology or social inheritance but still are efficient.

Finally, a few studies have been performed concerning the effects of inheritance. One shows that around half of the positive or negative economic effects of inheritance disappear in the next generation.[9] This is consistent with the notion that inheritance is far from the most important determinant of wage differences, leaving a broad scope for individual choice and initiative regarding how much we will earn.

UNEMPLOYMENT

There are reasons for wage differences other than those outlined earlier. These have to do with disequilibrium and the related phenomenon of unemployment. Human capital, home production, and hedonic wages all are facets of how wage differences emerge in equilibrium. Now, we turn to wage differences that largely are byproducts of the economy moving toward equilibrium (but not quite getting there). There are three major forms of unemployment in neoclassical economics: structural, frictional, and seasonal. We take these up in order, link them to wage differences, then look at the Keynesian challenge.

Structural Unemployment

Structural unemployment is caused by changes in the economy that make some jobs obsolete. These changes can stem from various sources: new technologies may re-

---

[8]See "The Billionaires," *Fortune*, September 11, 1989.
[9]See W. Stanley Siebert, "Inequality of Opportunity," in *Microeconomic Problems in Labour Economics: New Approaches.* Robert Drago and Richard Perlman, eds. London: Wheatsheaf, 1989.

duce the need for certain types of jobs, consumers may decide they no longer wish to purchase certain types of goods, firms may relocate production to low-tax or low-wage areas, or a new product with different production techniques may push aside old products. For example, a skilled typist could earn good money almost anywhere during the 1960s; in the 1990s, almost anyone can use a word processor (with a spell-checker) to accomplish the same results. When consumers decided they wanted more small, fuel-efficient cars and fewer gas-guzzlers in the 1970s and 1980s, tens of thousands of U.S. auto workers who produced the gas-guzzlers found themselves out of work while Japanese and German auto producers thrived. When compact discs came into the recording industry, producers of players for phonograph records found themselves out on the streets in a few short years.

Structural unemployment: Job loss resulting from changes in technology, consumer desires, or product innovation

---

Structural unemployment is painful but efficient. The pain felt by the thousands of auto and steel workers who lost their jobs in the 1980s is undeniable, so much so that the government provided extended unemployment benefits for many of them. On the other hand, any attempt to stem structural employment would mean holding on to inefficient technologies, producing goods that consumers have no interest in purchasing, and denying consumers access to new and better products. The government could have stopped consumers from switching to small, imported autos in the 1980s—and did through the import quotas discussed in Chapter 3. However, such policies were very costly and inefficient, slowing the development of small, fuel-efficient cars by U.S. auto makers.

Frictional Unemployment

Frictional unemployment stems from the fact that it takes time and money for firms to identify high-quality workers and for workers to find where they are most productive. Workers have an incentive to search for the job where their marginal revenue product is highest, because then their wages also will be highest. Firms have an incentive to identify potential employees with the highest marginal revenue product. Such searching by firms and workers is costly for society, because job searchers are not producing goods and they are using scarce economic resources in their search for new jobs. If a worker wants to quit a job and wait a few months before looking for another, this creates frictional unemployment (the firm searching for a replacement and the worker eventually for a new job), but this is efficient as both the worker and the firm are given the freedom to make these choices.

Frictional unemployment: Lack of employment caused by firms seeking high-quality workers and workers searching for high wages

---

Frictional unemployment sounds relatively painless in theory; in practice, it often is every bit as horrible as structural unemployment. Looking for work can be frustrating, especially when firms do not hire the first applicant because they too are searching. Further, once a job is taken, the firm may discover that it hired the wrong person, or the employee that the job was a mistake; in either case, the new job is quickly gone. Even a successful job search may conclude with a family moving from one state or nation to another, so the issue of home production is linked to frictional unemployment. Indeed, one study shows that among husband–wife pairs who switch states, the man's earnings rise by an average of $4254 and the woman's fall by $1716.[10] Because overall family income rises in this process, the move may be efficient, but it is not painless for the women involved.

Like structural unemployment, frictional unemployment is efficient—unless the government intervenes. Studies show that by providing unemployment insurance and training programs for the unemployed, the U.S. government has inefficiently lengthened the amount of time that individuals spend looking for work. There is less reason to take the first available job if the government will pay you to keep on looking.[11] This does not mean that unemployment insurance should be abolished, because it alleviates much real pain and suffering. However, there are costs for maintaining the system.

Seasonal Unemployment

Seasonal unemployment is exactly what it sounds like. Retail clerks can find virtually round-the-clock employment during the Christmas shopping season, as can peach pickers during the early summer in the southern United States. The rest of the year, some of the retail clerks and the agricultural workforce will be unemployed. Knowing they will be unemployed so much of the year, why would anyone take a seasonal job? The neoclassical answer is that individuals selecting this type of employment may value their leisure very highly. For example, a campground worker in the Catskills who winters in Florida might not complain too loudly about a low wage at the campground, or a worker with children in primary school might desire a job such as cafeteria worker, school teacher, or crossing guard, with work being scheduled around school attendance. Alternatively, the job might pay a compensating difference to make up for the lack of work during part of the year. This brings us back to the issue of wages.

Seasonal unemployment: Lack of certain types of jobs at predictable times of year

---

Linking Unemployment and Wages

Neoclassical economists view the three types of unemployment just discussed as efficient although painful. Unemployment of these types also can be viewed as fair—

---

[10]See Solomon W. Polachek and Francis W. Horvath, "A Life-Cycle Approach to Migration," in *Research in Labor Economics*. Ronald Ehrenberg, ed. Greenwich, CT: JAI Press, 1977.

[11]See Ronald G. Ehrenberg and Ronald L. Oaxaca, "Unemployment Insurance, Duration of Unemployment and Subsequent Wage Gains," *American Economic Review*, Vol. 66, December 1976.

in the sense that it may be random. No one knows who is going to lose his or her job, so we all take our chances. If we all buy lottery tickets, we view it as fair that one person wins, and this same argument can be applied to unemployment.

Unemployment also may be fair in a deeper sense—if the market pays us extra for being unemployed. Obviously, you do not receive a wage increase while you are out of a job, but what about after or before unemployment? In the case of frictional unemployment, the entire reason that workers search for jobs is to improve their wages, and firms who find the most productive workers available can afford to pay higher wages. In the case of seasonal unemployment, as suggested earlier, workers may receive a compensating difference as the job is temporary. Similarly, to the extent that structural unemployment is predictable, workers also should receive a compensating difference. For example, anyone taking a job at a U.S. automobile factory producing large cars during the 1980s could see the writing on the wall: the jobs were largely temporary. If more secure employment was desired, it had to be sought outside the auto industry.

THE KEYNESIAN CHALLENGE

While the three main types of unemployment as analyzed by neoclassical economists are efficient, and even fair to a limited extent, other neoclassical economists, called *Keynesians,* believe that some unemployment is both inefficient and unfair. With Keynesian unemployment, the government may need to intervene.

Keynesians such as Alan Blinder (1987) believe that people often experience *involuntary unemployment,* which means that people are willing but unable to find jobs at the market wage.[12] Other neoclassical economists see involuntary unemployment as an oxymoron. After all, how can workers claim they cannot find a job when all they have to do is to accept a lower wage, after which they will find plenty of work?

Involuntary or Keynesian unemployment: A lack of jobs because sales are down across the economy

---

Keynes and his followers believed that even if workers were willing to take wage cuts, jobs still might be unavailable. For example, suppose that consumers slow down their purchases, perhaps because they are worried about a recession. Producers see declining sales and lay off workers, and now we begin a process of *positive feedback.* With fewer people working, sales fall yet again. People may become fearful and, even if they have jobs, cut spending just in case they become unemployed. This leads to still more unemployment and lower spending; one bad event in the economy causes more.

Positive feedback: Where an adverse economic event causes more adverse events, or beneficial events cause more beneficial events

---

[12]Structural, frictional, and seasonal unemployment usually are not viewed as being involuntary in this sense.

What about wage cuts? According to Keynes, even if workers try to generate more demand for their labor by taking wage cuts, this may not work. Following a wage cut, workers have less money to spend, so sales may fall yet again. Keynesian unemployment with positive feedback effects can help to explain business cycles, where a small upward (or downward) movement in the economy leads to a larger upward (or downward) movement, so when economists discuss "cyclical" unemployment, they often mean Keynesian unemployment.

Because Keynesians see the economy as generating involuntary unemployment through positive feedback, they also see a role for an activist government in curbing unemployment. The problem of involuntary unemployment emerges from a lack of sales, and the government can increase sales by either buying more or taxing less.

Other neoclassical economists believe that market economies generate *negative feedback*. If unemployment occurs, the laws of supply and demand will work to return us to equilibrium, and in equilibrium, everyone who wants a job can find one. In other words, an adverse event such as increased unemployment sets in motion a process (*ie,* wage cuts) that solves the problem by increasing employment opportunities.

Negative feedback: Where an adverse or beneficial economic event is corrected by the economy to return us to equilibrium

---

THE FAIRNESS OF INEQUALITY: WAGE DIFFERENCES AMONG GROUPS

This chapter began by asking why firms hire people and people work for firms. Firms hire to make a profit, and they employ and pay people precisely according to their marginal revenue product. When people decide to seek a job, they make a labor–leisure trade-off, with people who value leisure less working more than those who value leisure more.

Then, we confronted a series of explanations for why some people make more money than others. First is the issue of time preference and general human capital. People who value the future have a low rate of time preference and are willing to sacrifice when they are young, by staying in high school or shelling out for college, so they are more productive and earn more later in life. Specialization in household production also may affect wages, because those who specialize are less skilled at paid employment. Nonetheless, such specialization is rational and efficient, perhaps more for women than for men, even if women's earnings suffer as a result. Other explanations for wage differences include firm-specific human capital, where the firm invests in a worker's skills and both the firm and worker benefit later. Firms also may pay higher wages in the form of compensating differences for jobs that are difficult, dangerous, or otherwise undesirable. Such differences may be small, however, because of hedonic wages: if enough people can be found who do not object to the seemingly undesirable conditions, then wages need not be higher than those for other jobs. Inheritance, whether in the form of money, biology, or socialization, may give some people an advantage when it comes to wages as well.

Finally, we examined unemployment. Some unemployment—frictional—leads to higher wages as people search for better jobs and firms search for better workers. Other types—structural and seasonal—also may be related to higher wages (when people work), which compensate them for the higher risk of losing their jobs and income. Keynesian economists challenge these arguments by suggesting that unemployment often is involuntary.

With this knowledge in hand, we consider the question of why some groups experience systematic differences in wages and employment even if there is no discrimination. Much of the earlier discussion regarding household production can help to explain such differences between men and women. If women have a comparative advantage or simply prefer household production relative to men, then we should not be surprised if women earn less than men. Part of this difference may result from women specializing in "training" that is less valuable in the labor market than in the home, another part may result from women's greater willingness to leave the workforce when wages fall, and yet another may result from women shunning higher education because it is not as valuable in the home as in the labor market.

Standard models of human capital suggest that over half the difference between the wages that men and women receive can be accounted for by educational achievement and experience on the job. Thus, if women wished to earn the same as men, around half the current difference could be wiped out if women switched their educational patterns to mimic those of men and did not interrupt their careers for childbirth. Recent evidence suggests this change is already occurring. While women were less than two-thirds as likely as men to attain a bachelor's degree as of 1960, women were more likely than men to achieve the degree by the end of the 1980s (Goldin, 1990). This change is reflected in the overall labor force, where the proportion of women with 4 years of college or more rose from 11.2% in 1970 to 25% in 1991, while the parallel male figures increased from 15.7% to 28.2% over that same period.[13]

The education gap between men and women is closing, so neoclassical economists would expect wage and employment differences to be disappearing as well. Evidence for this claim can be found by the drop in the male/female wage gap: men's median weekly earnings were 50% higher than those for women in 1983 but only 35% more in 1991. By historical standards, this is a rapid decline in inequality. Not only could women who worked expect to earn more, but the proportion of women in the labor force rose as well, from 49% in 1970 to 69.3% in 1991. Over that same period, the proportion of men in the labor force fell slightly, from 93.5% to 88.9%. In his model of household production, Gary Becker (1965) forecast precisely this sort of change: it became relatively cheaper to substitute store-bought goods for those produced in the home, so women went to work and rationally started acquiring the types of education that were rewarded by higher wages.

The discussion thus far has not addressed racial or ethnic divergence in wages, but it can. If a group of immigrants arrives in the United States, will they become

---

[13]See U.S. Bureau of the Census, *Statistical Abstract of the U.S.: 1992*, 112th ed., Washington, DC, 1992, for these figures and those reported in the next two paragraphs.

rich or poor? Does group membership tell us how they will perform economically as individuals? The neoclassical answer is that if group membership matters, it is at least partly attributable to culture and the economy from which the group derives. Indeed, to the extent that the group's culture emphasizes education, hard work, and savings, we would predict that the group would become wealthy precisely because the market is operating in a fair and efficient fashion.

The analogous story for black as opposed to white Americans is less heartening. In terms of education for whites, the proportion of labor force participants with 4 years of college or more rose from 14.8% in 1970 to 27.5% in 1991, but comparable figures for blacks show an increase from 8.3% to only 16% over that same period. Elevated educational levels for both groups were related to increases in labor force participation, which rose from 70.1% to 79.5% for whites but from 72% to only 75% for blacks. Labor force participation increased solely because of the dramatic shift of women from housework into wage work; participation rates for men actually fell, particularly for black men in what should be their prime-earning years. Most troubling, median weekly earnings for white and black workers showed a disturbing trend: whites earned 22% more than blacks in 1983 but 28% more by 1991.

Neoclassical economists focus on two major reasons for the very distinct trends affecting gender and race (both unrelated to discrimination). First, during the 1980s, the returns to education increased dramatically in the United States. No one really knows whether increasing returns to education have resulted from changes in the supply of college-educated workers, the disappearance of high-wage factory jobs, changes in technology, or other causes, but the facts are clear. For 25- to 34-year-old males, median real earnings for those holding a high school diploma fell by 12% between 1979 and 1987, while earnings for college graduates rose by 8% (Levy and Murnane, 1992). Because the educational attainment of women approached that for men while that of blacks remained far below that of whites, it is not surprising that the earnings gap by gender tended to close over the period while that by race increased.[14] Second, as women became more likely to work, their commitment to staying at work and, hence, their experience on the job increased as well. For example, the percentage of women working part-time actually declined between 1969 and 1988 (Tilly, 1992). If gender and racial differences in earnings and employment are caused in large part by differences in human capital, which in turn are related to formal education and experience on the job, then discrimination in the labor market cannot necessarily be blamed for these differences.

A third factor that also suggests the distinct labor market experiences for gender and race groups are not the result of discrimination concerns learning by these groups over time. For example, differences in education levels, occupations, and experience by group may appear to reflect differences in rates of time preference (as people with a high rate of time preference ultimately earn less because they invest less when they are young), which might in fact represent a response to historical and external con-

---

[14]Discrimination could play a role here if black Americans believe education is only rewarded if you are white. In other words, positive feedback effects could occur such that discrimination causes low wages and leads people to acquire less education, thus reducing wages even further.

ditions. If women specialize in homework, their absence from business courses might have nothing to do with time preference, instead signalling a rational response to the fact that knowledge of high finance does not pay off in the world of child-rearing. Similarly, individuals living in a society with an average life expectancy of 28 years usually would not live long enough to experience high earnings from obtaining a PhD. To the extent that immigrants carry the values from such societies into a developed economy, or that women who will be entering the labor market are socialized by mothers who did not, these groups may appear to be more present-oriented than males of the historically dominant ethnic group in the economy. Therefore, these groups will earn less. Nonetheless, over time, they will discover the value and returns for human capital. For immigrants to the United States, and women who have entered the U.S. workforce during the last several decades, Thomas Sowell (1983) and Claudia Goldin (1990), respectively, provide some evidence that over time, these groups do develop such expectations, and that their education and earnings improve accordingly.

Many neoclassical economists believe the labor market functions as an efficient and impartial mechanism for motivating individuals to contribute productively to the economy and to receive commensurate rewards. To the extent that this is true, the government should engage in laissez-faire policies with respect to both race and gender, permitting the market to work its magic. Other neoclassical economists, and probably a majority, believe that markets sometimes fail because of imperfect competition, externalities, and public goods. By extension, many of these economists believe that discrimination can exert real effects and, in some cases, persist in providing some groups with reduced economic opportunities. We analyze this possibility in the next chapter.

DISCUSSION QUESTIONS

1 Why is the demand for labor called a "derived demand"? Can you imagine a case where labor demand is *not* derived?

2 What are the opportunity costs for you to hold a full-time job (whether you already do or do not hold such a job)? What sorts of labor–leisure choices do you make on a day-to-day, week-to-week, or year-to-year basis?

3 What does it mean to say that men often "break the law of supply" in the labor market? Why would they not follow the law of supply?

4 Does the idea of a "rate of time preference" imply that individuals who choose to attend college usually will save more of their earnings? Does it imply they will save less?

5 What sorts of policies would a firm need to implement if it wished to reduce the extent to which women specialize in home production?

6 When families move from one city or state to another, does the theory of home production help us to predict how men's and women's wages are likely to change in the process?

7 Can you identify jobs where general human capital is important? Where firm-specific human capital is important?

8 Janitors perform many dirty and boring tasks. Should they be paid a compensating difference for these adverse conditions? Why might a neoclassical economist argue that no compensating difference should be paid?

9 If you have known someone who was unemployed for a time, do you think he or she was unemployed for structural, frictional, seasonal, or Keynesian reasons?

SUGGESTED READINGS

Becker, Gary. 1965. "A Theory of the Allocation of Time." *Economic Journal* 75, September.

Becker, Gary. 1975. *Human Capital,* 2nd ed. New York: Columbia University Press.

Blinder, Alan. 1987. *Hard Heads, Soft Hearts.* Reading, MA: Addison-Wesley.

Fuchs, Victor. 1988. *Women's Quest for Economic Equality.* Cambridge, MA: Harvard University Press.

Goldin, Claudia. 1990. *Understanding the Gender Gap.* New York: Oxford University Press.

Levy, Frank and Richard J. Murnane. 1992. "U.S. Earnings Levels and Earnings Inequality: A Review of Recent Trends and Proposed Explanations." *Journal of Economic Literature* 30, September.

Rosen, Sherwin. 1974. "Hedonic Prices and Implicit Markets." *Journal of Political Economy* 82, January–February.

Sowell, Thomas. 1983. *The Economics and Politics of Race.* New York: Quill.

5

DISCRIMINATION IN THE NEOCLASSICAL VIEW

INTRODUCTION: DIFFERENCE AND DISCRIMINATION

A white man works a fast-food restaurant that is part of a large national chain with standardized pricing, cooking machinery and methods, and standardized portions. This employee gives extra portions to white customers and the expected portion to black customers. Is this discrimination? Clearly, the answer is "yes."

This small story can be used to illustrate the neoclassical understanding of *discrimination*. The employee gave extra portions to whites, because he was averse to the skin color of the black customers. It didn't matter whether black customers were nicer, smarter, more honest, or more hard-working than the average white person; all that mattered was their skin color.

Discrimination: Adverse treatment of an individual based on group membership instead of productivity

---

Looking below the surface, a key that helps to unlock the neoclassical model of discrimination is the possibility that *both* parties suffer from the discriminatory act. Black customers get short-changed relative to whites, and the white employee may "pay" for his discrimination: if the boss finds out about the extra portions for whites, the employee likely will be fired.

Like all illustrative stories, this one is incomplete, because discrimination can have major impacts on the job, promotion opportunities, available housing, incomes, education, and health of those who are subject to it. Discrimination is inequitable. That is the bad news. The good news is that the story also suggests a way in which the ill effects of discrimination may be wiped out: even if the boss doesn't care about discrim-

85

ination, he or she can make more money by firing the discriminating employee and replacing him with someone who does not discriminate and hand out extra food for free.[1]

Let us be more specific about the meaning of discrimination for neoclassical economists. Discrimination occurs when the economic opportunities of some well-defined group are limited by virtue of their group membership rather than their potential or actual economic contributions. If "ascriptive" or unimportant characteristics of a group affect their position in the economy, discrimination may be the culprit.

As with household production and human capital, Gary Becker (1957) was at the forefront of explaining discrimination from the neoclassical perspective. Considering a story like the one described here, his logic suggests that we seek an explanation for such behavior through rational individuals maximizing their utility or, stated more simply, exercising their preferences. Those with preferences that generate discrimination must have a "taste for discrimination," and if you have a taste for any good (or here, "bad"), this should show up in a "willingness to pay."

Once discriminatory tastes are admitted, they enter the market in much the same way as any other taste. The market allows each of us to have unique tastes and to act on those tastes. In the neoclassical market economy—one that is populated by individual self-satisfiers—any individual consumer, worker, or business owner can make economic decisions based on discrimination. Anyone can choose products or services based on race, gender, ethnicity, religion, or sexual orientation, because the market permits them to do so. If people would benefit from ending discriminatory behavior, they would rationally do so.

Now we confront a puzzle. If markets allow each of us the freedom to discriminate at will, how can it be that competitive markets will stamp out the adverse effects of discrimination? While much of this chapter is devoted to putting this puzzle together, a hint at the solution lies in the fact that discrimination can occur in labor markets. As argued in Chapter 4, labor markets are unlike others, so tastes for discrimination within labor market settings may have unexpected effects.

We begin our analysis of the neoclassical model by explaining the results of labor market discrimination. Basically, discrimination in labor markets is inefficient and inequitable, and these problems show up in three ways: unequal wages, unequal employment opportunities, and occupational crowding. Then, we introduce neoclassical models of discrimination. Three of the models are based on tastes for discrimination held by consumers, employers, or employees; the other model concerns statistical discrimination. With these models in hand, we can solve the puzzle of how markets permit discrimination yet ameliorate its adverse effects. Further, if the "magic of the market" works to eliminate the effects of discrimination, the economy gains in terms of *both* efficiency and equity. We then examine measured discrimination, particularly regarding wages. Because studies almost universally find discrimination affecting wages and employment for women and minorities, we are left with another question: if competitive markets can solve the problems of discrimi-

---

[1]Notice the story still works if the employee gives white customers the standard portion and gives short portions to black customers. The latter are still short-changed, and the employee could be fired for driving away paying (black) customers.

nation, why hasn't it happened yet? We outline a variety of answers, then consider government policies to deal with discrimination.

The Inefficiency of Discrimination

In trying to understand the neoclassical approach to discrimination, it is important to separate market discrimination from differences in tastes, abilities, and effort. Neoclassical economics celebrates individual differences and diversity. It is precisely because we all have such different tastes and preferences that there is so much variety in consumer goods and occupations. Indeed, markets thrive in response to different tastes and preferences as producers strive to identify products that are desired by consumers and low-cost methods to produce those goods and simultaneously search for employment and personnel policies that will attract talented people.[2] Discrimination is a different kettle of fish altogether. Like most people, neoclassical economists condemn discriminatory practices that affect people on the basis of their gender, race, ethnicity, or religious background. Moreover, if discrimination exists in markets, this is an economic as well as a moral problem. Discrimination results in both inequity, such that opportunities and outcomes are unfair, and inefficiency, such that at least one person can be made better off without making anyone else worse off. With discrimination, there may be no trade-off between equity and efficiency, because both will improve if the effects of discrimination are eliminated.

The inequality of discrimination is obvious in unequal pay and unequal employment opportunities, but inefficiency is not so obvious. The inefficiency is seen most clearly when capable people are not allowed to hold certain jobs because of discrimination. Allow us to spin the following tale: imagine you are a talented fashion designer—one who can create the most beautiful and intricate gowns in the world. Because of discrimination, however, clothing manufacturers refuse to hire you or to purchase your designs. To support yourself and your family, you resort to working as a waiter. Unfortunately, you are a bad waiter, often forgetting orders and spilling drinks on customers; as a result, you receive virtually no tips. The reason this outcome is inefficient is that you suffer direct wage losses and society is robbed of your talents as a fashion designer, thus enjoying less total output than if you had been a fashion designer. *Both* you and those who purchase high-fashion clothing would be better off if discrimination were eliminated.[3]

Inefficiency of discrimination: Income for those experiencing discrimination is lower and commodities are more costly

---

Although discrimination is inefficient, ridding our economy of it is difficult. The problem is that labor markets generate substantial inequality in wages and em-

---

[2]Of course, some markets thrive on mass production, which provides similar goods to a large number of people (*eg,* McDonald's hamburgers). In these cases, technology may dictate similar products to achieve low costs. Even here, however, the market still permits diversity (*eg,* gourmet or vegetarian burgers), but at a price.

[3]We ignored the person who got "your" job as a fashion designer because of discrimination. Would that person be better off if discrimination were eliminated? Not directly, but in principle, the higher output resulting from eliminating discrimination could be redistributed so that, in fact, everyone would be better off afterward.

ployment which is efficient (see Chapter 4). In the neoclassical view, inequality generated by competitive markets is desirable, because it serves as a powerful motivator—providing incentives to save, invest, work, and locate the job in which you are most productive. These sources of inequality, which are efficient because they motivate people, will be fused in the real world with inequality which is inefficient because of discrimination. As it is so difficult to pull apart the efficient and inefficient sources of inequality, attempts to alleviate labor market discrimination might even reduce efficiency. Attempts to reduce or eliminate labor market discrimination may simply return us to the "trade-off" between equity and efficiency (see Chapter 3). We can make the economy more equal or more efficient, but not both.

For example, suppose that the government required "blind" hiring of all new employees and did not allow employers to know the name, age, work experience, education, or anything else about prospective employees. This would stop inefficient hiring discrimination and make the economy more equitable, but it would create new inefficiencies—the most qualified and productive employees often would be missed. In actual economies, it may be difficult to end inefficient discrimination without creating new inefficiencies.

Three Outcomes from Discrimination

Inefficiency because of discrimination in labor markets can take three forms: lower wages for some types of workers as opposed to others performing identical tasks, higher unemployment or underemployment rates for groups with similar characteristics, and job segregation or crowding of a group into a few jobs that pay less than other, comparable jobs.

Three results of discrimination: Lower wages, un- or underemployment, and occupational crowding

---

For an example of wage discrimination, return to our fashion designer. Suppose that a clothing manufacturer recognizes the value of your work and decides to hire you as a designer. Because your only other option is waiting on tables, the employer could offer you lower wages than those of other designers performing the same work. You have little choice other than to take the job at low pay. Further, the employer would not be maximizing profits if he or she paid you the going wage. You receive a lower wage because of discrimination.

The fashion designer might instead (or additionally) suffer from unemployment or *underemployment*. If no employer will hire you, you could end up without any job—you're unemployed. A more likely scenario, however, and the one depicted earlier, finds you taking a job for which you are less qualified—waiting tables—in which case you are underemployed. A different form of underemployment would occur if you cannot find full-time employment as a fashion designer and so either accept a part-time designer job or act as a part-time designer in your home. Whether you are unemployed or underemployed, you suffer, and consumers do too.

Underemployment: When a person is employed in a job where her or his abilities, skills, or preferred working hours are not fully used

---

A third outcome from discrimination is job segregation and *occupational crowding,* which is an idea developed by Barbara Bergmann (1974).[4] There is nothing inherently wrong with job segregation *per se.* If men wish to work with other men and women with other women, this is not necessarily a problem. Men and women may voluntarily "crowd" into different types of jobs and workplaces. What Bergmann noted, however, was that crowding may be involuntary and inefficient—discrimination may be at work. What if women or minorities are restricted to a few occupations because of a lack of promotion opportunities and employment discrimination in others? The supply of women or minorities to these few occupations then rises, and the wage must necessarily fall as we move down along the demand curve in response (recall from Chapter 3 that anytime supply increases, the equilibrium price will fall). This implies that for equally qualified workers, workers in crowded occupations will receive lower pay than those in other types of jobs. For example, if becoming a fashion designer and a skilled machinist require the same amount of training and effort, but members of your group are limited to a few occupations (*eg,* being a designer, waiter, or secretary), you will experience lower wages as a fashion designer than as a skilled machinist.

Occupational crowding: When a group is limited to a few occupations and so receives low wages

---

The key insight of Bergmann's crowding model is that voluntary segregation by gender or race does not explain wage differences between groups. After all, if you could change occupations and, given the same amount of human capital, make more money, wouldn't you try? Only discrimination can explain why women and minorities are limited to a few occupations and receive lower wages than others as a result. Stated differently, is it accidental that groups who are crowded into a few occupations today were legally prohibited from voting in the 1789 election of George Washington for president? Bergmann suggests that such crowding is not voluntary, but instead results from past and present discrimination.

Now that we have the outcomes from discrimination, let's go back to the causes.

MODELS OF DISCRIMINATION BASED ON PREJUDICE: CONSUMERS, EMPLOYERS, AND EMPLOYEES

Discrimination as an economic topic was introduced most forcefully into the neoclassical realm by Gary Becker in his 1957 work, *The Economics of Discrimination.* Using the central building block of neoclassical theory—self-interested, individual

---

[4]Earlier, Gary Becker suggested the possibility that discrimination might affect some occupations more than others, but Bergmann usually is credited with developing this idea.

behavior—Becker showed that different labor market outcomes based on prejudice against a group could fit into the neoclassical model of utility maximization. He argued that if individual consumers, employers, or employees exhibit a "taste for discrimination," then these prejudices could result in economic inequality. Having a *taste for discrimination* means that a person experiences disutility from association with people he or she doesn't like. As a result, people with the "taste" are willing to pay (in the form of shoddy goods and services, lower profits, or lost wages) to avoid contact with people in that group.

Taste for discrimination: A "willingness to pay" to avoid connections with members of a particular group

---

Becker argued that three distinct groups—consumers, employers, and employees—might engage in discrimination, and we analyze these three cases here. Another form of discrimination—"statistical discrimination"—is considered in the following section. A final type of discrimination exists outside of labor markets and is labelled "premarket discrimination." Because labor markets neither cause nor solve premarket discrimination, we relegate it to the end of this chapter.

Consumer Discrimination

Start with consumers who have a taste for discrimination. Assume, for instance, that you have a "distaste" for bald newscasters and refuse to watch them when they appear. If many others share your distaste for bald newscasters, TV stations who hire bald newscasters will lose a large portion of their audience. To satisfy advertisers who demand a large audience share, TV stations will hire only full-haired broadcasters. As a result of this widespread taste for discrimination, competent newscasters—who also happen to be bald—will not be hired. With the effective supply of broadcasters now restricted to the full-haired, wages will be higher than they otherwise would be. To pay these higher wages, the TV station has to show more insipid commercials or hire incompetent newscasters who are willing to work for lower wages. For consumers, the price of discriminating takes the form of less, or worse, news. For bald broadcasters, the cost is much higher—no jobs as broadcasters. Therefore, if discrimination is part of peoples' tastes and preferences, the economy will be both inefficient and inequitable.

Consumer discrimination: When those making purchases refuse to buy goods or services made or sold by members of certain groups

---

Two preexisting conditions must be met if consumer discrimination is to have economic effects. First, consumers must know who is on the other end of a purchase. While this is almost always the case with retail sales (except for those made over the phone or by mail), it will rarely, if ever, be true for manufactured goods or utilities such as water, sewage, or electricity. Second, a large group of consumers, with sufficient buying power, must have the same taste for discrimination. Residents of Montana might share a taste for discriminating against people and products from California, but there are too few Montanans to affect the market. These conditions help to explain when consumer discrimination may be relevant and who is in a position to discriminate effectively.

Employer Discrimination

Consumers are not the only ones who might have a taste for discrimination. When employers have the "taste," it can result in one group of workers receiving different wages than another group. For the sake of illustration, assume that the owner of a private hospital has a distaste for women doctors. This distaste is so strong that he is willing to pay male doctors a premium for working at his hospital. Further, assume that many hospital administrators feel this way—they share a distaste for women doctors. The result? Demand for women doctors will be low, and so will their wages. A taste for discrimination by employers can result in wage differentials, unemployment for female doctors, or women being crowded out of doctoring and into other professions.

Employer discrimination: When employers refuse to hire, or will only pay lower wages to, members of certain groups

---

In his 1957 work, Becker suggested that employer discrimination was more prevalent than consumer discrimination. The reason is not hard to find: consumers often do not know who produced the goods and services they purchase, but employers know for certain. Moreover, it is easy for most of us to see ourselves in a position where we would willingly engage in employer discrimination. How? Suppose you start a small business. Are you likely to employ your spouse, children, aunts and uncles, nieces and nephews? If you're like most people, the answer is "yes." However, when you do this, are you also likely to exclude individuals who are not of your own race or ethnicity? Unfortunately, the answer here also is "yes." Finally, returning to Becker's definition of discrimination, would you be willing to pay your mother or brother a little more than you might a stranger to perform the same quality of work? If the answer is "yes," then you would be discriminating. As a result, total output for society and wages for excluded groups will suffer, so the economy is both inefficient and inequitable.

There is a catch here, and one that is shared with the consumer discrimination story. For employer discrimination to be effective, most employers will need to share the same prejudices.

Employee Discrimination

Employees also may have a taste for discrimination. Again, take the case of doctors. Assume that male doctors have a distaste for working with women doctors. Male doctors may be willing to take a lower wage to avoid working with female doctors, or they may be willing to incur the cost of a long commute to an employer who only hires males.

Employee discrimination: When skilled employees of one type prevent people of an-other type from obtaining those skills and jobs

---

In this situation, neither employers nor consumers have any incentive to oppose employee discrimination. If employee discrimination prevents you, as an employer, from hiring the most qualified employees, then your discriminating employees must be willing to accept lower wages to make up for their lack of productivity (*ie,* they must be "willing to pay"). From a profit standpoint, employee discrimination is not a problem. By the same logic, products that are generated by discriminating employees will come into the market with the same price and quality as they otherwise would. Indeed, the effects of employee discrimination should be wiped out by competitive markets through the creation of segregated workplaces. In our medical example, unless the male doctors can collude to keep women out of the profession, some hospitals will hire only male and others only female doctors, so the wages for both female and male doctors should be equal.

If the market can solve employee discrimination, then where are the inefficiencies? The answer lies in skill monopolies. If male doctors refuse to train female doctors and there are few, if any, female doctors to begin with, or if male carpenters refuse to train female apprentices or male professors to train female graduate students, then inefficiency rears its ugly head. In this case, the *only* people who are available for hiring are male, and they need not suffer low wages when exercising their prejudices.

The example of doctors is no accident. Male doctors successfully kept women out of the prestigious American Medical Association until 1915—and out of Harvard Medical School until 1945.[5] As a result, women's position in the medical profession was minimal for many years. In theory, the result of this discrimination is poor medical care—consumers suffer from shoddy products as some of the most potentially productive individuals are kept out of an occupation.

Some evidence regarding discrimination by consumers, employers, and employees is provided in Box 5.1.

A final note on tastes for discrimination is that regardless of whether it is consumers, employers, or employees who have the taste, actual discrimination almost always will look like the employer's fault. After all, it is employers who hire people and set wages, even if they are responding to consumer or employee discrimination. For example, Daniel H. Hamermesh and Jeff Biddle (1994) found evidence that "beautiful" people are favored and "homely" people experience discrimination in wages, but it is difficult to know whether such "looks" discrimination results from employers, employees, consumers, or all three!

---

[5]See Blau and Ferber, 1992; 157–158.

BOX 5.1

DISCRIMINATION IN MAJOR LEAGUE SPORTS

Lawrence Kahn (1991) summarized the results of neoclassical studies concerning discrimination in professional sports, and he uncovered evidence consistent with each of the three types of discriminatory outcomes described earlier. Until the 1940s and 1950s, blacks were banned from all major professional sports in the United States (*ie,* unemployment). Nonetheless, after the color barrier was formally broken, studies found blacks receiving lower wages for identical productivity, particularly in basketball (*ie,* wage discrimination) and being relegated to less prestigious positions, particularly in hockey, football, and baseball (*ie,* occupational crowding).

The tough question is *why* the latter two types of discriminatory outcomes still exist. Kahn suggests that in many ways, the situation has improved, because the market has slowly worked its charms against discrimination, leading to relatively equal salaries for equivalent black and white players in baseball, for example. Employee discrimination has occurred, but it now is believed to be rare. For example, when Jackie Robinson broke the color barrier in 1947 and entered major league baseball, a white team member requested—and was granted—a trade to an all-white team. This sort of extreme and obvious behavior is now rare.

The most well-accepted neoclassical explanation for discrimination based on tastes pins the blame on consumers. The evidence suggests that spectators are far more willing (and able) to shell out big-ticket money to watch white rather than black basketball players, and that they prefer to watch white athletes hawking products in advertisements.

Employer discrimination may be rarer, but it still occurs. For example, at Wimbledon, men play tennis for higher stakes than women, although television ratings have been *highest* for women. Of course, this last example does not concern a perfectly competitive market. (Try to start your own version of Wimbledon, and see how many people come!)

There is some reason to be suspicious of no employee discrimination being found, because men's and women's sports are highly segregated. Would the males of football, basketball, and baseball take kindly to the presence of women in their locker rooms? The experience of female sportscasters suggests the answer often is "no."

STATISTICAL DISCRIMINATION

In the 1970s, some neoclassical economists developed alternative explanations for discrimination. These explanations require that we relax one of the basic assumptions of competitive markets—that there is complete and perfect information—to see if it alters the predicted outcomes. Under conditions of imperfect and incomplete information, there is uncertainty in economic transactions, which can induce economic instability and discriminatory outcomes.

The Transaction Costs Problem

Transaction costs is the term that economists give to the expense of entering into and conducting market exchanges. These costs include those for discovering relevant information. Consider the following example: you have decided to buy a TV.

Of course, you want the best one in your established price range. Because a TV is a relatively big purchase in your budget, you decide to do a little research—read *Consumer Reports,* scour the circulars in the Sunday paper for sales, and actually go and look at TVs in the store to compare their performance. All of this takes time—perhaps even time away from studying (a costly way to spend your time!)—and, in effect, increases the price of a TV to you. And, if you decide to purchase a used TV through the newspaper or at a flea market, you are likely to incur additional costs in terms of the time it takes to negotiate the selling price.

Transaction costs: Time or money that is spent trying to identify and negotiate the price, quality, or location of commodities, employers, or employees

---

When the notions of incomplete information and transaction costs are applied to labor markets, there may be fairly large information gaps between employers seeking qualified employees and potential employees searching for the best jobs, then negotiating wages, benefits, and working conditions. Efforts to overcome this information gap impose large transaction costs on both employees and employers. When looking for a job, you require information on where the jobs are, who to talk to, and what skills are needed for each one. You need to line up recommendations and make sure you know the appropriate clothes for a particular interview. This quest for information makes your job search longer and costlier. Further, you need to think about what sort of package you might negotiate or demand in terms of wages, health and dental care, training opportunities, pensions, and so forth.

Most immediately, this information problem creates "frictional" unemployment, because it requires time for employers to identify good employees, for employees to identify good jobs, and for both to negotiate an employment contract. With people out of work in the meantime, frictional unemployment occurs. Such information problems also can generate statistical discrimination, which is the problem we turn to next.

The Problem of Statistical Discrimination

Given the information problem, rational employers will use whatever information on potential productivity they can find, and efforts to use all relevant information can produce *statistical discrimination.* This type of discrimination is not based on tastes or prejudice. Instead, it occurs when employers judge an applicant's abilities based on known characteristics of the group that individual belongs to rather than on the applicants' individual abilities (Aigner and Cain, 1977). An employer is especially likely to do this when there is imperfect information about prospective employees or the cost of obtaining more information is high. So, instead of conducting extensive and expensive tests, the employer ascribes what he or she knows about similar applicants in making hiring decisions.

Statistical discrimination: Applying group information to an individual member of that group

---

Education provides a case of statistical discrimination. Here, economists have found that for one extra year of schooling when you are young, you earn around 4 to 5% more when you obtain paid employment. However, graduation from high school provides an extra wage kick of 4%, and graduation from college yields an additional 10%. It seems likely that you do not learn more in your senior as opposed to junior year of either high school or college. Therefore, economists take the extra earnings from graduation as an example of statistical discrimination, because the diploma signals you are a member of an elite group (*ie,* graduates) and may signal stick-to-it-iveness on your part.[6]

The good news with the case of high school or college graduation is that as an individual, you exert some control over whether you are in or out of the high-wage group. When it comes to race or gender, there is less choice. In the 1960s, it was common for a married woman in her twenties to be denied a job, because employers assumed she was going to get pregnant and leave.[7] Employees who quit cost firms money—especially if the job requires skills that the firm must provide to the worker (*ie,* the "firm-specific skills" discussed in Chapter 4). So, employers who invest in workers' firm-specific skills have a profit motive for hiring workers who likely will stay with the firm for many years. In the 1950s and early 1960s—the height of the "Baby Boom"—most young, married women had children and left the labor force. While any particular woman may not bear children, or has no intention of leaving work once a child is born, this makes little difference if statistical discrimination is at work. As long as the statistical average points to women quitting more often than men, employers will assume that any individual woman also is likely to quit. Young or married women will have a hard time finding a job, and their wages will be lower or their unemployment rates higher—just as predicted by Becker's very different theory of discrimination.

An additional source of statistical discrimination, which is similar to that associated with education, also can affect women. Suppose that you have a child right after college and work as a homemaker for the next 10 years. Then, you decide to enter the workforce but find you have little information to give to employers regarding your skills. You might be either extremely competent or extremely slow, but as it will be costly for the employer to find out, you will face difficulties obtaining a good job.

These two sources of statistical discrimination represent two general types. In the first case, an employer may know that on average, one group is less productive than another and therefore avoids hiring members of the less productive group. In the second case, the employer knows that, on average, both groups are equally productive, but he or she has less information about one of the groups, and so again avoids hiring from that group.[8]

---

[6]See Dale Belman and John S. Heywood, "Sheepskin Effects in the Returns to Education: An Examination of Women and Minorities." *Review of Economics and Statistics,* November 1991.

[7]Even earlier, women in many occupations were required to quit if they so much as got married, because their role as a "wife" demanded it (Goldin, 1990).

[8]For those with a statistical bent, the average productivity-difference case concerns different *mean* productivity, while the less-knowledge case concerns different productivity *variance*.

Two sources of statistical discrimination: 1) One group is less productive on average, or 2) less is known about one group

---

For a simpler example, suppose you are taking applications for a job managing a group of clerical workers when two rather unusual candidates show up. The first is a 10-year-old girl; you immediately think, "She's too young to do this job." On average, this assumption would be correct, so you reject this applicant based on her membership in a low-productivity group (by age). Next, you find a Martian has applied for the job. You are polite to the visitor from outer space but cannot quite bring yourself to hire "it," because you know so little about Martians. In each of these cases, you statistically discriminate—but for very different reasons.

There has been much speculation about why and how statistical discrimination occurs. For women, even if a young woman promises an employer that she will not quit to raise children, the employer might believe that if she does give birth, she is more likely than a man to be absent because of a sick child or might put more effort into working at home and, hence, be less productive on the job. Concerning minorities, employers may believe that nonwhites in general—and blacks who grow up in the inner cities of the United States in particular—receive an inferior education or are more likely to experience problems at home or in their communities, thus reducing their expected job performance in either case. For either minorities or women, if managers who make hiring decisions are white males, it is possible that they find it easier to pick up relevant information from white males during the interview process. The manager might be less comfortable with—and so pick up less information from—interviews with women or minorities.

Statistical discrimination often is efficient. Employers simply are using all available information in a case where the costs of eliminating statistical discrimination by gathering more information outweigh the benefits in terms of hiring more productive employees. To end statistical discrimination in these cases would mean reducing total output to pay for additional tests and interviews. In this circumstance, society loses in terms of efficiency if we try to eliminate statistical discrimination.

There are two cases where statistical discrimination is inefficient, however, and so should be eradicated on grounds of *both* equity and efficiency. First, there may be externalities or public goods aspects of testing. If all prospective employees have taken a particular type of test, then employers will know what a certain score implies, but if a single employer gives the test, then she or he may not know how other prospective employees might score. Further, once a test has been taken, if the scores are held by only one employer, then inefficiency occurs as the economic cost of giving the score to other firms is close to zero. Here, there is a clear efficiency gain if the government steps in, pays the costs of testing, and then distributes results to all interested employers.

A second case where statistical discrimination is inefficient occurs when group behavior changes but employers do not know. For example, when an immigrant group enters a country, they may bring their cultural values and previous patterns of behavior with them. If these values and behaviors are not very productive, then statistical discrimination will follow. Now, what if the next generation of the immigrant group adopts native ways? They still may experience statistical discrimination even though it is unwarranted. If these values and behaviors do not match those that employers want, then statistical discrimination will follow.

Because of the two possibilities outlined here, statistical discrimination may be efficient or inefficient. To complicate matters further, it often will be difficult to tell whether such discrimination is efficient and the government should stay out, or whether it is inefficient and the government could improve matters by gathering and disseminating better information on prospective employees.[9]

Comparing Prejudice and Statistical Discrimination

A central difference between statistical discrimination as outlined earlier and Becker-type models of discriminatory tastes lies in their implications for efficiency. Statistical discrimination by employers sometimes is efficient, but discriminatory tastes always lead to inefficient discrimination.

Discrimination and efficiency: Consumer, employer, and employee discrimination are _inefficient;_ statistical discrimination _may be efficient_

Recall that in the cases of consumer, employer, or employee discrimination, *the discriminator pays.* Discriminating consumers end up with low-quality or over-priced products, discriminating employers end up paying higher wages than they could or should, and discriminating employees receive lower wages than others. With statistical discrimination, *employers profit* from discriminating, and this is where transaction costs come in. If a 10-year-old child applies for a managerial position and you as the employer try to avoid statistical discrimination, you will spend time and money on testing, interviews, reading job applications, and so on that you could have avoided. It is inefficient for you to do so, because you know beforehand that few, if any, 10-year-old children are capable managers.

Statistical discrimination may be inefficient from society's view if testing has externalities, such that the total benefits of all interested employers receiving the results outweigh the costs of administering the test but the costs to the *individual* firm of giving the test are greater than the benefits. Similarly, statistical discrimination is inefficient if group characteristics have changed but employers do not know.[10] In either case, there may be an efficiency-improving role for government. Discrimination because of prejudice, however, is always inefficient.

---

[9]In theory, prospective *employees* could engage in statistical discrimination against firms. For example, if prospective employees know that promotion opportunities are more limited in small firms, they may target their job search at big, Fortune 500 firms—even if a particular small firm might provide greater promotion opportunities.

[10]This argument follows standard treatments of statistical discrimination, such as those found in Ehrenberg and Smith (1991) or Hamermesh and Rees (1993). A different form of "statistical discrimination," where initial employer prejudices become inefficient, self-fulfilling prophecies, is discussed by Stephen Coate and Glenn C. Loury in "Will Affirmative-Action Policies Eliminate Negative Stereotypes?" *American Economic Review* 83(5), December 1993.

THE MAGIC OF THE MARKET TO THE RESCUE: ENDING DISCRIMINATION

Now we are ready to solve the puzzle posed earlier: if everyone is free to discriminate in a competitive market economy, how does competition erode the adverse effects of discrimination? The answer takes us back to the "magic" of the market first discussed in Chapter 3. Basically, because the market is impersonal, it penalizes those who discriminate and rewards those who do not.

Initially, we look at how models of prejudice break down in the presence of competition. Then, we consider how the market erodes statistical discrimination.

Ending Discrimination Because of Prejudice

At first glance, it appeared that Gary Becker successfully explained why discrimination persists: as long as consumers, employers, or employees are willing to pay to exercise their prejudices, discriminatory outcomes will be sustained. Consumers with the taste for discrimination end up paying more for goods or services (or getting less of the good than one might have without discrimination), discriminating employers must pay a higher wage to employees, and employees with a taste for discrimination conceivably could end up with a lower wage.

As Kenneth Arrow (1973) and others have argued (and as Becker later recognized), there is an inconsistency in Becker's model: if there is just one employer who does not have a taste for discrimination, then Becker's original model of employer discrimination cannot hold in the long run. Wage discrimination will be bid away. Arrow argued that if there is one employer who is indifferent to whether black, white, or even green people are hired, and there are no skill differences according to skin color (or gender or religion), then the nondiscriminating employer will be able to hire cheaper workers and make higher-than-average profits (because costs are lower than the industry average). The existence of super-high profits for employers without a taste for discrimination will mean that more and more nondiscriminating employers will enter the market and/or that those with a "taste" for discrimination will be forced out of business (the stock market does not like firms with low profits!). Eventually, employers will have to raise the wages of workers facing discrimination (as the demand for these workers rises) until, in the long run, wages will be equal for equally productive workers. Indeed, as a practical matter, if an employer does not wish to associate with certain groups, he or she can achieve this end while still making average profits by investing on the stock market, where he or she will not have to associate with anyone beyond his or her broker. In the long run, there's just no money to be had by employers who discriminate.

Erosion of effects of prejudice: Competitive markets reward consumers, employers, or employees who have no taste for discrimination

---

Somewhat differently, if employees are discriminatory, this need not result in adverse outcomes for anyone. Instead, firms could operate segregated workplaces, with some for black women, others for white men, and so forth. The separate groups could exercise their prejudices but no one group would receive lower wages for identical levels of productivity, because in that case, employers would build more factories to employ these low-wage workers and increase their demand for workers in this group until wage equality exists. Further, if training is a problem such that members of certain groups cannot enter a field, then open admissions policies at both schools and for apprenticeship programs should block this avenue for employee discrimination (as eventually happened with the American Medical Association and Harvard Medical School).

Concerning discrimination by consumers, because of our highly integrated and global economy, consumers typically have no idea who has produced the goods they buy. Even with services such as health care, education, and security, the consumer often does not know exactly who is providing it, and if you do not know who is providing goods and services, discrimination will be difficult or impossible.

Even when consumers can identify employees, consumer discrimination should still break down over time. Assume there are two labor markets, one for women and one for men, where because of consumer discrimination, equilibrium wages are higher in the men's market and lower in the women's. Now, introduce a small group of nondiscriminating consumers (this might be younger people). They will be able to purchase women-produced goods at a lower price and so should drive up the demand in the women's labor market. At the same time, if some traditional consumers (these might be older people) drop out of the market, then demand in the men's labor market should fall. In the long run, the wages should be equal. At most, one might find segregated workplaces, but not wage differences.

The point here is that coupled with competition, differences in tastes and preferences ensure that the unequal and inefficient economic effects of discrimination on wages among equally skilled workers will be bid away. Because of self-interest in better and cheaper consumer goods, higher profits, and higher wages, discrimination that results in wage differentials or unemployment will dissipate over the long run if markets are competitive. Indeed, if all else fails, those who experience discrimination should be able to start their own firms, produce at substantially lower costs, and receive higher profits than firms that permit discrimination.

This argument has become so pervasive in neoclassical economics that many often argue for competitive markets as the cure for discrimination—precisely because discrimination is *not* profitable. Milton and Rose Friedman bring home this point through a discussion of the production of pencils in their treatise, *Free To Choose* (1979). They describe a pencil assembly process that brings together lumberjacks and woodcutters from California, miners extracting graphite in Ceylon, and rubber tappers from Indonesia. "These people live in many lands, speak different languages, practice different religions, may even hate one another—yet none of these differences prevented them from cooperating to produce a pencil" (1979;13).

Ending Statistical Discrimination

Although statistical discrimination may be efficient and exist even if no one is prejudiced, it need not last forever. Firms have an incentive to come up with better and cheaper predictors of individual productivity, or better tests to gauge the qualifications of job applicants. Firms that do so will make more money for two reasons: 1) they can cheaply identify and then hire highly productive women or minorities who are passed over by firms that perform less extensive tests, and 2) as long as statistical discrimination still exists, the employer can pay women or minorities less than equally qualified whites or males receive. Therefore, we should see fewer and fewer instances of statistical discrimination over time.

Erosion of statistical discrimination: Competitive markets reward employers for finding productive individuals in groups subject to statistical discrimination

---

While there is little direct information on the employer side regarding elimination of statistical discrimination, there is evidence on the employee side. First, evidence suggests that women or minorities who are willing to spend the money to signal their value to the firm experience much larger returns than whites or males do. Women and minorities experience larger increases in earnings from college graduation than white males, suggesting there is less wage discrimination against women and minorities who graduate from college (Goldin, 1990). By improving the information that is available to employers, these individuals themselves act to stamp out the adverse effects of statistical discrimination. Presumably, employers also have an incentive to improve the quality of their information on job applicants and, thereby, to ameliorate statistical discrimination.

Second, and perhaps of greater importance, a study by Light and Ureta (1992) suggests that employers *did* have good cause for statistically discriminating against women but *do not now*. Light and Ureta used the types of information that employers typically obtain from job applicants (*eg*, schooling, prior experience, and so on) and analyzed whether it was more difficult to predict if women as opposed to men would quit their jobs. They found that women born in the mid-1940s were indeed less predictable than men, so employers rationally and efficiently discriminated against this group. For women born in the early 1950s, however, employers could predict women's behavior just as well as men's. If employers are rational, as neoclassical economists assume, then statistical discrimination against women should now be on the wane.[11]

Have competitive markets effectively combatted discrimination? Gallup polls from 1993 suggest that whites and males believe this to be true: 70% of whites believe that qualified blacks have as good a chance as whites to get any kind of job, and 50% of men believe that women have job opportunities equal to those for men. On the other side, however, perceptions of discrimination persist: only 30% of blacks believe that qualified blacks have as good a chance as whites to get any job, and 69% of women agree they do not face job opportunities that are equal to those of men.[12]

Who should we believe? To get an answer, let's look at some numbers.

---

[11]A special issue of the *Journal of Human Resources* (Spring 1994) brings home this point. Many of the studies in this issue show that there now are basically two types of women—those who rarely work for wages, and those who almost always do—and that it is relatively simple to figure out which group a woman falls into.

[12]*The Gallup Poll Monthly*, no. 337, October 1993.

MEASURING WAGE DISCRIMINATION

How much discrimination actually occurs in labor markets? Thousands of studies have attempted to answer this question. Here, we examine how typical studies are performed, look at some representative findings, and finish by examining some problems associated with this line of research.

How to Measure Wage Discrimination

For neoclassical economists looking at the issue, wage discrimination is measured by taking actual wage differences between groups and breaking these down into those that are and those that are not caused by discrimination. Economists do this with regression analysis, using a technique called the *residual method*. The idea of a regression is that we can use some characteristic of people to predict an outcome for those same people. For example, a regression analysis might show that people who live in the suburbs of large cities earn 25 cents an hour more than those who do not, and that people with prior military service earn 10 cents an hour more than others. This does *not* mean that everyone who has served in the military earns exactly 10 cents more than the average. Many individuals will earn more, and many will earn less. It is the average we are talking about.

Discriminatory wage differences: What is left over (the "residual") after accounting for human capital and other market-generated wage differences

---

Now, we come to residual part. Suppose that on average, young workers receive 50 cents an hour less than older workers, but that more older workers live in the suburbs and have served in the military. Calling the 50-cent differential "discrimination" would miss the possible influence of these other factors. After accounting for the fact that some older workers have never served in the military or lived in the suburbs, we could use the regression to show that 15 cents of the differential results from suburban residence, and that 5 cents results from different military service experiences. The final result is that 30 cents (*ie*, the residual) of the difference between what young and old workers receive can be attributed to discrimination.

This example is a bit silly. On the one hand, young workers likely have less work experience (hence, less firm-specific capital), so much of what looks like discrimination (30 cents) may result from productivity characteristics we did not account for. Discriminatory differences then are overstated. On the other hand, it is possible that real estate agents in the suburbs discriminate against young home buyers, so part of what looks like an objective factor (*ie*, suburban home ownership) is really caused by discrimination. Further, just having a regression does not ensure that causality is correct. If workers with higher wages move to the suburbs (rather than suburban residence influencing wages), then the entire model is wrong. Regardless of these problems, neoclassical economists typically view the residual from a wage regression as basically capturing the effects of discrimination.

Looked at slightly differently, a regression partitions wage differences between people into those that result from discrimination and those that result from differences in productivity. Drawing on Becker's work on human capital, neoclassical economists first partition off productivity differences associated with education. Wage studies usually control as precisely as possible for levels and types of education, and this explains much (although far from all) of the wage differences that usually are identified. If education indeed makes people more productive (as the theory of human capital holds), then such differences should not be attributed to discrimination.

A related source of wage differences concerns experience on the job—or job tenure. As discussed in the previous chapter, there are two reasons why individuals with lengthy job tenure receive higher wages. First, investments in firm-specific training may occur over time, thus increasing the worker's productivity and, hence, wages. Second, once a firm has invested in a worker's human capital, it has an incentive to pay workers who stay with the firm more than others so that the workers do not quit.

An additional cause for workers to receive higher or lower wages stems from compensating differences. If some workers desire flexible hours and "no heavy lifting," they will pick occupations that pay less money but offer these advantages. Again, we might not want to attribute related wage differences to discrimination.

A final cause of wage differences that neoclassical economists focus on has to do with the specific labor market that a worker is in. Workers in the southern United States typically earn less than workers in the northeast (and pay less for consumer goods as well), but this may have nothing to do with discrimination. Similarly, wages may be higher in urban areas or for employees of Fortune 500 firms, and again, discrimination may not play a role. If such factors are unrelated to discrimination, they should be included in regressions so that their effects are excluded from the discriminatory residual.

How Severe Is Wage Discrimination?

Francine Blau and Marianne Ferber (1992) presented a representative study of gender wage differences that used the methodology outlined earlier. Here, they sought evidence on the "gender gap" in wage differences, or why men earn more than women. Table 5.1 presents their results.

The table deals with three groups of men and women: those who have not graduated from high school, those who graduated from high school but not college, and those who received a college diploma. Looking at the bottom row of numbers, we find that among those who do not complete high school, the average man earns 29.7% more than the average woman, while among college graduates, the average man earns 28.2% more than the average woman.

Using regression analysis, the study partitioned these differences into percentages that add up to 100% for each schooling group. For the group who has not graduated from high school, formal schooling explains none of the gender gap, experience on the current job and others explains 13.9%, and holding a skilled trade job accounts for 12.9% of the gap. If we take experience and skilled jobs as indicators of human

TABLE 5.1

THE GENDER GAP IN WAGES

Percentage of the Wage Gap Between Men and Women Explained by Differences in Characteristics

Characteristic	Non-high school graduate (%)	High school graduate (%)	College graduate (%)
Formal education[a]	—	0.8	12.7
Experience[b]	13.9	22.2	22.6
Skilled trade[c]	12.9	—	—
Gender composition of occupation[d]	30.3	30.0	17.4
Other characteristic[e]	2.4	7.1	12.8
Unexplained	40.5	39.9	34.5
Total	100.0	100.0	100.0
Wage differential (%)	29.7	31.0	28.2

[a]Includes the type of high school program; the number of math, science, and foreign language courses in high school; whether the high school was public or private; the highest degree attained; and the field of study for college graduate.

[b]Includes number of years with current employer, years of work experience less years in current occupation, whether the individual usually worked full-time during work years, and length of time between current and previous job.

[c]Whether in precision production, craft, or repair occupation.

[d]Includes percentage of persons in occupation who are female.

[e]Includes marital status, type of geographic area, whether covered by union contract, size of firm, class of worker, whether involuntarily left last job, race and Hispanic origin, disability and health status, and presence of children.

Source: Francine Blau and Marianne Ferber, 1997, *The Economics of Women, Men, and Work.* 2nd ed., New York: Prentice-Hall, p. 193, with permission.

capital, then over one-quarter of the gender gap results from differences in human capital. Because the gender gap for workers who did not graduate from high school is 29.7%, one-quarter of this difference is approximately 7.5%, so experience and the difference in who holds skilled jobs causes a 7.5% wage gap between men and women without a high school education.[13]

There is a potential problem with viewing these figures as capturing productivity differences instead of discrimination. The definition of "skilled trade" occupations was invented by men and typically applies to male-dominated jobs. It might well be that a precision machinist requires greater skills than, say, being a skilled seamstress or a parent. This is not obvious, however. Instead, biases in the definition of skills may be involved, so we may understate the extent of discrimination in the gender gap.

The gender composition of the occupation is the percentage of women who work

[13]Note that the regressions included both blacks and whites, but the results basically result from whites as they are the vast majority of the U.S. working population.

in the type of job (*eg,* for secretaries, welders, or any other occupation). Here, we find that over 30% of the gender gap for non-high school graduates results from gender composition. Is this discrimination at work? Possibly, if the gender composition reflects occupational crowding because of discrimination, as suggested by Bergmann (1974). On the other hand, if women prefer a few, select, "nurturing" jobs, then discrimination is not an issue. Similarly, if jobs that women hold typically exhibit good working conditions, such as flexible hours, these jobs would generate low wages because of compensating wage differentials.

After partitioning all other characteristics, including occupational differences, Blau and Ferber found that over 40% of the gender gap for non-high school graduates is unexplained in the regression analysis. This residual can be attributed to discrimination. Looked at differently, women who do not have high school diplomas would experience a 12% earnings increase if discrimination were eliminated (this is 40% of the 29.7% wage gap).

As mentioned, it could be that discrimination—in the form of the definition of skilled jobs or through occupational crowding—may cause us to understate the size of the discriminatory wage differential. Instead, the discriminatory gap may be overstated if sources of productivity differences are ignored. For example, the types of data that are used in these studies rarely distinguish between workers who attended Harvard University or a community college, or even between "A" from "C" students, but employers often use this sort of information to gauge the likely productivity of a prospective employee.

For men and women with diplomas from high school but not college, the numbers are quite similar. However, experience counts for much more and skilled trade jobs for less of the gender gap.

For college graduates, the reasons why men earn more than women are quite different. Human capital (*ie,* formal education and experience) now accounts for over one-third of the gender gap, and the gender composition of occupations accounts for only 17.4% of wage differences, with other characteristics playing a stronger role. Of greatest importance, as argued earlier, women with high levels of education experience less wage discrimination, because the unexplained part of the gender gap is only 34.5% for college graduates but hovers around 40% for less educated women. (For a parallel analysis of the black–white wage gap, see Box 5.2.) The lesser (although still substantial) discrimination against women who obtain college degrees may be a byproduct of statistical discrimination. Women who signal their high commitment and potential productivity to employers by going to the expense and time of getting a college degree may be rewarded accordingly. At the opposite end of the spectrum, employers may assume that less educated women are likely to quit paid employment to raise children.

Problems with Measures of Wage Discrimination

There would not be a mini-industry devoted to studies of wage discrimination if everyone believed the numbers in Table 5.1. Indeed, there is much disagreement as to the accuracy of such studies, and most centers on two issues. First is a reverse

---

BOX 5.2

HOW DO YOU MEASURE DISCRIMINATORY WAGE
DIFFERENCES FOR WHITE AND BLACK MEN?

A problem for measuring wage discrimination is knowing what wages would be if discrimination were eliminated. Would blacks be paid like whites? Would whites be paid like blacks?

In a 1973 paper, Ronald Oaxaca argued that we could view these two approaches as providing boundaries for the extent of discrimination. In a more recent study, Oaxaca and Michael Ransom compared white and black men in the United States during 1988. To get at productivity differences, they controlled for education, experience, occupation, industry, government employment, and other variables. If we assume that eliminating discrimination would cause white men to be paid the same as black men are now, then white men would experience a 12.5% decrease in earnings, although they would still earn approximately 11% more than black men because of higher productivity. If instead we assume that everyone would be paid like white males, then black male wages would rise by 14.6%, but black men would still earn approximately 9% less than white men because of productivity differences.

There is an alternative approach, developed by David Neumark, that assumes everyone already receives what they are worth—but only on average. This approach implies that discrimination causes a dollar-for-dollar movement of money from black to white males, so if discrimination disappeared, white male employees would simply "give the money back" to underpaid blacks while employers would pay the same average wages. Under this assumption, white males are overpaid by 1.1% because of discrimination, while black males are underpaid by 12% in wages. (The black figure is much higher, because the money is taken from a small number of blacks and spread across a large number of whites.) In this case, white men would still receive approximately 10.2% higher wages than black men because of productivity differences.

Regardless of the method that is used, the evidence suggests serious disadvantages to being black and working in America.

Sources: Ronald Oaxaca, "Male-Female Wage Differentials in Urban Labor Markets." *International Economic Review* 14(3), October 1973; Ronald Oaxaca and Michael R. Ransom, "On Discrimination and the Decomposition of Wage Differentials." *Journal of Econometrics* 61(1), March 1994; and David Neumark, "Employers' Discriminatory Behavior and the Estimation of Wage Discrimination." *Journal of Human Resources* 23, Summer 1988.

---

causality problem, which causes us to understate discrimination. For example, suppose we believe that as people become more experienced on a job, their productivity rises, and so should their wages. Following this logic, we would control for experience and might find that part of the male–female or black–white wage difference results from males or whites having more experience on the job. However, what if you as a woman or a black find it hard to obtain a job in your preferred field due to discrimination, or find that you are subject to discrimination in promotions or layoffs? Because of any or all of these forms of discrimination, you are less likely to gain as much experience as whites or males, so it will look like you "choose" to be less experienced when in fact discrimination was at work.

The second problem with the residual method is that we might ignore real differences in productivity that are not measured. In this case, we would overstate discriminatory wage differences. For example, suppose that men work harder than women because of women's greater commitment to home production, as Becker (1985) suggests. If Becker is right but we have poor measures of how hard people are working, it will look like discrimination is present when in fact productivity differences are responsible for the wage difference.

Most neoclassical economists resolve this issue—the understating of discrimination because of reverse causality, and the overstating of discrimination because of unmeasured productivity differences—by arguing that some discrimination exists and that we need better indicators of individual performance to be more precise about effects. The studies of wages in sports (see Box 5.1) go a long way toward resolving this problem, because measures of productivity are readily available for that industry.

In sum, even with all the problems that afflict studies of discriminatory wages, most neoclassical economists believe the problem is real. However, if competitive markets can eliminate the ill effects of discrimination, why hasn't it happened yet?

WHY DISCRIMINATION PERSISTS

If the market should eliminate the effects of discrimination, why do we still encounter evidence of the phenomenon in today's economy? Basically, four general arguments have been used by neoclassical economists to answer this question:

1 *Discriminatory effects are apparent only and are not real.* As Becker's theories of human capital and home production suggest, it may be that observed differences in the economic circumstances of different groups result entirely from objective differences in productivity among these groups (Sowell, 1983; O'Neill, 1990). For example, blacks may inhabit a culture with little emphasis on training and careers and, hence, earn less as they are less productive than whites. Women may be efficiently emphasizing home production at the expense of market wages. There may indeed be discrimination in a society, but the market has already stamped out any economic effects.

2 *Discrimination is disappearing, but this takes time.* While markets may be acting to stamp out the effects of discrimination, the market may be sluggish or slow (Goldin, 1990). For example, if women began entering business schools in record numbers in the 1980s, we might not expect to see them evenly represented in high-level management positions for another three or four decades.

3 *Consumer discrimination can persist.* In markets where employees are highly visible to the public, consumers can easily identify and discriminate against those they dislike. If most people in an economy dislike bald newscasters, a TV station will never hire anyone with less than perfect hair. (Check this on your local station, and see if we are right.) The key to this persistence is that the discriminating group must have substantial purchasing power (money or majority status in the population) and the ability to monitor whether their will is being enforced. Evidence from professional sports is largely consistent with this possibility (see Box 5.1).

4 *Monopoly power can sustain discrimination.* If a group controls some product or input that others cannot provide, that group will be able to translate monopoly power into discriminatory outcomes. For example, if workers in a labor union prevent others from gaining skills that are needed to perform the job, the workers can keep their wages high by limiting the supply of skilled workers to one firm, industry, or area and crowding all other workers into other jobs. (The American Medical Association does this by limiting the number of students who are permitted to enroll in medical school.) Typically, the remaining jobs require fewer skills and, hence, pay less (Bergmann, 1989).

This last case is important, because it suggests that unions may use their monopoly power to discriminate unfairly. Evidence from the U.S. trucking industry suggests that such behavior has indeed occurred. Until the late 1970s, interstate trucking was limited by the U.S. government to a few large companies, virtually all of which had collective bargaining agreements with the powerful Teamsters union. Then, the government deregulated the industry, allowing anyone to enter the market. As a result, the Teamsters lost power, its membership waned, and wages for truck drivers fell. Most important, the wage difference between black and white drivers narrowed dramatically, suggesting that the union had been discriminating against black drivers (Peoples and Saunders, 1993).[14]

In general, most neoclassical economists agree with one or more of the four arguments presented here: either discriminatory effects are already gone, gradually disappearing, prevalent only in a few occupations where consumer discrimination persists, or exist in only a few select occupations where employees, unions, or government permit discrimination to continue.

This general view does not, however, mean neoclassical economists believe that discrimination no longer exists, nor does it imply that nothing should be done about it (*ie,* that laissez-faire policies are needed). After all, "gradually disappearing" could take a long time. Neoclassical economists who do believe that government intervention is warranted make their case on the empirical grounds that the costs of intervention are low and the benefits high.

We return to the question of costs and benefits shortly when looking at affirmative action and comparable worth. For now, we turn to the arena where most, if not all, neoclassical economists agree that discrimination *is* a problem: outside the labor market.

Discrimination outside the labor market cannot be solved by competitive labor markets, because the market is not involved. Logically, such discrimination occurs before an individual's entry into the labor market, so it is called *premarket discrimination*. From a strict neoclassical viewpoint, "discrimination outside of the labor market is beyond the scope of labor economics" (Hamermesh and Rees, 1993; 471). We discuss these issues now because many social scientists who basically work within the neoclassical framework do, but it is worth warning you that the waters we move into are murky.

One way to view group differences resulting from factors outside the labor mar-

---

[14]There also is direct evidence in that the U.S. government sued the Teamsters during the 1970s for discrimination against minorities.

ket is to view them as *supply-side factors*. Discriminatory tastes mean that identically qualified women or minorities are treated differently in the labor market; the demand for equally qualified women and minorities is less than that for white males. Supply-side factors mean that women and minorities actually are different from males and whites when they enter the labor market. Hamermesh and Rees place these supply-side differences outside of labor economics in part because even a perfectly fair, perfectly competitive labor market could not possibly alter these things: if women are less productive than men, the market will consistently and efficiently generate lower pay for women. On the other hand, if equally qualified women are paid less than men (*ie,* demand-side discrimination), then market competition should alleviate the problem, as occurred in the interstate trucking industry.

Supply- vs. demand-side differences: Discrimination in labor markets affects the demand for labor; external differences (including premarket discrimination) affect the supply of labor

---

The supply-side factors that we look at fall into two categories. The first is labelled *premarket discrimination*. This is real discrimination, but it occurs outside the labor market. The second is *cultural* or *biological differences among groups*. This second set of factors has nothing to do with discrimination, but it could generate outcomes that look an awful lot like those produced by discrimination. An amalgam of these arguments appears in literature on the *underclass,* the final topic in this section.

Premarket Discrimination

Premarket discrimination occurs when a group of people are denied opportunities because of discrimination in the form of laws or attitudes.[15]

An example of premarket discrimination is the "Jim Crow" laws that existed in the United States from the late 1800s until the 1960s. These laws sanctioned "separate but equal" facilities for black and white Americans. As a result, many colleges and universities refused to accept black students, and because of this premarket discrimination, blacks were denied opportunities to improve their human capital.[16]

Unequal access to human capital would explain how blacks might have lower earnings based on lesser educational attainment. Another example is that girls receive less attention in the classroom than boys. For whatever reason (*eg,* individual teachers may prefer boys to girls, boys act up more than girls and require more attention),

---

[15]We use the term *premarket discrimination* because it is accepted. It is not quite accurate, however, because it covers more than just young people "before" they enter the labor market (*eg,* Jim Crow laws affected adults as well).

[16]The Jim Crow laws were one of many legal challenges by southern whites to the abolition of slavery in the 1860s. By 1883, the U.S. Supreme Court overturned legislation guaranteeing blacks equal access to public accommodation. Then, in 1898, the principle of "separate but equal" was accepted by that same body. See Teresa Amott and Julie Matthaei, *Race, Gender, and Work.* Boston: South End Press, 1991.

if less attention translates into less learning, then girls will be at a disadvantage relative to boys once they enter the labor market.[17]

Somewhat differently, Linda Grant found evidence from elementary schoolrooms that black girls typically are expected to be "helpers," ignoring academic pursuits to help keep the classroom clean, help students locate materials or lost items, or help teachers maintain order in the classroom.[18]

Premarket discrimination: Unequal treatment or opportunities in nonmarket settings that cause unequal labor market opportunities

---

Regarding the gender gap specifically, premarket discrimination can take the form of discriminatory tastes or instead be a rational response to discrimination. Causality could go either way. The discriminatory-tastes argument fits the stereotyping found in schools and discussed earlier. There also is evidence that women respond to discrimination when they are young through their choice of, for example, college major.[19]

If you believe that men will make life as a female engineer difficult, why even try to enter that field? Therefore, part of the phenomenon of premarket discrimination could be discrimination proper—women being discouraged from becoming engineers—and part could really be a response to labor market discrimination—giving up before the career game even begins as the labor market is stacked against you.

This reverse causality problem makes our understanding of home production, as outlined in Chapter 4, look somewhat naive. For example, part of the gender earnings gap could result from women specializing in home production and receiving appropriately lower wages through the mechanism of statistical discrimination; this is discrimination that is more apparent than real. Extending this argument, Becker (1985) suggested that employers might efficiently pay women less (*ie,* statistically discriminate) for reasons beyond the likelihood that women will quit to have children. Even women with ongoing careers may be more likely to miss work because of an ill child, parent–teacher conferences, or the like, and they might be less focussed on the job or work less hard because of a relatively greater concern with children. On the other hand, if discrimination in the labor market implies that women will earn less than men for the same skills and education, it is rational (but inefficient) for women to specialize in home production.

Many neoclassical economists argue that premarket discrimination should be eliminated. For example, laws that promote discriminatory behavior could be over-

---

[17]See Bernice R. Sandler, "The Classroom Climate for Women," or Rita Kramer, "Are Girls Shortchanged in School?," both in *Race and Gender in the American Economy.* Susan F. Feiner, ed. Englewood Cliffs, NJ: Prentice-Hall, 1994.

[18]Linda Grant, "Helpers, Enforcers, and Go-Betweens: Black Females in Elementary School Classrooms," in *Women of Color in U.S. Society.* Maxine Baca Zinn and Bonnie Thornton Dill, eds. Philadelphia: Temple University Press, 1994.

[19]Thomas N. Daymont and Paul J. Andrisani, "Job Preferences, College Major, and the Gender Gap in Earnings." *Journal of Human Resources,* Summer 1984.

turned. Once premarket discrimination is gone—for example, if schools are deseg-regated and all students admitted and treated based on merit, not gender or skin color—then economic outcomes should converge. In fact, many neoclassical econ-omists point to the fact that the wage gap between blacks and whites has narrowed since the 1950s (see Chapter 2), and they take this as evidence that the removal of legal restrictions on education for blacks in the United States has indeed alleviated much premarket discrimination.[20]

Somewhat differently, Claudia Goldin (1990) argues that part of what appears to be premarket discrimination may be reverse causality at work, particularly in terms of choosing whether to attend college and choice of major while there. Goldin ex-plains that markets eliminate discriminatory effects only slowly, because it takes time for young people to see that opportunities are opening. Eventually, the market opens opportunities for all productive individuals, but this may take a long time because of past discrimination.

Cultural and Biological Differences

Some neoclassical economists question whether premarket discrimination exists at all, or if instead lower wages for women and minorities are really caused by differ-ent preferences or abilities. These are the cultural or biological differences among people, which may in turn create inequality in the labor market (although *not* because of any discrimination). Take the case of boys receiving more attention than girls in school. It is possible that on average, boys are biologically more active and aggres-sive than girls. Boys then "command" more attention from their teachers. In our so-ciety—where education and attention from teachers pay off—boys' biological traits lead to higher-paying jobs.

Cultural or biological differences: Differences that are not discriminatory, but can cause different group outcomes in labor markets

---

Biological or cultural differences can carry into the neoclassical understanding of wage differences because of factors considered in Chapter 4: time preference, human capital, and compensating wage differentials. If women or minorities have higher rates of time preference relative to white males, this could result in white males ul-timately earning more as they are more future-oriented. Concerning human capital, cultural or biological differences can explain why women or people of color choose not to invest in themselves. Time preferences for cash today versus in the future, an ethnic group's historical emphasis (or de-emphasis) on education, and the knowl-edge that one will need to leave the labor force to raise children have all been pro-moted as explanations for differences in self-investment. Once in the market, indi-viduals are solely responsible for their economic position, but outside the market,

---

[20]See Robert Higgs, "Black Progress and the Persistence of Racial Economic Inequalities, 1865–1940," in *The Question of Discrimination: Racial Inequality in the US Labor Market.* Steven Shulman and William Dar-ity, Jr., eds. Middletown CT: Wesleyan University Press, 1989.

gender or race could determine what an individual desires from or is capable of in the market. The culture and community that one grows up in also could alter those desires and abilities. Thomas Sowell (1983) argues that immigrants from China typically exhibit a high level of interest in obtaining education and frequently become entrepreneurs. As a result, this group often holds some of the most prestigious jobs and earns more than natives, even in countries like Malaysia, where the government has passed laws that explicitly discriminate against the overseas Chinese.

Whether differences in group behavior (*ie*, supply-side differences) result from biology or culture determines whether we, as individuals or through government policy, can improve matters. If we are poor because of bad genes, there is little that can be done. If we are poor because of our culture, however, this can be changed. (Whether it *should* be changed is another question.)

Regarding racial differences in earnings, Richard J. Herrnstein and Charles Murray argued in their 1994 work, *The Bell Curve,* that genes largely determine earnings, so social programs to improve education or job opportunities for the poor are both misguided and inefficient. While the media trumpeted their results, social scientists quietly went to work to discover whether Herrnstein and Murray's research was accurate and their conclusions logical. The unanimous decision is that the research was fundamentally flawed and the conclusions misguided.[21] The major reasons for this decision are that IQ (Herrnstein and Murray's indicator of genetic inheritance) can be changed through schooling and socialization and that even if IQ is completely hereditary (which it is not), education and socialization still exert a major impact on earnings. There is substantial room for social and educational programs to improve the lot of the poor. This conclusion does not imply that culture or biology don't matter, rather that environment and government programs to improve the education and productivity of minorities or women can make a difference.

Regarding male–female differences in earnings, recall from the last chapter (see Box 4.2) that anthropological research found the division of labor between men and women to be fairly stable across a large number of societies. This suggests that biology may play a role: inherent mental or physical differences between men and women may help to explain the gender gap. If this is the case, then the gender gap will always be with us in a competitive market economy.

More recent research, summarized by Blau and Ferber (1992), suggests that biology plays at most a minor role in determining the division of labor between men and women. For example, studies of primates find that among chimpanzees, which are the most socially advanced primate aside from humans, females do not occupy subordinate positions. Moreover, more recent studies of people suggest that the sexual division of labor varies widely across societies. Blau and Ferber conclude that the division of labor found today, as in the crowding of "female" occupations, is "not shaped by biology alone." Instead, they suggest we look at "the interaction of tech-

---

[21]For an early, critical response to *The Bell Curve,* see Stephen Jay Gould, "Curveball," *The New Yorker,* November 28, 1995. Careful review articles by Robert M. Hauser, Howard F. Taylor, and Troy Duster appear in the March 1995 issue of *Contemporary Sociology,* or try instead James J. Heckman, "Cracked Bell," *Reason,* March 1995, as well as Arthur S. Goldberger and Charles Manski, "Review Article: *The Bell Curve,*" *Journal of Economic Literature,* June 1995.

nology, the role of women in production, and a variety of social and political factors" (1992; 31). Not surprisingly, one of the factors which Blau and Ferber consider to be relevant is discrimination.[22]

The Underclass

The logic of premarket discrimination and cultural or biological differences comes together in recent discussions of the *underclass*. The underclass was described many years ago by Edward Banfield in *The Unheavenly City* (1970). He argued that the underclass typically is concentrated in urban ghettos, is poor, black, and lives for the present. Underclass arguments suggest that what looks like discrimination against blacks may in fact include important elements of premarket discrimination (*eg,* geographic isolation), culture (*eg,* living for the present), or biology.

Underclass: A group that is defined by persistent poverty, social and geographic isolation, and antisocial behavior

---

Until the recent Herrnstein and Murray work discussed earlier—and already abandoned—the biology explanation for the underclass was ignored. The premarket discrimination approach is found, although with a twist, in an earlier work of Murray's, *Losing Ground* (1984). There, Murray argued that the underclass is a product of the welfare state. People become locked into a vicious cycle of poverty and welfare dependency, because the government rewards them for doing so. Race-conscious government policies like affirmative action (discussed later) make the problem particularly severe for black Americans, because even in the workplace, it is not hard work but skin color that is rewarded. Murray's answer? Abandon welfare programs and affirmative action policies so that the magic of the market can work. The *government,* working outside of the labor market, has engaged in premarket discrimination, creating the underclass and concentrating blacks within that group.

The cultural explanation for the underclass was used most forcefully by William Julius Wilson in *The Truly Disadvantaged* (1987), in tandem with a depiction of structural economic changes that are occurring in U.S. cities. Wilson argued that inner cities suffered during the 1960s through the 1980s in large part because of the shrinkage of industrial jobs and the flight of middle-class blacks from inner cities to the suburbs. A black underclass remained in the inner cities with few job opportunities, declining housing and educational resources, and a lack of community institutions to keep children out of trouble and give them middle-class values. Wilson answers that universalistic policies such as full employment are the answer to these problems, and he believes that the race-blind nature of such policies can appeal to a majority of voters in part by returning us to the notion of equality before the law. Further, such policies can directly respond to supply-side problems by providing greater opportu-

---

[22]Blau and Ferber's textbook cited here is explicitly neoclassical. However, much of their other work arguably falls between the neoclassical and political economy views presented here.

nities for ghetto youth, and they can help with demand-side discrimination as the costs of discriminating are high when it is difficult for firms to find qualified employees.

To the extent there is such a thing as an "underclass" (and there is much debate here),[23] it means that much of what appears to be discriminatory wage differences, particularly against poor blacks and single mothers, largely may result from supply-side problems. Competitive labor markets cannot solve problems coming from the supply side: if you are less productive, competitive labor markets recognize this and reward you accordingly. Nonetheless, as we will see, most neoclassical economists believe that demand-side problems—tastes for and statistical discrimination—are real and deserve treatment.

POLICIES AND PRESCRIPTIONS

As argued in previous chapters, the general neoclassical prescription for social problems is for the government to take a laissez-faire stance, allowing impersonal market forces to sort out matters. This same argument usually is applied to the labor market. If discrimination results in serious inefficiencies, however, then virtually any neoclassical economist would agree that the government should move to correct the situation. Therefore, it is crucial to determine if discrimination really is at work and causing inefficiencies or if, instead, different labor market outcomes result from productivity differentials among groups. Which is it?

Most neoclassical economists who have addressed the question of race and gender wage differences believe that some labor market discrimination exists (see pages 106-107). The most celebrated and cursed government policies that directly get at such labor market discrimination are affirmative action and comparable worth. Affirmative action affects the demand for labor (who the employer can hire), while comparable worth directly affects the price of labor (wage rates). Because both policies have been seen as legal cornerstones in combatting discrimination in labor markets, let's take a closer look at them. Afterward, we summarize this chapter.

Affirmative Action

Antidiscrimination laws were ushered in under Title VII of the Civil Rights Act of 1964, which prohibited employment discrimination based on a person's sex, race, national origin, or religion. Almost all aspects of employment are covered by Title VII—wages, benefits, firing, hiring, and promotions. Executive Orders in 1965 and 1967 required affirmative action by employers with federal contracts or subcontracts toward groups (or classes) of workers who had faced discrimination in the past. Employers with federal contracts therefore needed to address the underrepresentation of specific groups in their workplaces. Typically, only large firms, or those that rely heavily on federal money (*eg,* the defense industry and universities), are required to comply with the executive order, although many firms comply voluntarily. At the

---

[23]See, for example, William A. Darity, Jr., and Samuel L. Myers, Jr., *The Black Underclass: Critical Essays on Race and Unwantedness.* New York: Garland Publishing, 1994.

same time, there have been a series of court cases suggesting that affirmative action results in reverse discrimination.

You might expect neoclassical economists to focus on the reverse discrimination angle. Affirmative action legally forces employers to limit the pool of job candidates, a restriction that will have the same inefficient effects as when employers, consumers, or employees discriminate and permit only members of a certain group to be hired. With a smaller pool—one that is restricted by law—employers are left with a less talented workforce and, because of the Equal Pay Act of 1963, these employees must be paid the same as other—perhaps more qualified—workers who are already employed. As a result, affirmative action causes some workers to be paid more than their marginal product, an outcome that is both inefficient and unfair to other workers and, particularly, workers who might have won the job but were not permitted to compete. So, in the case of affirmative action, the intent of eliminating discrimination can result in causing it—hardly an appropriate solution. More important, to the extent that affirmative action reduces the potential pool of applicants, productivity and, ultimately, wages will decline. These would be the results if affirmative action is inefficient.

While the reverse discrimination logic may be correct, it may not be as important as the capacity of affirmative action to correct real discrimination, which itself is inefficient. In this view, affirmative action acts to *expand* the hiring pool, because employers who otherwise would discriminate and exclude qualified women and minorities are forced to include them. If this argument is correct, then productivity, wages, and efficiency (as well as equity) all may benefit from affirmative action. Perhaps surprisingly, this is the current conclusion of mainstream neoclassical economists. Neoclassical texts such as Blau and Ferber (1992), Ehrenberg and Smith (1991), and Hamermesh and Rees (1993) are consistently, if mildly, supportive of affirmative action. Admitting that the programs have problems, each of these authors concludes from the evidence that affirmative action effectively confronts genuine problems of discrimination on the demand side of the labor market. Eventually, such policies should be unnecessary, because the people doing the hiring—who historically have been mainly white males—will begin to look more like the rest of society, male and female, and of different races, ethnic, and religious backgrounds. Even strong believers in the magic of the market, such as Solomon Polachek and Stanley Siebert (1993) have little bad to say about affirmative action.

Comparable Worth

In the late 1970s, comparable worth policies were proposed by women's rights advocates. The logic for comparable worth hinges on the claim that women earn less than men in part because the jobs that women hold pay less. In other words, the crowding of women into a few occupations is a cause of low wages for women. Equal-pay policies require employers to pay the same wages to men and women in the same occupation, but such policies cannot respond to wage differences caused by crowding. Comparable worth policies require employers to offer comparable wages to individuals with comparable skills, job requirements, and so on *across* occupations. This policy was the original intent of the framers of the Equal Pay Act of 1963.[24] For example, public school custodians typically earn higher wages than cafeteria workers in the same schools. Under comparable worth, the employer must adjust wages for the cafeteria workers to reflect equal pay for similar work. For comparable worth policies to be implemented, employers must perform detailed job evaluations to quantify and rate the skills that are employed in various jobs.

Comparable worth policies have been pursued in court and in collective bargaining agreements. In the courts, female workers have argued successfully that Title VII of the Civil Rights Act can be interpreted to include pay equity through comparable worth policies, while several public sector unions have negotiated comparable worth studies and provisions in their contracts.

Comparable worth has generated far more controversy among neoclassical economists than affirmative action, and the reasons are not hard to find. Suppose there are separate labor markets for women and men, and that men's equilibrium wages are higher because women are crowded into a few occupations. Now, increase the wage for women through comparable worth. The result should be that employers will wish to hire fewer people into women's occupations (*ie,* excess supply will result), so a policy that is designed to help women's wages may in fact hurt their employment opportunities. This is nothing more than an application of the law of demand. For example, if female-dominated occupations in government agencies were to be given a 20% comparable worth wage increase, Ronald Ehrenberg and Robert Smith estimate that 5.5 to 6.0% of women with government jobs before the increase would lose their jobs as a result.[25] In other words, not only would employment decrease because of comparable worth, it would decrease most for the group that comparable worth is supposed to help, because wages are being artificially inflated in female-dominated occupations.

Another adverse outcome that comparable worth might cause is an increase in segregation. For example, suppose the recent entry of women in large numbers into managerial and professional occupations is driven partly by a simple search for higher wages. If wages in female-dominated jobs are increased, then the incentive for women to seek employment in male-dominated occupations is reduced. The result will be an increase in segregation.

While many neoclassical economists such as Mark Killingsworth (1989) view comparable worth as inefficient (because wages are too high in some occupations) and inequitable (because women lose jobs and may be increasingly segregated as a result), others argue that the effects may be more complicated than the law of demand suggests. These economists, such as Blau and Ferber (1992) or Richard Perlman and Maureen Pike (1994), also have some evidence on their side. While the arguments are somewhat complicated, we can get a flavor for the defense of comparable

---

[24]The scope of the Equal Pay Act eventually was narrowed through court decisions merely to require that employers provide equal pay for men and women in the *same* jobs.

[25]Ronald Ehrenberg and Robert Smith, "Comparable Worth in the Public Sector." *Journal of Labor Economics,* January 1987.

worth by asking whether *men* will wish to enter women's jobs once those jobs pay more, and by asking whether *women* might seek traditionally male jobs once employment in female-dominated occupations starts to decline. Moreover, it is possible that women are crowded because of inefficient discrimination, so productivity and efficiency could even *rise* under comparable worth policies. For most neoclassical economists, the response to such issues is to look at data to identify the actual costs and benefits of comparable worth. These data show that employment opportunities, at least in the governmental sector, have sometimes *increased* following a comparable worth pay increase, and that segregation has *declined* (Kahn, 1992). Nonetheless, other studies, such as Ehrenberg and Smith's, suggest that comparable worth will harm the economy in general and women in particular.

Because the evidence goes both ways, most neoclassical economists currently are taking a "wait and see" attitude (Ehrenberg and Smith, 1991; Hamermesh and Rees, 1993) on comparable worth, waiting to see further evidence before viewing it as a good or bad policy.

SUMMARY

This chapter opened with a puzzle: if free markets allow you or anyone else to discriminate against anyone or anything else, how can it also be that free markets eliminate the ill effects of discrimination? Part of the answer is that outcomes from discrimination inside of the labor market are inefficient. Whether groups experiencing discrimination are paid less, unemployed, underemployed, or crowded into a few occupations, we would all (potentially) benefit from ending such discrimination. Four types of discrimination exist inside the labor market: as Becker argues, consumers, employers, or employees may have a "taste for discrimination"; and statistical discrimination may occur. Statistical discrimination itself takes on two forms: one group is on average less productive than another, or less is known about one group than another. The solution to our puzzle lies in the magic of competitive markets rooting out inefficient discrimination. Consumers without a taste for discrimination will be able to purchase better products at lower prices, nondiscriminating employers will earn higher profits, nondiscriminating employees will earn higher wages, and employers who are able to overcome statistical discrimination through better testing and interview procedures will earn higher profits.

The vast majority of studies to date reveal continuing wage discrimination, although debate about its extent continues. Some of this difference may result from premarket discrimination, such as laws or attitudes that restrict opportunities for women or minorities outside the labor market. Competitive labor markets cannot solve premarket discrimination; only government or community action can deal with it. Some of this difference also may result from biological or cultural differences among groups. The vast majority of neoclassical economists discount biology arguments, but some believe that culture indeed plays a role. Some neoclassical economists believe premarket discrimination and cultural differences have combined to create an underclass, which is largely black, poor, and located in our inner cities. If we believe the underclass arguments (and many do not), at least some of what looks like discrimination inside the labor market is not caused by labor markets and cannot be solved by labor market policies.

At the end of the day, many neoclassical economists believe that some discrimination *does* exist inside of labor markets and seriously harms women and minorities. The simple view of supply and demand in competitive markets suggests that the effects of discrimination either have been, will be shortly, or will eventually be wiped out, because markets reward people who do not discriminate, whether they are consumers, employers, or employees. In this case, laissez-faire government policies are the appropriate response to discrimination. Other neoclassical economists believe that markets do not always operate in a competitive fashion, so government intervention, such as affirmative action or comparable worth policies, may be warranted depending on whether the benefits outweigh the costs.

DISCUSSION QUESTIONS

1 Suppose you started your own business and hired only family members. Why would this strategy be inefficient?
2 Have you ever been involved in a situation where you believe that you experienced discrimination because of someone's taste or prejudices? Because of statistical discrimination?
3 Suppose a car salesperson charges a higher price to black than to white customers. Is this likely to result from discriminatory tastes or statistical discrimination? How would it change your answer if the salesperson was black?
4 If people voted in national and local elections only for candidates of their own race, would this be inefficient? If so, how might the "market" for votes solve the problem?
5 Many whites and males believe there is "reverse discrimination" and, as a result, receive fewer opportunities than minorities and women. How can they believe this when the vast majority of studies show continuing discrimination against minorities and women?
6 A problem with measuring wage discrimination using the "residual method" is that part of the residual may result from unmeasured productivity differences. Can you imagine a test that would solve this problem?
7 If a parent purchases a Barbie doll for a young daughter and a Mighty Morphin' Power Rangers doll for a young son, is this an act of premarket discrimination?
8 Thomas Sowell believes cultural differences explain the different economic experiences of various minorities. If this is true, what effects would you expect from antidiscrimination policies such as affirmative action or comparable worth?
9 If affirmative action can eventually and effectively root out discrimination in the labor market, how far should such policies be extended? To quotas on hiring pools (*ie,* a specific proportion of women and minority applicants must be identified)? To hiring quotas (*ie,* a specific proportion of women and minority applicants must be hired)? To promotions (*ie,* a specific proportion of women and minority employees must be managers)?

SUGGESTED READINGS

Aigner, Dennis J. and Glen G. Cain. 1977. "Statistical Theories of Discrimination in Labor Markets." *Industrial and Labor Relations Review,* January.

Arrow, Kenneth. 1973. "The Theory of Discrimination." In *Discrimination in Labor Markets,* Orley Ashenfelter and Albert Rees, eds. Princeton: Princeton University Press.

Banfield, Edward. 1970. *The Unheavenly City: The Nature and Future of Our Urban Crisis.* Boston: Little, Brown.

Becker, Gary S. 1957. *The Economics of Discrimination.* Chicago: University of Chicago Press.

Becker, Gary S. 1965. "A Theory of the Allocation of Time." *American Economic Review* 75, September.

Becker, Gary S. 1985. "Human Capital, Effort, and the Sexual Division of Labor." *Journal of Labor Economics* 3(1, Supplement) January.

Bergmann, Barbara. 1974. "Occupational Segregation, Wages and Profits When Employers Discriminate by Race or Sex." *Eastern Economic Journal,* April-July.

Bergmann, Barbara. 1989. "Does the Market for Women's Labor Need Fixing?" *Journal of Economic Perspectives,* Winter.

Blau, Francine and Marianne Ferber. 1992. *The Economics of Women, Men and Work.* 2nd ed. New York: Prentice-Hall.

Ehrenberg, Ronald G. and Robert S. Smith. 1991. *Modern Labor Economics, Theory and Public Policy.* 4th ed. New York: HarperCollins.

Friedman, Milton and Rose Friedman. 1979. *Free to Choose.* New York: Harcourt, Brace, & Jovanovich.

Goldin, Claudia. 1990. *Understanding the Gender Gap.* New York: Oxford University Press.

Hamermesh, Daniel S. and Jeff E. Biddle. 1994. "Beauty and the Labor Market." *American Economic Review,* December.

Hamermesh, Daniel S. and Albert Rees. 1993. *The Economics of Work and Pay.* 5th ed. New York: HarperCollins.

Kahn, Lawrence M. 1991. "Discrimination in Professional Sports: A Survey of the Literature." *Industrial and Labor Relations Review,* April.

Kahn, Shulamit. 1992. "The Economic Implications of Public-Sector Comparable Worth: The Case of San Jose, California." *Industrial Relations,* Spring.

Killingsworth, Mark R. 1989. *Comparable Worth: Analyses and Evidence.* Ithaca, NY: ILR Press.

Light, Audrey and Manuelita Ureta. 1992. "Panel Estimates of Male and Female Job Turnover Behavior: Can Female Nonquitters Be Identified?" *Journal of Labor Economics* 10(2), April.

Murray, Charles. 1984. *Losing Ground: American Social Policy.* New York: Basic Books.

Murray, Charles and Richard J. Herrnstein. 1994. *The Bell Curve: Intelligence and Class Structure in American Life.* New York: Free Press.

Okun, Arthur. 1975. *Equity vs. Efficiency: The Big Tradeoff.* Washington, D.C.: The Brookings Institution.

O'Neill, June. 1990. "The Role of Human Capital in Earnings Differences Between Black and White Men." *Journal of Economic Perspectives* 4(4), Fall.

Peoples, James and Lisa Saunders. 1993. "Trucking Deregulation and the Black/White Wage Gap." *Industrial and Labor Relations Review* 47(1), October.

Perlman, Richard and Maureen Pike. 1994. *Sex Discrimination in the Labour Market: The Case for Comparable Worth.* New York: Manchester University Press.

Polachek, Solomon W. and W. Stanley Siebert. 1993. *The Economics of Earnings.* New York: Cambridge University Press.

Sowell, Thomas. 1983. *The Economics and Politics of Race.* New York: Quill.

Wilson, William J. 1987. *The Truly Disadvantaged: The Inner City, the Underclass, and Public Policy.* Chicago: University of Chicago Press.

PART THREE

THREE

THE POLITICAL ECONOMY APPROACH

6

THE BASICS OF
POLITICAL ECONOMY

INTRODUCTION: A DIFFERENT WORLD-VIEW

In the political economy world-view, people are not simply rational, calculating individuals. They are members of groups, and membership in particular groups predicts whether any particular individual will get a fair shot in the labor market or elsewhere in the economy. From the moment you are born, you enter an economy with an unlevel playing field. Each of us may have the opportunity to try hard and be the star player on our respective teams, but overall, the teams do not have equal resources and the rules of the game favor some over others.

This chapter begins our exploration of political economy. Parallel to our overview of neoclassical economics in Chapter 3, we overlook some important differences among political economists for the sake of simplicity of exposition. Nonetheless, we believe this material will give you an accurate understanding of the basic principles that unify this school of thought (see the Appendix to this chapter for more on differences among political economists).

This chapter first introduces the lens through which political economists view society: the "Four C's" of political economy—context, collective behavior, conflicting interests, and change. The Four C's are key concepts that provide a way to examine society and help to distinguish political economy from neoclassical economics. We then focus this lens on three critical divisions in society: class, race, and gender. These divisions are used by political economists to inform their analysis of almost any economic issue, whether it is air pollution, economic development, raising children, or in our case, discrimination and wage inequality. In political economy, these divisions are directly connected to different forms of oppression and particular places (*ie,* sites) where that oppression primarily occurs. We explore the issue of why such divisions continue if they are unfair, immoral, and inefficient by first asking whether market competition can break down these barriers and, second, by asking how social change occurs in general. Chapter 7 discusses work and wages in the political economy view, then we apply the tools of political economy directly to the question of discrimination in Chapter 8.

THE FOUR C's: CONTEXT, COLLECTIVE BEHAVIOR, CONFLICTING INTERESTS, AND CHANGE

What is "political" about *political economy?* Why is it not just called "economics"? Neoclassical economists use markets and competition to analyze not only economic phenomena but also institutions such as the family and government as well as behaviors such as crime and divorce. For neoclassical economists, society as a whole can be explained directly by market behavior and competition, or indirectly as an analogy to markets and competition.

Political economists argue that behavior is not only individual but social as well. We are both individuals and members of social groups—such as blacks, women, or workers—and our behavior represents a response both to what we as individuals value *and* to what the groups we are affiliated with value. "Political" enters here because political economists perceive important social groups within our society as being related to each other by unequal power and uneven access to resources. Whites hold power over blacks, men over women, and capitalists over workers. When one group holds power over another, one group controls another, and one group can say "yes" or "no" and have their decision stick, political economists call those relations oppressive. It is this group control or power that explains the "political" in political economy. To understand how such inequalities are played out and contested in an economy where actors are both individuals and members of social groups, we introduce the Four C's that link the thinking of political economists: context, collective behavior, conflicting interests, and change.

Political economy: An approach to studying societies that emphasizes unequal economic power

---

Context: It Isn't Just the Economy

As our discussion of the word "political" suggests, political economists believe that a narrow focus on markets and competition cannot explain how the economy works. Instead, we need a broader view of economics, one that includes the social and political context for economic decisions. In the simplest view, *context* means that the past influences the present—history matters.

Now hold on, you say. If I decide to buy a package of chewing gum, how is this influenced by the past? First, whether you can afford to buy the gum can be loosely predicted by how much money you have, which in turn depends on how much money your parents had, which can be predicted by their race, gender, and class. Sec-

ond, before you purchase the gum, you will probably think about where you can c\
it. If you have a big meeting or are on your way to church, maybe chewing g\
wouldn't be appropriate. Where do the rules for what is appropriate originate? They
emerge from history.

Context: The history and institutions that shape and constrain behavior

---

For political economists, however, context is broader than simply saying "history
matters." Context includes customary beliefs about social roles, such as whether
women should work outside the home. It includes institutional configurations, such
as the size and role of government; popular ideologies, such as the celebration of
wealth or consumption; and property rights, such as the private ownership of capital. Context also includes the distribution of wealth and power in society, which determines far more than who can afford chewing gum. So, for political economists,
markets do not operate in a vacuum; rather, they vary with, and can only be understood within, the historical and cultural contexts in which they occur.

Let's look at a more substantial example. Consider how a family with two adults
and young children decides to acquire the goods and services it needs. Certainly, the
family will try to "economize" by selectively looking for items on sale, and when
looking for employment to pay for the items, lower-pay jobs will be avoided if possible. These aspects of decision-making are shared by the neoclassical and political
economy views.

The political economist, however, argues that many other components enter into
this decision as well. The cultural and customary standard of living will determine
how much a family thinks it needs to consume (*eg,* one car or two?). The role of shopping and acquiring goods and services in society as a whole will matter. As economist Juliet Schor notes, "Americans spend three to four times as many hours a year
shopping as their counterparts in Western European countries" (1991; 107). As part
of U.S. society, this family also is likely to want to shop until they drop, so they will
need a lot of money (and a credit card or two). The need for money to do all this buying may dictate that the children be placed in day care so the two adults can work
for pay. However, this strategy may run up against cultural stigmas attached to
women working outside the home while their children are young. As journalist
Susan Faludi (1991) argues, the media often signal women that they should feel guilty
for having a career at such times, while a man is supposed to feel better to the extent that he can earn more and more money. A woman's desire for economic independence also may be a factor, which in turn is influenced by whether her friends or
female relatives are economically independent. None of these issues can be taken as
"given" unless we are willing to abstract from the most concrete questions concerning
the decision to work.

If political economists are correct that the context of social life largely determines
human behavior and not the other way around, then the sources of tastes and preferences, as well as the constraints on behavior, take the center stage in economic
analysis (Box 6.1).

While context may sound abstract, many of its results are easily understood. If

BOX 6.1

CONTEXT MATTERS: NEOCLASSICAL ECONOMICS VS. POLITICAL ECONOMY ON UTILITY, TASTES, AND PREFERENCES

To see an important difference between political economy and neoclassical economics, consider the most basic of assumptions in the neoclassical model: that people are by nature out to satisfy their individual desires; people are self-satisfying and individualistic (*ie,* utility and profit maximizers). Political economists argue that people are not inherently selfish and greedy. Instead, they believe that our economic system rewards self-satisfying behavior and those who promote it, hence encouraging people to act selfishly.

The differences parallel the two views' starting points (*ie,* individuals vs. groups). Political economists stake their view on humans' desires to be members of and identify with groups (*eg,* classes, races, genders) and to want to transform nature into useful things. Once in a group, collective effort brings its rewards, but the rewards are not always, or even necessarily, monetary.

For example, people who put a lot of time into volunteer organizations such as Habitat for Humanity (where people build or reconstruct housing for the poor) may find it a very emotionally rewarding experience, and it certainly is necessary. However, there are few economic rewards and increasingly less and less time to perform such activities. Even so, the fact that people do often join volunteer organizations and donate money, time, or materials to these groups implies that people are not consistently selfish. Indeed, it is hard to imagine how a society could function if everyone—in the home, community, or workplace—strives to do whatever it takes for her- or himself to get ahead. Political economists go further and argue that a different economic system—one that rewarded cooperative behavior—might create an entirely different set of behaviors that we call "human nature." There is a small neoclassical literature on altruistic giving, but the vast majority of neoclassical models assume that people behave selfishly. How bad is the problem? So bad that students who study neoclassical economics tend to become more selfish in the process!

Perhaps a bigger difference in the two models, however, is the assumptions of why people want what they want (*ie,* where tastes and preferences come from). In the neoclassical model, an individual's desires are just that—individual. They are not influenced by what other people want or made in tandem with other people's desires. In fact, in the neoclassical model, where desires come from is not of much interest—it is assumed to be determined "exogenously" (*ie,* outside the purview of the economist's world). Political economists, on the other hand, argue that outside influences are perhaps the most important determinant of what people want to purchase. In sum, context is everything.

As an example of this last point, think about the attire you purchase. While this is an individual choice—no one made you buy jeans instead of running clothes—your desires are intimately connected with society. Today, young men often have pierced ears, but for young men during the 1950s, wearing an earring was to invite derision at best or even a fight (hardly "individual" decisions). Many of the young men who desire and purchase earrings would not have done so during the 1950s and, arguably, wouldn't have wanted the earrings even if they were handed over on a silver platter!

Corporations are well aware that what you want is in large part socially determined. In 1992, U.S. corporations spent over $30 billion on advertising services and another $2.9 billion on "public relations." That same year, they spent only $24.7 billion on research, development, and testing services. Corporations know there is more money in convincing you to buy their mouse trap than in building a better one.

Sources: U.S. Bureau of the Census, Current Business Reports BS/92, *Service Annual Survey: 1992,* Washington, DC; U.S. Government Printing Office, 1994; Table 4.1, and Robert H. Frank, Thomas Gilovich, and Dennis T. Regan, "Does Studying Economics Inhibit Cooperation?" *Journal of Economic Perspectives* 7(2), Spring 1993.

your parent or parents were nice to you as a child, you likely will be nice to your children as well. If your grandparents lived in a society where forks, spoons, and knives were common eating utensils, then you probably will, too. And, to get a bit ahead of our story, if blacks and other minorities (as well as women) experienced discrimination historically, they likely will today as well.

It follows from the notion of context that political economy is very broad. The danger here is that we might end up arguing that "everything causes everything." Nonetheless, if you follow the story, a pattern emerges. It is not as precise as neoclassical economics, but political economists believe these patterns provide believable and, ultimately, powerful explanations for how economies function. By recognizing that history and institutions are important in explaining and understanding economic phenomena, political economists believe they provide a more complete basis for interpreting (or misinterpreting) the consequences and causes of economic actions.

Collective Behavior: Who We Are Is What We Are

All social theories must begin by making some assumption about the categories through which causality occurs. This assumption largely determines how a theory "explains" the world around us. Theories that begin with the individual will produce explanations that are rooted in individual motivations. Theories that begin with groups will produce explanations that are rooted in group relationships. The problem of choosing an analytical unit cannot be avoided, but it is a chicken-and-the-egg situation. Are groups merely the sum of individual actions, or do groups determine what individuals want and do?

Neoclassical economists have many disagreements among themselves, but they all agree that economic behavior can be understood best in terms of the decisions of rational, self-interested individuals. They dismiss the notion that groups are more fundamental for the simple reason that groups do not make decisions, individuals do. Only the individuals who compose groups can be called decision makers. Group behavior therefore is perceived to be a function of the decisions made by many individuals, and it is those decisions that neoclassical economists perceive to be the most fundamental.

Collective behavior: Actions resulting from group influence or membership

---

The neoclassical perspective has an intuitive appeal, so it is worth pausing to explain why political economists reject it. In political economy, individuals cannot be taken as the basic unit of analysis, because their tastes, interests, knowledge, judgement, and ultimately, their actions largely are the product of their social experiences and circumstances. Their "choices" frequently are self-interested, but self-interest is context dependent. After all, individual decisions are influenced by factors such as advertising, community standards, job expectations, the judgements of friends and relatives, and ideologies such as consumerism or religion. In other words, individual decisions are no more basic than the context in which they occur. To use our earlier analogy, you as an individual can strive to be the best member of a team, but the "team" that you are assigned to by your race, class, or gender is equally important for predicting your success or failure. Political economy focuses on the structure and dynamics of that context, and it emphasizes the ways in which people jointly influence economic outcomes.

For example, Judith Lorber (1994) argues that individual behavior is not "prior" to group behavior, because groups predate individuals. Would a rational male choose to wear a suit and tie? Like high heels for women, ties are uncomfortable, yet men as individuals continue to buy them and put them on in the morning. Only the long-standing, group practice of wearing a tie can explain such apparently irrational behavior.

For most of us, most of the time, we will share much of our identity and desires with members of our family, neighborhood, apartment complex, village, town, or country, and we often will confront collective concerns or decisions as members of these groups. We consist of those relationships in the sense that our thoughts, feelings, and actions take place in terms of them. Nothing we do is—or could be—separate from them. Just try going out to the woods sometime and *not* thinking about other people, or try buying clothing without thinking about how other people might respond. Each of us exists in a web of relationships. Instead of focusing on the individual, political economy focuses on the relationships that comprise and sustain the individual and the role that *collective behavior* plays in motivating economic behavior and outcomes.

The final reason why political economists choose groups as the basic unit of analysis stems from an understanding of unequal power in our society. Political economists believe that disparate power relations are based on differences in access to the political and cultural resources and institutions of our society, and gaining control of economic and other resources requires more than individual action. It requires the concerted action of many people with shared interests. Only groups can gain and maintain power.

Conflicting Interests: Winners and Losers

Political economists argue that society combines different groups with *conflicting interests*. These are not conflicting interests in the simple sense that if you can talk your grocer into a 10-cent discount on a loaf of bread, then he or she loses the 10 cents you gain. Following our discussion so far, you should guess that these conflicting interests in political economy instead exist between groups.

Conflicting interests: Group goals that, if met, mean one group gains at the expense of another

---

The significance of conflicting interests stems from political economy's analysis of groups and emphasis on group dynamics. Serious conflicts often result from one group having power over another group.

Conflict in political economy may take many forms, and political economists sometimes disagree over what constitutes real (as opposed to perceived) conflicts. One conflict that all political economists see as important, however, is that based on people's relationship to production. Those who own the means of production, such as land, rights to natural resources, plant, and equipment (called *capitalists*), have distinct goals and interests in terms of how these forces are used compared with those who only own their own labor power (called *workers*) and must obtain a job from those who own the resources. Workers want the highest wages they can get, while capitalists want to pay the lowest wages possible. Capitalists want workers to be as productive as possible, while workers may perceive few, if any, rewards for doing so.

You might believe that competitive markets will wash away the effects of conflicting interests, but this will only be true in some cases. As economist John Roemer (1988) argues, if one group has more money at the beginning of an economic game, then that group is likely to end up much richer at the end, even if the "game" is perfectly fair or competitive.

Going further, conflicting interests often destabilize markets. An obvious example is when workers go out on strike. Another is plant closings in developed countries that undercut the markets for a firm's products when they move to a low-wage country for production. Economic activities become games in which we cannot know the outcome beforehand, because we cannot know which strategies will be employed. (Indeed, making sure that others do not know your strategy before a game starts often is a key to winning.) Political economy views such conflicts as being inherent in most economic systems.

There are many other important conflicts: those among different types of capitalists, such as financial vs. industrial, goods-producing vs. service-producing industries, and small vs. large; and between different types of workers, such as high-skill vs. low-skill and male vs. female. Further, there are conflicts that exist between capitalists and those outside the production process that also are important, such as those concerning environmental protection. Finally, there are conflicts that exist both inside and outside production, such as those between men and women, whites and blacks, gays and lesbians and straight people, and between Jews, Moslems, and Christians.

In this book, we have chosen to highlight the conflict between workers and capitalists (*ie,* class conflict), between whites and people of color, and between men and women. We believe that these three conflicts help to explain both wage levels and inequality in a way that other conflicts do not. And while we see these conflicts as being somewhat separate, they are very much shaped by the same context—the historical development of an economic system in which a relatively few, propertied white men have wielded the lion's share of control over productive resources and people.

Change: It Wasn't Always This Way

The final unifying component of political economy is the importance of change. Political economists emphasize that collective behavior in a conflict-ridden context can only result in struggles and, with it, change. In other words, the nature of unequal power generates conflict, which leads to change. All varieties of political economists view society as a dynamic entity. *Change* is the one thing on which there is always certainty, although the direction and the outcome of that change is never certain.

Change: Instability created by conflicting interests

For political economists, inequality is built into the economic system. It is an inevitable byproduct of the ownership of most productive resources by a relatively small number of capitalists. In addition, as we argue later in this chapter, such inequality is systematically linked to race and gender as well as to class. This inequality is based on group membership rather than individual efforts and, as such, creates group conflicts over the rules that govern distribution of resources and power. In turn, these conflicts create the impetus for economic and political change.

Consider something as simple as income taxes. The old saying is that "the only certain things in life are death and taxes." In the political economy view, however, it also is certain that income tax rates will change in your lifetime. The rich will seek limits on income tax rates, while middle-income workers may wish to see income taxes overall reduced. On the other hand, those who use public schools or believe in antipoverty programs, national defense, parks, roads, and so on will want the government to collect enough taxes to pay for these things. These groups will constantly strive to improve their position and, as they discover new tactics, put together different coalitions. As related events unfold, they will be in stronger, or weaker, positions to change income taxes. The result is guaranteed change, because these conflicts will not go away.

The Four C's of political economy provide general guidelines for understanding an economy or society and for distinguishing political economy from neoclassical economics. However, for political economists, further context is required before examining concrete issues such as wages and discrimination. That context is provided by looking at three key social relations—class, race, and gender—that political economists view as central to understanding our economy.

CLASS, RACE, AND GENDER

Historically, working people with no or little wealth, people of color, and women are oppressed groups in the United States. Their position at the bottom of the totem pole today is nothing new. Men have dominated women, whites have dominated blacks, and the rich have dominated everyone else ever since Europeans first landed on these shores.

Class, race, and gender are *social* categories. This does not mean they cannot have other interpretations, nor does it mean all people are biologically identical. It does mean, however, that differences by class, race, and gender take their meaning primarily from society rather than biology. Therefore, it is the ways in which societies *treat* biological differences that matter and make race or gender a social category.

Some people believe that race combines both social and biological components; however, it is worth considering that other societies do not define "black" and "white" as we do. In Brazil, for example, a person with any amount of white ancestry is considered to be white, while in the United States, a person with any amount of black ancestry is considered to be black. Only sometimes are human beings purely black or purely white; many of us are something in between. Thus, people cannot be neatly divided along racial lines on a strictly biological basis. There must be a social determination on the issue, and how this determination is made and affects the groups thereby delineated is the question that interests us.

Class, race, and gender are groups into which an individual fits at birth. They are what economist Nancy Folbre (1994) labels as "given." You are born into a given group but can join a "voluntary" group like the Red Cross. The significance of these groups may shift over time as a result of political, ideological, technical, or economic developments. Further, unlike race or gender, class is not completely "given" at birth and can be changed by the occupational mobility of a relative or a marriage. Nonetheless, each of these categories will have a great deal to do with the resources (social as well as financial) that are available to us as individuals, the reactions that we will face from other individuals, and our self-image. This is true for all of us, white as well as black, male as well as female.

Groups exist in relation to other groups. This is intrinsic to the very idea of the "group." White implies black, male implies female, and wealthy implies poor. To analyze group behavior means to analyze a group's relation to its *counterpart group.* The phrase "social relation" expresses this inherent connection between counterpart groups. By implication, we also can explore the group's relationship to noncounterpart groups. For example, we might be interested in the economic circumstances of women. To construct an explanation, we would begin by pointing out what is unique about women's circumstances by comparing them with the circumstances of men (*ie,* the counterpart group). Then, we could complicate the picture by bringing in the other relationships that intersect gender, such as class and race (*ie,* noncounterpart groups), by showing how women's circumstances are influenced by their distribution between class and race groups. We will explore these connections further after examining class, race, and gender in relative isolation.

Counterpart groups: Where the definition of one category implies, and is implied by, another

---

Class, race, and gender relations in the modern United States are marked by different types or forms of oppression. To see why, we might start by arguing that capitalists exert their power over workers to receive money or profits, but this cannot explain a holy war between nations, where one group wishes to eliminate another (not much profit there). In addition, neither profits nor hatred can explain why a man might wish to keep "his wife" at home and provide for her financially. Nonetheless, the wife in this case may be oppressed, controlled by her husband, and limited in her opportunities.

To conceptualize these diverse relations, we use the term *forms of oppression.* The basic idea is that oppression can be for purposes of one group making money from another (*ie,* exploitation), achieving submissive behavior from another (*ie,* domination), or limiting the location or opportunities of another group (*ie,* exclusion). We define these terms more carefully later.

The relationship between counterpart groups also occurs in a particular context. In other words, relations of class, race, and gender are associated with practices (*ie,* behaviors) that occur at *sites* (*ie,* locations).[1] A site gives us a very general notion of which aspects of context are most important for interpreting social relations. The idea of sites allows us to analyze counterpart groups by first examining their individual sites and then looking at the impact of one site on others. For example, the community is the primary site of race relations in the United States largely because of geographic segregation. We also can look at the connections between sites and, particularly, how practices are carted between sites. The transportation of practices is one way in which oppression can be maintained, but it also can provide a method for creating social change.

Sites: The primary physical locations where social relations are played out

---

Class: The Rich Get Richer . . .

Karl Marx and Frederick Engels wrote about classes in capitalist societies.[2] For them, class was the most important social and economic category of analysis. A *class* is a group of people who have the same relationship to the "means of production" and the generation of surplus. The means of production are what people need to produce goods and services—machinery, communications equipment, buildings, and the know-how to successfully market a product as well as finance and manage the firm. *Surplus* is the amount of product left over after enough is set aside to assure reproduction of the people and equipment that produced the product.

Surplus: Output above that needed to replace the capital and labor used in the production process

---

In capitalism, there are two primary classes: the capitalist class, and the working class. The capitalist class is defined as the group that owns the means of production and, by virtue of that ownership, holds property rights to the surplus, which in capitalism means profits. The working class is the group with nothing to bring to market except its capacity to work; it produces the entire product but receives only a portion of it as wages. This is not to say that capitalists do not play an important function in the production process, or that they do not necessarily work. Capitalists typically make investment decisions. Some work in managing the day-to-day operations of work; others do the work of hiring managers. The point is that capitalists have control over productive resources while the workers do not (except their own ability to do work).

In this view, creation and struggle over the surplus is at the heart of the economy.

---

[1]The notion of sites and practices comes from Samuel Bowles and Herbert Gintis (1986).

[2]Marx's most famous work is *Capital* (1967), which was first published in 1867. Much of his work with Engels appears in Tucker (1978). Among many biographies, see David McLellan (1973).

In turn, conflict over surplus sets into motion a process of constant struggle and change. While some political economists argue that classes are not so neatly defined, they nonetheless still assign an important role to the decision-making power that capitalists, as a group, have over workers and other groups in society.[3]

Surplus isn't all bad. If a society produces more than is needed to replace worn out machinery and keep workers fed, clothed, and housed, that sounds like a pretty good society. We could take the remaining surplus and use it to put a woman on Mars, build pyramids, or commission great works of art. However, if one economic *class* controls the surplus, then inequality and oppression are bound to follow. That class may be a group of slaveowners, government officials in a dictatorship, or a group that decides whether workers can have a job—capitalists. In any of these cases, those who produce the surplus do not get to keep it, so they have no long-term incentive to keep producing it.

Class: Relationships defined by control vs. production of surplus

---

Another slant on this relation is found by arguing that capitalists *exploit* workers. While we look more closely at this issue in the following chapter, the basic logic is simple. Capitalists have all the options that workers have—to purchase any consumer goods on the market, to seek employment anywhere, and in democratic societies, to vote. However, capitalists also have more options than workers—the ability to hire and fire people, survive without employment by others, and the money to contribute to political campaigns. These extended options provide capitalists with the power to strike an unequal bargain with workers. Capitalists benefit quite a bit by receiving and controlling the surplus that workers produce.

An important site where exploitation occurs is inside the firm. Class relations influence communities and families, but the act of creating surplus as well as struggle over that surplus mainly occur in the arena that connects employers to employees (*ie,* the firm). Class aspects of community development (*eg,* capital flight) are unlikely to make sense unless we first understand what is going on inside of firms.

Exploitation: Control by one group of another's work for monetary or material gain

---

To pin these ideas down, let's ask where you fit. Do you (or your parents) receive enough income from owning stocks or bonds so that you will never have to work for someone else? Do you work for someone else who has the money to hire you? If you're like most people, you are in the *working class* and not a capitalist.[4] Assuming that you're a member of the working class, will you be *exploited?* That is, when you get a job, is the owner of the firm likely to make money off your work? And, fi-

---

[3]For a discussion of the various interpretations of economic classes, see Erik Olin Wright (1994).

[4]Of course, you may receive *some* money from ownership of stocks and bonds, as this is how many workers save for retirement. The key point is whether you have much choice about whether to seek employment.

nally, where will this exploitation take place? Like a small but growing number of people, you may find yourself working with a computer, modem, and phone line from home, but for most people, you are likely to go to work inside a firm.

Race: Exclusion and Solidarity

While race and ethnicity often are thought of as relating to biological differences in skin color or the shape of facial features, it is the transformation of these features into race or social relations that is important here. The United States was colonized by Europeans in the 16th and 17th centuries. Since that time, racial differences have been used to justify the appropriation of land, labor, and wealth from a wide range of racial and ethnic groups. In extreme cases, it has even justified genocide.

Race: Social relations that are associated with cultural or ethnic divergence

---

When people of color go to work in a firm, they are as likely to be exploited as any white worker, and possibly even more so.[5] As workers, they are members of the group of all workers, so they share common interests with other workers, such as in higher wages and obtaining control over the surplus. These interests are not identical, however, because white Americans have systematically sought to *exclude* people of color.

Gary Becker's notion of a "taste for discrimination" captures an element of exclusion: whites may seek to avoid contact with blacks. In the political economy view, however, acts of exclusion generally have a broader basis in collective behavior and context. Regarding context, political economists believe that the shadow of slavery can indeed stretch into the present (Darity and Meyers, 1994). Regarding collective behavior, whites may perceive it as "normal" to exclude blacks (*ie,* "everyone does it").

Exclusion: Physical or social isolation of a group to diminish their roles and opportunities

---

The process of exclusion has led most directly to residential and geographical segregation. As a result, community or regional location is key to understanding the establishment of race relations in the present-day United States. Stated differently, communities are an important site where race relations are played out because of segregation: whites and blacks overwhelmingly live in separate communities, primarily resulting from the refusal of whites to accept integration (Massey and Denton, 1993). By dividing communities along color lines, whites have been able to restrict use of their tax dollars to their own communities, particularly with respect to schooling and other public services. Segregation establishes residential and voting

---

[5]As the black scholar W.E.B. DuBois put it: "The Negro is exploited . . . and that exploitation comes . . . from the white capitalist and equally from the white proletariat." (From "Marxism and the Negro Problem," *The Crisis* 40(5), 1933: 104.

patterns that divide the tax base and electoral districts, which in turn allows whites to concentrate resources in their own communities.

Given segregation and unequal resources, conflict is certain to follow. These conflicts, both between and within communities, often concern the distribution of public resources: white communities have the good schools, white communities are near the areas of greatest job growth, white communities provide social networks that inform the residents about job openings, white communities have the votes to influence local and state politicians, white communities have basic public services. Black, Latino, and Asian communities in general have few or none of these amenities, nor are they likely to get them in an era of budget cuts and urban fiscal crises.

We do not minimize the importance of race within the site of the firm or family (discussed later). Nonetheless, in the political economy view, we cannot hope to understand racial differences in jobs or incomes without considering the impact of geographical segregation.

The flip side of exclusion and segregation is group identity and solidarity. This too distinguishes race relations from the class relations (discussed earlier) or gender relations (discussed later). Managers at work and men at home make it difficult for workers to gather as workers or women to gather as women, respectively. This is not as big a problem for minorities in the United States, who are constantly bombarded with the message that they should stay with "their own kind." For all its ill effects, exclusion also facilitates group culture, whether it is the passing of Native American languages and religious practices from generation to generation or the development of gospel music, blues, rhythm and blues, jazz, and rap music in the black community. Similarly, it is doubtful that the election of so many black officials in major U.S. cities would have occurred without geographical segregation (Orfield and Ashkinaze, 1991).

Exclusion is not required for the development or maintenance of distinct ethnic cultures, nor should it be a prerequisite for minorities to exercise a political voice. A society that valued and celebrated the richness of experiences, ideas, and cultures ethnic and racial diversity make possible would, however, look very different from what we see in the United States today.

In sum, race is a social relation that in the present-day United States, as in the past, is largely based on the processes of excluding minorities socially, politically, and physically. As a result, the site of the community is largely segregated in the United States.

Gender: "A Woman's Place"

Everyone knows that men and women *are* different, but for political economists, the important aspect of gender is that men and women often *do* different things that are, at most, only loosely connected to biology. This view stems from the argument that what men as opposed to women do varies from generation to generation (*ie,* change) and across societies (*ie,* context). Most societies exhibit a sexual division of labor— women perform very different tasks than men—but the tasks vary according to the social context. What does this division look like in the United States?

Gender divisions appear in wages and occupations (see Chapter 2), but they are crucially linked to roles that are established inside the family. They have an important impact on firms and communities, but their roots lie in the sexual formation of identity and division of labor within the family (Bergmann, 1986). In other words, parallel to class and the firm and to race and the community, our understanding of gender relations will be enriched greatly when we examine the site of the family.

Gender: Socially created distinctions between men and women

Gender relations inside the nuclear family—with a wife, husband, and child or children—often do not look like exploitation or exclusion. Typically, neither women nor men marry just for the money, nor do women and men often live in segregated communities. Instead, we apply the term *domination* to relations of oppression between men and women. Domination in this case refers to the ability of men to assert their authority or to rule over the women in their lives.

Domination: Social roles or forms of coercion which assure that one group is submissive to another

---

Domination can take many forms. Practices such as foot-binding in East Asia, pornography, or wife-beating are obvious examples of domination. Domination also might appear as sexual harassment in the firm, where specifics might include wolf-whistles, love letters, or men expecting women to make coffee, take notes, be quiet at meetings, or just not giving much credence to women's suggestions. Domination also could be embodied in the wealthy husband discussed in Thorstein Veblen's *Theory of the Leisure Class* (1973), who neither wishes his wife to take paid employment nor perform household tasks nor wear comfortable clothing, any or all of which would reflect poorly on the man's ability to make money and "properly" show off his wife to the rest of society. The shared aspect of all these cases is the control of women by men and submission by women to male authority—in short, domination.

Domination of women is different than both race and class, because women and men often are combined within families. When a woman lives with a man, she will have the same legal access to public and private resources. However, her access is dependent on her family connection. If she leaves her husband or he leaves her, she is likely to experience a drastic fall in her standard of living. Indeed, recent studies suggest that on average, the standard of living for a woman drops by 33% following a divorce (Faludi, 1991). Within the family, it is typical for the woman to spend far more time than the man cleaning, cooking, and raising children. Thus, men have physical and financial leverage over women as well as access to free female labor in the household.

Until the last four decades, women's economic status in capitalist societies has been severely restricted. White married women were not expected to work and, in many cases, were barred from jobs. The types of jobs that any particular woman could hold were very limited and also delineated by race. Further, women's wages have always been lower than men's and usually not enough to support a single person, let alone a family. Since the 1950s, women's position in the economy has changed dramatically, and women have more economic independence from men. However, some things still remain true: women are primarily responsible for providing caregiving in households, and women still make considerably less than men when they do work for wages.

Further, things have not necessarily become better for women as they have gained independence from men through their massive entry into paid employment during the last three decades. As Juliet Schor has documented, the average employed woman worked 145 hours less in the home in 1987 as compared to 1969 but also worked 305 hours more in the firm, so total working time rose by 160 hours per year—or almost a full month's worth of work at a full-time job (1991; 35).

Connecting Relations and Oppression

The good news about the political economy story thus far is that it expands our vision of the economy beyond the workplace and simple economic explanations for behavior. While capitalists exploit workers in the firm, whites exclude blacks from communities, and women are dominated by men in the home. The bad news is that to this point, the story is seriously incomplete.

The idea of connecting class, race, and gender to the respective sites of the firm, community, and home fits white, male, middle-class stereotypes and experiences. Ask such a person about work, and he thinks about getting up in the morning, kissing his spouse and children goodbye, and going to the *firm*. Ask him about women, and he is likely to think about his wife or mother in the *home*. Ask him about race relations, and he is likely to conjure up images of blacks in the inner city or the *community* (although not "his" community).

These stereotypes obscure the fact that the majority of each relevant counterpart group participate in activities at all three sites. Most adult men and women—and adult blacks and whites—work for wages, have some type of family life, and live in communities. These stereotypes also hide the possibility that men can exclude women, bosses dominate workers, and whites exploit blacks.

To think about the variety of processes that people engage in, consider the "Matrix of Oppression" in Figure 6.1. In it, we see how the three relationships of interest—class, race, and gender—intersect with the three forms of oppression discussed earlier—exploitation, exclusion, and domination.

First, consider exploitation. In the subsection on class, we discussed ways in which capitalists exploit workers. Now, we extend that to include the possibilities that men exploit women and that whites exploit blacks. The potential for men to exploit women in the home is obvious; if men work fewer hours and control decisions about what the household will consume or how leisure time will be used, then men exploit women at home. Men also may exploit women at work if women receive lower wages for the same work as men and thus subsidize men's wages or contribute to profits (we call these "job competition" effects in Chapter 8). Similarly, whites may exploit people of color at work. In the community, whites might use their control over resources to ensure that amenities located in the city but often used by whites

FIGURE 6.1
FORMS OF OPPRESSION: CLASS, RACE, AND GENDER.

	Exploitation	Exclusion	Domination
Class	Low wages, job loss threats	Legacy preferences at elite colleges	Rewards for worker obedience, status perks for managers
Race	Low minority wages, lack of employment	Housing segregation	Minorities limited to service jobs
Gender	Unpaid housework, women's low wages	Marriage bars, occupational segregation	Male control over household decisions

from the suburbs (*eg,* museums, ball parks, convention centers) are maintained while public expenditures are diminished for the public schools and roads used by predominantly minority city residents.

Second, consider exclusion. While blacks typically are excluded from white neighborhoods and white jobs, it also is true that many workers often are excluded from the opportunities and activities of the wealthy. With few exceptions, most readers of this book can be confident that neither they nor their children will ever be admitted to elite prep schools such as Deerfield Academy or Exeter; to Ivy League schools such as Yale, Princeton, or Harvard; or to exclusive country clubs. Women also are excluded from many activities, such as male occupations, many big-money sports activities, and (to date, at least) the presidency.

Third, consider domination. Women may be dominated in the home or at work, but workers and people of color may, by virtue of group membership, also experience domination. If a worker does not voice her ideas for improving quality or reducing unnecessary paperwork, exploitation cannot provide an explanation (the firm makes less money than it could), but domination can. If she feels that her male colleagues don't take her seriously because she is a woman, she might not feel comfortable speaking up. Similarly, whites often may try to exclude blacks from society, and the occupations where black employment is relatively easy to find are those where the worker is subservient to the (typically white) customer—from shining shoes to serving meals to cleaning houses or buildings. While there may be elements of exploitation in such jobs, it also is clear that domination in the sense of submission enters the mix as well.

We have not introduced the sites of the firm, community, and home into the matrix of oppression. If we did, it would form a third axis (we do not show this in Fig. 6.1, because it yields 27 cells in the matrix!). Domination, exclusion, and exploitation can occur at any of the three sites (*ie,* the firm, home, or community), while relations of class, race, and gender also exist at all three sites. If you look back on the examples just used, you will see some of these interconnections.

While we omitted the notion of sites from the matrix of oppression, it is used extensively in the remaining discussion of political economy section in this book. To see why, go back to the Four C's. Now, we can flesh these out a bit. *Collective behavior* concerns the actions of various counterpart groups—capitalists/workers, whites/blacks, and men/women. Forms of oppression, such as exploitation, exclusion, and domination, are the source of *conflicting interests* between these groups, and these forms of oppression and counterpart groups form part of the *context* for analyzing a society. Nonetheless, the simple matrix of oppression does not capture *change*. In fact, it looks static, as if men have always—and will always—dominate women. When we add the notions of practices occurring at sites, we admit that practices can change, whether because of conflicting interests or because practices can, and often are, transported from one site to another.

COMPETITION TO THE RESCUE, NOT

A neoclassical economist might respond to the material just presented by saying, "But what about the market?" If markets are competitive, why can't workers stop exploitation by threatening to switch employers or, better yet, by starting their own firms? Why can't women and people of color invest in their own education, get jobs and incomes equal to those of white males, and refuse to deal with men or whites unless domination and exclusion are halted?

The political economy answer is rooted in a different understanding of what *competition* means. Drawing from the work of Joseph Schumpeter, political economists view competition as a battle or a contest with winners and losers.[6] Suppose that you are selling a used car. You look in the newspaper to get some idea of the advertised price of similar cars. In the neoclassical view, the story ends with you selling the car at the market price. With many such cars and buyers on the market, you are anonymous. In the political economy view, however, you are engaged in a contest to sell your car. Whoever does buy from you (*ie,* the winner) doesn't buy from someone else (*ie,* the loser). Further, you are unlikely to charge exactly the "market price." You might set your price a few dollars lower than others, hoping for a quick sale, or set your price higher, hoping to locate a hapless fool who will pay your price.

Competition in political economy: A dog-eat-dog process with winners and losers

---

What does this have to do with exploitation, exclusion, and domination? Regarding exploitation by capitalists, capitalists have resources (*ie,* money), which give them an advantage in the labor market. Another advantage for capitalists in the labor market game is that there are relatively few capitalists but many workers. In most games, having more members on your team would be better, but in the labor market, the op-

---

[6]Schumpeter was not a political economist, but his vision of competition is used by many political economists. See Schumpeter's *Capitalism, Socialism, and Democracy,* New York: Harper & Row, 1942.

posite holds true. Regarding exclusion and domination, it means bringing less power to market relationships, especially when there is competition. For example, one recent study found that new-car salespeople offer lower final prices to white men than to women or blacks (Ayres and Siegelman, 1995).

Does competition mean that you could become a successful capitalist and escape exploitation? Let's see. In 1993, the Fortune 500 largest industrial corporations earned over one-quarter of all after-tax profits in the United States ($71 billion out of a total $260.9 billion).[7] That same year, U.S. consumers spent almost $4.4 trillion, and the Fortune 500 sold over one-half as much, receiving $2.4 trillion in revenues. Do you have a chance to start a business that might someday join the prestigious "500"? As of 1990, there were over 20 million businesses in the United States,[8] so if all else were equal, your chances of making it into the Fortune 500 are approximately one in over 40,000. All else is not equal, however, because the chances of actually making it have declined over time. As economist Joseph Bowring (1986) finds in a careful study of competition in the United States, economists in general now agree that big firms have continued to get much bigger and stronger relative to small firms during the 20th century.

If dog-eat-dog competition favors those with money, it follows that not only capitalists, but whites and males (who typically have more money than their counterparts), are favored as well. This gives us some idea of why exclusion and domination are not eroded by markets, but a more complete explanation requires an additional distinction.

In addition to the *market competition,* there also is *firm-generated competition* (Box 6.2). Market competition occurs when players, such as corporations, are forced into attempts to weaken or eliminate their market opponents. Someone is going to lose, and so each side strives to win. Firms that do not attempt to play the game of market competition, or who are not terribly successful, go bankrupt. Firm-generated competition occurs when a corporation (instead of the market) creates a game played by those who can help the firm financially (*eg,* employees, subcontractors, local governments, consumers). Here, one group of, say, employees wins while everyone else loses, one local government "wins" a plant while others lose, or one subcontractor receives work while others do not. Firm-generated competition is central to the idea of "divide-and-conquer," wherein capitalists divide workers along racial, ethnic, or gender lines and play each side off against the other. (We delay further discussion of divide-and-conquer tactics until the next chapter.)

In the political economy view, competition might tend to level the playing field in certain arenas, but this is not a general tendency. Where there are winners and losers, competition can turn slight differences in power and resources into larger ones. If men dominate women at home, they may be able to translate this into wage advantages in the firm, and competition may help them to do so. If whites can exclude

---

[7]Information on the Fortune 500 is from *Fortune,* April 18, 1994. Other information (except as noted) is from *Economic Report of the President, 1994,* Washington, D.C.: Government Printing Office, 1994.

[8]Figures from the U.S. Bureau of the Census, *Statistical Abstract of the United States: 1994,* Washington, D.C.: Government Printing Office, 1994.

BOX 6.2

MARKET COMPETITION AND FIRM-GENERATED COMPETITION

You see examples of competition every day. Coca-Cola Corporation continues to advertise at a breakneck pace even though it controls over 40% of the U.S. soft-drink market, selling a mere 79.2 *billion* containers of soda per year. Their continued advertising suggests they are very concerned that someone is going to take away their market share (*ie,* market competition). At the same time, soft-drink and beer manufacturers often generate competition by allowing consumers to enter contests with winners going to Disney World or the Super Bowl. Of course, the latter type of competition seems pretty innocuous to most of us, but the firms would not generate this competition unless they thought that money could be made in the process.

Market competition can be brutal. When Folgers wanted to enter the market for coffee in Syracuse, New York, during 1974, it came in with guns blazing for Maxwell House, which controlled 33% of the market. The two battled with coupons, which ultimately reduced the price of coffee in Syracuse by almost 50%. After the smoke cleared and prices returned to normal, Folgers had gained 25% of the market, but Maxwell House *still* controlled 33% of the market. The losers? Small coffee producers like deLima, who saw their market share drop from 15 to 7% in the process.

The logic of firm-generated competition (*ie,* divide and conquer) is close to that for a game called the "prisoner's dilemma." In this game, the police capture two thieves, separate them (*ie,* divide), and encourage them to confess. The prisoners would benefit from keeping their lips sealed, but if one confesses, then the other is in serious trouble. The result is that both confess (*ie,* conquer). The prisoners lose, while the police get their confession.

In the real world, a manager can do much the same thing to get more work out of workers than they otherwise would provide—and for less money. The classic case is one where management enforces a strict policy that employees cannot discuss salary with each other. When it comes time for raises, each employee is told that she or he is receiving an above-average raise because of her or his exemplary performance. Only one problem here: everyone can't be above average (but everyone can work hard).

Sources: Soft-drink industry figures for 1992 from Standard and Poor's *Industry Surveys,* New York: Standard and Poors, 1994. Other material from Samuel Bowles and Richard Edwards, *Understanding Capitalism,* 2nd ed. New York: HarperCollins, 1993.

---

blacks from their communities, this may give whites an "edge" in the labor market, which competition may reward heavily. If capitalists can draw more and more workers into labor markets, competition between workers helps the firm to become larger, more powerful, and better able to exploit workers. In other words, competition is unlikely to rescue groups from the oppression of exploitation, exclusion, or domination.

CHALLENGING OPPRESSION: IT AIN'T OVER TILL IT'S OVER

If people with power are a product of the context surrounding them and act collectively to maintain and extend that power, then where is the room for change? Are whites, males, and capitalists doomed from birth to oppress blacks, women, and workers? By the same token, are women, minorities, and workers bound to be oppressed? Will the "matrix of oppression" exist forever? Political economists respond with a resounding "no," because change is inevitable in an economy with inherent conflicts of interest.

The primary reason why change that reduces oppression occurs is that oppressed groups have no interest in maintaining their subordinate status. Over the centuries, workers have struggled to contain and control capitalists by joining labor unions, forming labor and socialist parties, and pressing for minimum wage, maximum hours, and occupational health and safety laws. Women have fought for equal access to voting, property, education, and jobs. Black Americans fought for freedom from slavery and equal access to public accommodations, jobs, and housing. For each of these groups, oppression has not been eliminated. The war has not been won, but this does not mean that battles are always lost—or that the battles are not worth fighting.

Related to the fact that oppressed groups have an interest in change is that market economies generate constant turbulence. People are moved in and out of jobs, new products are always under development, new technologies are being tried, and so forth. With such dramatic disturbances in the economy, opportunities are regularly opening and closing. For example, black and white women now work in much more similar jobs than was the case several decades ago, so there now are greater opportunities for these groups to organize under the same union or feminist organizational umbrella.

Marx provided another reason why people would ultimately abandon oppressive social relations: they are alienating.[9] Marx used the concept of *alienation* to express capitalism's separation of people from the results of their work (which is owned by the capitalist) and from control over their work. Marx also wrote about how capitalism reduced social relationships to money and things, and how this reduction inhibited people from fully developing their human potentialities. More generally, political economists view alienation as a sense of irrelevance and fragmentation caused by compartmentalizing one's life into "work" and "everything else." In this view, we are all victims of oppression, regardless of whether we are rich or poor, black or white, male or female, because relations of trust, love, loyalty, and friendship are undermined by the overwhelming importance that is placed on money by capitalism. Why else would people have to sign "prenuptial agreements" that guarantee a certain split of the money following a divorce from a marriage that is *yet to occur?* Why else would students fight—and even kill—fellow students over expensive basketball shoes or jackets?

Alienation: A sense of meaninglessness and the fragmentation of life

---

In Marx's view, such alienation can be eliminated only by abandoning oppressive relations. In other words, when men meet women and blacks meet whites as

---

[9]See Rosemary Tong (1989) for a discussion of the various meanings of "alienation."

equals, we will each have greater opportunities for meaningful relationships. This view also provides a strong defense of democracy. Democracy is not simply our right as citizens; it also is necessary for our development as human beings. Democracy matters not just as a set of formal procedures, such as the right to vote, but also with respect to our ability to control the circumstances of our lives. Worker-controlled firms, for example, are seen as a positive alternative (both with respect to equity and efficiency) to the authoritarian organization of traditional, capitalist-controlled firms. Community-based organizations that strive to accommodate the needs of those who live in the community through representative and just mechanisms are an important part of the fabric of an enriched life. Similarly, valuing the work of families (rather than admiring family values) by recognizing and socializing the costs of child-rearing enhances our lives and enables all of us to be more effective participants in our families, communities, and workplaces.

The idea of alienation means that groups have more than just dollars driving them to act collectively to end oppressive relations. It expands our understanding of why people fight oppression—whether through the union movement, feminist movement, or the civil rights movement. As highlighted in this chapter, oppression is not only about exploitation for profit, and groups that strive to end oppression often are concerned with more than monetary aspects of oppression.

Liberatory knowledge: Information that helps both oppressed and oppressors understand the benefits of eliminating inequality

---

Also connected to the idea of alienation is the concept of *liberatory knowledge,* which is further linked to the notion of "institutional discrimination" that is discussed in Chapter 8.[10] Liberatory knowledge focuses on facts and social connections that explain the benefits of eliminating oppression. The notion of alienation may help to form the basis for liberatory knowledge, but there are other types of liberatory knowledge and other reasons to end oppression as well. For example, if a young girl is taught that she can perform mathematics as well as boys, or someday become the president or the pope, this would be a form of liberatory knowledge. Relatedly, many whites do not consider themselves to be discriminatory and will, if some discriminatory action is pointed out, be perfectly happy to change their behavior.

Finally, for a dose of reality, political economists recognize that oppression has existed for a long time and will not disappear overnight. In the political economy view, as opposed to that of neoclassical economics, capitalists, men, and whites have a powerful economic interest in maintaining inequality. It will take more than gentle philosophy and presentation of a few facts to change that.

SUMMING UP

We began this chapter with the Four C's of political economy. Context reminds us that the past and the society in which we live are important for understanding both

---

[10]See Amott and Matthaei (1991) for a more complete discussion of this idea.

the present and the future. Collective behavior reminds us that although we may "feel" like isolated individuals, we are not only individuals; we are parts of larger groups that act and influence people's thoughts and actions. Conflicting interests stem from unequal power relations between groups and, in turn, drive change.

With the Four C's in hand, we turned to three sets of counterpart groups: capitalists and workers, whites and blacks, and men and women. We began by examining these in isolation, arguing that capitalists exploit workers in the firm, whites exclude blacks in communities, and men dominate women in the home. A richer approach permits all three forms of oppression to occur at all three sites and affect all three sets of counterpart groups. Then, men can exploit women at home or in the factory, whites can dominate blacks inside the firm or in the community, and capitalists can exclude workers in the community or the firm.

Counterpart groups—according to class, race, and gender—are those who act collectively, and the forms of oppression—exploitation, exclusion, and domination—are the primary reason for conflicting interests between groups. The particular groups that we examine, and the particular forms of oppression today, act as a backdrop or context for what follows.

Finally, we examined change. Looking at competitive markets, we asked whether these might break down forms of oppression. The answer generally is "no," but competition in markets of the political economy type—with winners and losers—does tend to cause dramatic changes in the economy. We finished by asking whether oppression will last forever and again answered "no," partly because of conflicting interests, partly because market economies are constantly changing, and partly because oppression is in many ways bad for everyone (but worse for some).

DISCUSSION QUESTIONS

1 Recall the last item that you purchased. Did context play any role in your decision? Do you think that other people in your class, race, or gender groups are more likely than those in other groups to buy the item?

2 Suppose that the audience for the "Rush Limbaugh Show" was mainly white and male. Would this imply that these white males are acting collectively (as "ditto-heads")?

3 Do you see conflicting interests in terms of class, race, or gender on your college campus? If so, what particular "battles" have occurred? Have these led to changes on campus?

4 Do you plan to or already have children? In making a decision, did you consider solely economic factors, or were you also influenced by others, such as family or friends?

5 Have you ever been exploited in the sense of producing more than you were paid? If so, was this in the firm, community, or home? Why was the other party able to get away with exploitation?

6 Could one person both dominate and exclude another at the same time? Try to find an example where this would be true.

7 Given their understanding of market competition and oppression, how do you think a political economist would respond to a government program such as WIC (Women, Infants, and Children) that improves average nutrition by providing free milk, bread, and other necessities to poor children?

8 If you were a white male, would you have any interest in seeing women and minorities receive job opportunities equal to your own? What if this meant that you would not get a good job or a promotion?

9 Are managers part of the working class? Why, or why not?

SUGGESTED READINGS

Amott, Teresa L. and Julie A. Matthaei. 1991. *Race, Gender and Work.* Boston: South End Press.

Ayres, Ian and Peter Siegelman. 1995. "Race and Gender Discrimination in Bargaining for a New Car." *American Economic Review,* 85(3).

Bergmann, Barbara. 1986. *The Economic Emergence of Women.* New York: Basic Books.

Bowles, Samuel and Herbert Gintis. 1986. *Democracy and Capitalism.* New York: Basic Books.

Bowring, Joseph. 1986. *Competition in a Dual Economy.* Princeton, NJ: Princeton University Press.

Darity, William A., Jr. and Samuel L. Myers, Jr. 1994. *The Black Underclass.* New York: Garland.

Faludi, Susan. 1991. *Backlash: The Undeclared War Against American Women.* New York: Crown.

Folbre, Nancy. 1982. "Exploitation Comes Home: A Critique of the Marxian Theory of Family Labour." *Cambridge Journal of Economics* 6, December.

Folbre, Nancy. 1994. *Who Pays for the Kids?* New York: Routledge.

Hartmann, Heidi I. 1979. "The Unhappy Marriage of Marxism and Feminism: Towards a More Progressive Union." *Capital and Class* 8, Summer.

Humphries, Jane. 1991. "The Sexual Division of Labor and Social Control: An Interpretation." *Review of Radical Political Economics* 23, Fall & Winter.

Keynes, John Maynard. 1936. *The General Theory of Employment, Interest and Money.* New York: Harcourt, Brace.

Lorber, Judith. 1994. *Paradoxes of Gender.* New Haven, CT: Yale University.

Marx, Karl. 1967. *Capital, Vol. 1.* New York: International Publishers Co.

Massey, Douglas and Nancy Denton. 1993. *American Apartheid: Segregation and the Making of the Underclass.* Cambridge, MA: Harvard University Press.

McLellan, David. 1973. *Karl Marx, His Life and Thought.* New York: Harper Colophon Books.

Myrdal, Gunnar. 1944. *An American Dilemma: The Negro Problem and Modern Democracy.* New York: Harper & Brothers.

Orfield, Gary and Carole Ashkinaze. 1991. *The Closing Door: Conservative Policy and Black Opportunity.* Chicago: University of Chicago.

Robinson, Joan. 1962. *Economic Philosophy: An Essay on the Progress of Economic Thought.* New York: Doubleday.

Roemer, John. 1988. *Free to Lose: An Introduction to Marxist Economic Philosophy.* Cambridge, MA: Harvard University Press.

Schor, Juliet. 1991. *The Overworked American.* New York: Basic Books.

Smith, Adam. 1976 (originally 1776). *An Inquiry into the Nature and Causes of the Wealth of Nations.* Oxford: Clarendon Press.

Tong, Rosemarie, 1989. *Feminist Thought: A Comprehensive Introduction.* Boulder, CO: Westview Press.

Tucker, Robert C., ed. 1978. *The Marx-Engels Reader.* 2nd ed. New York: W.W. Norton & Co.

Veblen, Thorstein. 1973 (originally 1899). *The Theory of the Leisure Class.* Boston: Houghton Mifflin Co.

Wright, Erik Olin. 1994. *Interrogating Inequality: Essays on Class Analysis, Socialism, and Marxism.* New York: Verso.

APPENDIX: Political Economy's Roots

Political economy combines several different traditions within economics and politics. Although many traditions in political economy differ in important respects, they are united in their belief that supply and demand are inadequate tools with which to understand economic dynamics and outcomes. Instead, they focus on forces such as conflict, power, and culture.

Political economy has its roots in four very different schools of thought. These four "legs" of political economy include the works of Marx, institutionalism, Keynesianism, and the protest movements of the 1950s to 1970s, which included the civil rights, anti–Vietnam War, and feminist movements. We focus on these four, because they embodied theories of economic activity and advocated change as well.

The Point of Departure

Neoclassical economists justifiably claim Adam Smith as their founder, because he was the first to articulate the principles of a self-regulating market economy. However, Smith also is considered to be the founder of political economy, because he did not limit his discussion of economics to supply and demand. In *The Wealth of Nations* (1976), Smith raises three themes that lie at the core of political economy today: class conflict, wealth production, and human needs.

Smith's great intellectual breakthrough was his belief that labor, as opposed to agriculture or trade, was the source of national wealth. This belief allowed Smith to envision the process of economic growth in general without reducing it to any particular sector.

From Smith's notion of the wealth of nations, it follows that profits represent a deduction from the value that is produced by labor. The profit that capitalists receive is a *surplus,* an amount of products and services generated above and beyond the wages that are received by workers. This surplus theory of profits was later discarded by neoclassical economics in favor of the argument that profits are a return to the productivity of the capitalist. The dispute about the origin of profits continues today. Unfortunately, it cannot be resolved empirically, because there is no agreement on how to define or measure the productivity of capitalists.

Smith argued that the division of income between wages and profits was governed by a struggle in which the interests of owners and workers were diametrically opposed. "The workmen desire to get as much, the masters to give as little as possible. The former are disposed to combine in order to raise, the latter in order to lower the wages of labour."[11] Of course, other factors, such as the growth rate of the economy and the population, also influenced wages, but it was Smith's doctrine of class struggle between workers and owners that proved to be especially influential for political economists. His attention to the impact of worker and owner organizations introduced political and ideological elements into his economic analysis. It presented a picture of the economic system that was grounded in conflict rather than harmony, and it contributed to the more radical theories of Karl Marx.

Marx: Class Systems

Marx wrote during the mid-19th century, when England was experiencing the Industrial Revolution. He saw that small manufacturers were being swallowed up and displaced by large corporations. Technological change had become very rapid and, in conjunction with the expulsion of peasants from their land (called the "enclosure" movement), was contributing to widespread

---

[11]Quoted in Robert Heilbroner, ed., *The Essential Adam Smith,* New York: W.W. Norton, 1986; 195–196.

unemployment. Child labor, poverty, and industrial exploitation existed side-by-side with great wealth. Financial capital had become intertwined with industrial capital, making the economy more prone to speculative booms and busts. Therefore, Marx was much more critical of capitalism than Smith was; Marx believed it should be overthrown and replaced with socialism. He explained all of these developments in terms of domination by the capitalist class and subordination of all other aspects of society to its needs. Today, political economy follows in his footsteps with its focus on class relations and the domination of society by the wealthy, the transformation of competitive capitalism into monopoly capitalism, the destabilizing impact of technology, and the tendency of the economy to generate recurring unemployment.

Marx's other major contribution to political economy came from his philosophical training. As a young student, Marx studied philosophy in Germany. The first major contribution to political economy is Marx's method, referred to as *historical* or *dialectical materialism,* which developed out of both his attraction and repulsion to Hegel's theories about the role of ideas in transforming the world. The materialism part of dialectical materialism came from Marx's rejection of the emphasis of German philosophy on ideas as the agent of social change. Marx argued that social life springs from, but also is changed by, the way that humans purposefully transform nature—not by their ideas about the world. In short, Marx thought that all of history could be understood by examining the ways in which people perform economic activities such as work, management, or the selling and purchasing of goods and services. The dialectical portion of dialectical materialism is the integration of Hegel's philosophy of the nature of change—that conflicts and contractions clash, resulting in change. For Marx, the fundamental contradictions of a society in which ownership of the tools used in production is divorced from the people who perform that production result in constant struggles and conflicts, which in turn produce change. The outcome of this process is never predetermined; instead, it depends on the relative strengths and effectiveness of the strategies of the groups in conflict.

The analysis of capitalism comprises almost all of Marx's work. Despite common misperceptions, he rarely wrote about socialism or communism. He believed that capitalism drained people of their most creative energies, and that economic exploitation was unjustified, unfair, and inefficient. As part of his analysis of classes, Marx and his coauthor, Frederick Engels, argued that the conflict and inequality that are inherent in a class society lead to collective action on the part of classes—or class struggle. Their hope and political project was that the working class would triumph in its struggle to create a more equitable and humane society.

Modern political economy continues to draw from Marx its emphasis on the importance of economic classes and how these classes struggle and conflict in a capitalist society. Nonetheless, over a century of further work and attempts to create nonclass societies have revealed serious flaws with Marx's approach. As experience in the Soviet Union, the Eastern Bloc, and the People's Republic of China revealed during the 20th century, simply eliminating capitalist class distinctions is no guarantee that race and gender oppression will be eliminated, or that democracy will flourish. For these reasons as well as others, political economists strove to broaden their analysis in ways to which we now turn.

Including Institutions and Customs

In the late 19th and early 20th centuries, some political economists began looking at the roles of customs and socially constructed institutions in the economy. Inspired by late 19th-century anthropological accounts of the evolution of humans and of cultures, early institutionalists developed theories of economic activity that, like Marx's, were concerned with social relationships and human needs along with systematic inequality. This approach was based largely on an appreciation of the importance of culture in both explaining and in changing social, political, and economic relations. Culture (*eg,* a society's religious practices, treatment of children, rituals and celebrations, sexual division of labor, and consumption customs) provides norms for social (*ie,* communicative) interaction. The person who most often is credited with establishing institutionalist thought is Thorstein Veblen, a U.S.-born, German-trained economist who taught in the political economy departments of several major U.S. universities in the late 1800s and early 1900s.

While neoclassical economists are most interested in the outcome of the exchange process (*ie,* the price of the good as determined by the supply and demand), institutionalists like Veblen argued that the exchange process itself is of as much, if not more, interest in explaining economic phenomena. For example, where do people meet, and what important rules or customs are followed there (think about malls!)? What social and technical relations are necessary to produce the goods coming to market? What cultural and/or social relations exist in society that help to determine what kinds of goods people want to buy and how much they are willing to pay for them? Why do women perform most of the child-rearing work in society? In other words, institutional analysis is interested in the cultural, social, and political context in which economic activity occur.

Institutionalists analyze the status differentiation that is created by the cultural uses of economic behavior, such as Veblen's famous analysis of conspicuous consumption in *The Theory of the Leisure Class* (1973). Later, the institutionalist Gunnar Myrdal, who won the Nobel prize, wrote a classic analysis of race relations entitled *An American Dilemma* (1944), which showed how discrimination was a vicious circle that resulted from and reinforced status distinctions between blacks and whites. Status distinctions also can explain the rigidity of wage patterns, job ladders, and other phenomena (see Chapter 7). Institutionalists have used concepts such as these to dismiss the neoclassical notion that each person's utility is independent of other people's utility. In their view, the interdependence that is expressed by culture and enshrined in institutional structure is most important for understanding economic behavior.

John Maynard Keynes

It was not until the 1930s, and particularly the publication of John Maynard Keynes' *The General Theory of Employment, Interest and Money* (1936), that "macroeconomics" emerged as a distinct field within economics. Keynes argued that the neoclassical interpretation of single markets being "added up," or aggregated, to explain the entire national economy was wrong. He believed that the market system as a whole was not self-regulating, and that it was possible for the economy to stagnate for long periods of time. Some economists, such as Paul Samuelson, argued that Keynes' theories were only modifications of the standard, equilibrium framework, which concluded that capitalism was efficient and equitable. However, others rejected this interpretation and pointed to Keynes' argument that profit is a return to the scarcity of capital that is available for investment, not a return to the productivity of capital.

An important component of Keynes' theory is the role of uncertainty in explaining economic decisions. Because no one knows the future, there is an inherent uncertainty to economic decision-making (especially investment) when an individual must predict future rates of return. Given this uncertainty, it is futile to try to understand economic systems in terms of adjustment to a stable equilibrium. Further, Keynes believed that the determination of national wealth had more to do with the behavior of groups than of individuals, and that individual and social interests rarely coincided. He showed that economic problems can become self-perpetuating and, in particular, that the market system may be unable to eliminate unemployment. So, while individual markets may work fine, there may be *too* many goods being produced such that individuals will not purchase them all and firms will lay off workers as a result, meaning that even fewer goods will be purchased and produced, and so forth. This process results in unused resources. Further, Keynes believed that once down, the economy would not be able to pick itself up again on its own. All of this suggested that capitalism cannot be efficient.

Joan Robinson, who worked with Keynes, described his impact when she stated that "Economics once more became Political Economy" (1962;77). Keynes' contribution to political economy today is the concern that unfettered markets will be insufficient to create prosperity for all.

Expanding Rights: The Protest Movements in the 1950s to 1970s

The fourth major influence on the development of political economic thought is the integration of race and gender dynamics into economic models of conflict and change.

In the 1950s, the civil rights movement called the nation's attention to the racial ordering of economic, social, and political institutions in this country. Jim Crow laws, which were established in the South after Reconstruction, sanctioned separate educational and public facilities. However, separate was anything but equal. Using the powerful arguments of democratic rights and opportunity, black men and women organized to confront white individuals and institutions that had legally and illegally excluded them from equal participation.

The economic implications of racial inequality always have been a focus of the civil rights and later black nationalist movements. The role of people of color since colonial times, allocation of physical and human capital, and access to publicly provided goods and services all have played crucial parts in the history of racial inequality in the United States.

Feminists also have focused on the importance of culture, politics, psychology, and the language of rights in understanding economic behavior. Their contribution has been to dissect the belief system that differentiates male and female, one which is largely situated in the home and not the firm per se, and to analyze the impact of patriarchy on the division of labor within the family and the firm. The concept of patriarchy—the system of male domination—sharply distinguishes this view from the neoclassical perspective that the sexual division of labor is efficient and gender differences in occupational attainment equitable. Feminist economists such as Heidi Hartmann (1979) argue that the free female labor that benefits men in the household has important implications for the relationship between men and women, both in the home and at work. As a result of this and other work, gender now is recognized to be as fundamental as race and class in the determination of economic outcomes (Folbre, 1982; Humphries, 1991).

The contributions of the civil rights and feminist movements to political economy emerged from the fact that these were political movements calling attention to problems of inequality and conflict by appealing to the importance of democratic participation in all realms of life. Because these movements highlighted the dynamic of power and conflict, many in them looked to political economy for help in explaining—and transforming—a system of racial and gender economic inequality. In doing so, political economy's vision was broadened to explain the inequality so clearly demarcated not just by class but by skin color, gender, and native language as well.

7

WORK AND WAGES IN THE POLITICAL ECONOMY

INTRODUCTION: MORE THAN A PAYCHECK

The neoclassical analysis of labor markets outlined in Chapter 4 started with the fact that labor markets are different from other markets: people are hired in the labor market, and people often have different tastes and preferences. Additionally, those who hire labor do so because of the "derived demand" for labor services; people are hired for their productivity, not their looks or personality quirks. Political economists also highlight the fact that people rather than things are involved in labor markets. Beyond this commonality, the two approaches diverge.

In political economy, wages and the world of work are embedded in the social and political fabric of life, as well as in economic mechanisms. In many ways, looking at wages and labor markets is a perfect example of applying the Four C's discussed in Chapter 6. Working for a wage is a relatively new phenomenon in world history. It evolved with the rise of capitalism and therefore needs to be understood within this historical context. In the last chapter, we argued that workers are exploited in capitalism. Exploitation implies conflicting interests between workers and capitalists. In addition, wages are determined by an array of "extramarket" activities, including the ability of workers to be organized and demand higher wages. Workers' wages fluctuate with the business cycle and the relative strength of workers' organizations, but wage levels also are influenced by society's definition of a "fair wage for a fair day's work," particularly as these are written into minimum/maximum wage laws.

Political economists also argue that the labor market and wage levels are important beyond the exchange between workers on the one hand and firms on the other. Wages are the major source of income for families and are influential in shaping communities' economic well-being. Therefore, wages are an important component of an entire distribution mechanism that depends on the cultural organization of families and firms, race relations, and the role of government in providing income and services.

We begin our discussion of work and wages in political economy by examining the concept of the customary standard of living. Political economists argue that at the most abstract level, wages must be sufficient for people to survive. We approach wages from two angles. First, we look at the labor theory of value, and then we examine the role that customs and institutions play in wage determination. However, because the customary standard of living is influenced by the ways in which income is shared within families and by the level of goods and service that the government provides, we broaden the concept of wages to encompass the role of families and of government in wage determination. Then, we outline the political economy view of unemployment and business cycles, as these too exert a strong influence on wages. Later, our focus turns to two specific ways that firms are able to exploit workers over a long period of time: the cost of not having a job (*ie,* the threat of unemployment) as a motivator, and management practices in controlling the labor process. Finally, we look at the way in which political economists understand wage differences among workers: labor segmentation and tradition.

WAGE DETERMINATION

The factors that govern wages—and with it, wage inequality—are difficult to measure. Political economists believe there is little question that productivity differentials provide a very incomplete explanation for wage levels and differences in the economy. The assumption of competition that is required by the productivity explanation clearly is violated by labor market rigidities such as long-term contracts, minimum wages, worker immobility, and persistent unemployment.

If the touchstone for the neoclassical understanding of wages is supply and demand, that touchstone for political economists is the labor theory of value and the constraints of customs and institutions. The theory of political economy (outlined shortly) explains the prices that we expect to see in the economy, whether for cars or bubblegum or in labor markets, and tells us how workers are exploited. The theory is modified substantially, however, by looking at work in the home and at government income supports, because these change the terms or context under which capitalists and workers struggle over wages. We take up these modifications after considering the labor theory of value and the role of custom and institutions.

The Labor Theory of Value

Early economists, such as Adam Smith, David Ricardo, and Karl Marx, believed that wages were set equal to the customary standard of living for workers. When these economists envisioned wages, they thought about the entire wage bill—the total amount going to all workers, not to a particular individual. In this case, the wage bill is the value of the total output that must go to all workers for them to avoid starvation.[1] Capitalists had to pay workers their subsistence wages and all other costs of production (*eg,* rent, raw materials, depreciation of equipment); what was left over—the surplus—was profits.

Karl Marx, extending the arguments of Smith and Ricardo, developed a labor theory of value. He argued that the value of any good or service was the amount of labor time that it customarily takes to produce the product.

Labor theory of value: Commodities are worth the total amount of labor that is required to produce them

---

In Marxian economic theory, the value of anything is the amount of time it takes to make something within the technical, social, and cultural context of that society. The level of technology, skills, equipment, and work habits all will influence the value of goods and services. Marx argued that every commodity exchanges at its value—equivalent for equivalent. So, for example, if it takes me 3 hours to make a vest using the current level of technology and I have what is considered to be the average skill in the industry, then I should be able to trade that vest for a chair that takes the same amount of time to make.

If equivalent exchanges for equivalent, then how could workers be exploited? The first trick to answering this question is to ascertain what is actually exchanged in the labor market. The exchange is not as simple as it would be if the question referred to the apple market, for example. Apples can be owned and eaten by the buyer, and apples rarely complain in the process. Workers, however, are *not* exchanged in labor markets, because workers cannot be owned (this distinguishes capitalism from slavery). Nor are labor services the commodity that is bought and sold, because for most jobs, each and every specific task the worker must perform would be difficult, if not impossible, to specify (Box 7.1). Instead, workers offer their time—or more precisely, their potential to work within that time. In exchange, they receive a wage. Labor time is the actual commodity that is bought and sold in the labor market.

Next, put the idea of workers selling labor time together with the labor theory of value. Labor time must be worth the amount of time that it takes to "produce" a worker given the current context (*ie,* the amount of time needed to support a worker and his or her family at the customary standard of living). The amount of time required to produce a worker is then a social and cultural relation, a matter of conflict over the customary standard of living. If the customary standard of living requires a VCR (and, of course, the TV attached to it!) and a car, then the wage bill will reflect that. The wage rate is not simply tied to productivity and the price of the good. The wage—or the amount of time that is devoted to producing workers—depends on context and will change over time. Now, we can get at the major source of conflicting interests between workers and capitalists.

Marx noted that the labor theory of value seemed to leave exploitation as a "mys-

---

[1]Historically, economics was known as the "dismal science," because early economists like Thomas Malthus were convinced that population would grow faster than the food supply, resulting in mass starvation—pretty dismal.

BOX 7.1

LABOR FOR SALE?

If workers are exploited, why don't they just sell their work to capitalists? Piece rates, where individuals are paid for the number of "pieces" that are produced (or units sold, or telephone calls completed, and so on), would seem to do exactly this. While some jobs—sales representatives who travel from house to house—almost always are associated with piece rates or commissions, capitalists prefer to pay either hourly wages or salaries. The latter systems allow managers to compete more effectively, because they can more easily control workers and increase output while reducing wages.

In Bolivar, Tennessee, Sidney Harman decided to let his workforce participate in managerial decisions, and they created a system much like piece rates called "Earned Idle Time." When the workgroup completed its assigned projects for the day (*ie,* making rearview mirrors for automobiles), they could go home. This made it difficult for managers to increase output, because workers would demand more pay. It also made participation difficult, because workers wanted to leave (rather than manage) the plant when they had a chance. The program ended after Sidney Harman sold the plant.

At a small clothing operation in New England, the (female) stitchers operated under piece rates, but this created managerial difficulties. If allowed, the women would work very hard some, but not all, of the time, so when the manager needed an order completed quickly, the piece rate did more harm than good. Nor could he lower rates on existing work to improve his costs vis-à-vis his southern U.S. competitors. His solution? The women worked in rooms of 50 each, where the supervisor could see them at all times; supervisors harassed workers who seemed to be idle; talking was prohibited; and for many years, workers could not even go to the bathroom without the supervisor's permission. In addition, whenever new work came in, the rate was reduced.

Sources: On Bolivar, see John Simmons and William Mares, *Working Together,* New York: Alfred Knopf, 1983, and Appelbaum and Batt (1994). On the clothing case, see Robert Drago, *Success and Failure in Quality of Work Life Programs,* Unpublished PhD dissertation, University of Massachusetts–Amherst, 1983.

---

tery." How can a capitalist make money if everything exchanges at its value? Where do profits come from? The secret to this mystery lies in the special nature of labor time, because it is the only commodity that exchanges at its value but produces more than its value following the exchange. Stated differently, the capitalist pays for *labor power* (*ie,* the cost to produce the worker), but the capitalist receives, or hopes to receive, *labor* (*ie,* actual work that is worth more than the value of labor power).

Labor: Actual work that is performed
Labor power: The potential to work (*ie,* labor time)

To understand how exploitation works, consider an example. Every worker (including managers) in a meat-packing factory works 8 hours a day and produces an average of 32 pounds of packaged meat per day. Thus, each work-hour worked is equivalent to 4 pounds of meat. To buy all the raw materials and equipment used everyday, the owner of the meat-packing firm pays the equivalent of 4 pounds of packaged meat per day (or approximately 1 hour of an average day's work). The customary standard of living is equivalent to 24 pounds of packaged meat per day (or approximately 6 hours of an average day's work). The owners get whatever is left over—the surplus—the value of 4 pounds of packaged meat. Everything exchanges for its value, yet the owners end up with a profit. The secret of profit is that workers produce 8 hours' worth of commodities but are only paid their value—which is less than 8 hours' worth of commodities. After the capitalist pays for all the raw materials and the depreciation, the rest is profit—or surplus labor. In other words, the capitalist purchases the potential for work (*ie,* labor power), but then sets the employee to doing actual work (*ie,* labor).

The labor theory of value implies that workers produce all commodities for exchange in a capitalist economy—but are only paid a portion of it. A portion must be preserved to purchase raw materials and account for depreciation of machinery (labor goes into these, too). What's left over is profit and belongs to the capitalist because she or he owns the means of production—not because he or she did any work. Remember, the capitalist puts up the money (she or he usually does not manage work) and then sits back and "clips coupons."[2] Marx called the extraction of surplus labor (*ie,* the labor time during which workers are generating profits) exploitation. Any level of profit-taking exploits workers.

The production of profit and exploitation of workers can be simply illustrated. Consider a work day broken into two time segments, A to B, and B to C:

$$A \text{————————————} B \text{————————} C$$

The amount of time that is represented by the distance from A to B is the amount of time for workers to produce an amount equivalent to his or her day's wage. The amount of time that is between point B and C during the day is the surplus. Workers want the amount of wages they receive to increase and/or want to work less for the same amount (on the A-B-C time line, this would be represented by pushing B closer to C or pulling C and B closer to A). Workers can do this by organizing and demanding more pay or a shorter work day. Capitalists, conversely, want to increase the B-C portion of the working day and/or reduce the A-B portion. This can be done by making the workers work harder or smarter, so that they produce a day's worth of work in a shorter period of time, or by increasing the standard length of the working day.

As argued in Chapter 6, political economists stress the notion of how collective action and change are generated by conflict. In other words, those who are oppressed do not take it lying down. They struggle against oppression and, in the process, change the economy. In terms of wages and exploitation, this argument implies that workers will strive both individually and collectively for higher wages. How do they do it? Going in as an individual and demanding a raise from the boss usually doesn't work—especially if there are a hundred more just like you dying for a job. If there is no one else out there with your training, however, you will have a much better shot at getting a raise. When unemployment is low and workers difficult to replace,

---

[2]"Clipping coupons" refers to the way in which bondholders are paid for lending money. Each bond has a set of coupons attached that, periodically, bondholders clip and redeem for money.

wages tend to rise; when unemployment is high and workers are a dime a dozen, wages tend to fall. We return to this phenomenon when discussing the business cycle later in this chapter.

A much more forceful and sustained way to improve wages, however, is to get all your coworkers to go to the boss and ask for a raise at the same time. In other words, acting collectively—organizing workers into groups, demanding that everyone receive higher wages, and signing a contract to this effect—is an important way that workers improve their wages. Indeed, since the beginning of capitalist production in the early 19th century, workers have organized themselves in trade and craft unions as well as workers' associations. Workers were successful in reducing the length of the working day in advanced industrial countries and improving the standard of living for many. These changes often have come out of direct conflict and confrontation.

The reason that capitalists and workers maintain conflicting interests now should be apparent: those that do all the work only claim a portion of the bounty. Further, the higher the wages, the lower the profits. Class struggle, then, is a fight over the surplus, and class struggle is tied closely to wages.

The Role of Customs and Institutions

Nonmarxist political economists do not rely on the labor theory of value to explain how wages are determined, but they do rely on an argument about the customary standard of living. In this argument, wages are in large part determined by social, historical, and cultural influences. What people earn and what firms are willing to pay are determined by what people consider to be "fair" in a particular context.

The role that custom might play in wage determination is hard to model but very easy to understand. Economist Albert Rees, who taught neoclassical labor economics for 30 years, after which he served on several wage stabilization boards, as a corporate director, as a university provost, as a foundation president, and as trustee of a liberal arts college, found this out for himself. Here are Rees' conclusions from comparing his real-world experiences with the theory he had faithfully taught:

> In none of these roles did I find the theory I had been teaching for so long to be the slightest help. The factors involved in setting wages and salaries in the real world seemed to be very different than those specified in the neoclassical theory. The one factor that seemed to be of overwhelming importance in all these real world situations was fairness, and fairness always seemed to be judged by making some kind of wage comparison: with another union, with another employer, or with another person . . . I cannot recall ever being involved in any dispute or controversy in which any party to the dispute questioned the criterion of fairness as the basis for settling the controversy. Even employers never argued that supply or demand conditions in the labor market should be taken into account. The question was always which wage or salary comparison was appropriate . . . and of course each party would always contend that the comparison favorable to its cause was by far the most relevant one.[3]

Wage determination is largely influenced by collective behavior, which makes us concerned about where we stand relative to others, while what is specifically considered to be fair at any point in time can be traced to the social context.

[3]Albert Rees, "The Role of Fairness in Wage Determination," *Journal of Labor Economics* 11(1), 1993.

Rees goes on to argue that neoclassical theory is not so much wrong as incomplete: "The most it can do is set the stage for players such as personnel directors, union officers and individual workers. It cannot write their lines."[4] In other words, supply and demand may create loose limits on where wages can go, but within those limits, ideological and institutional factors must be invoked to explain the levels that actually are set. Beliefs about issues such as fairness and custom as well as organizational characteristics such as internal labor markets and unions work alongside the supply and demand considerations to determine wages. Consequently, productivity differentials cannot be the entire explanation for wage differentials.

Nobel Prize winner Robert Solow also believes that ideological factors such as fairness are crucial to the understanding of wages and unemployment. The title of his 1990 book, *The Labor Market as a Social Institution,* reveals a marked similarity of perspective with that of political economy. Solow agrees that labor markets are unlike other markets, because labor time is unlike other commodities. Labor market behavior involves social interactions and perceptions as well as traditional economic motivations. Workers not only react to the price paid for their own services but also to the wages received by others (Dunlop, 1979). Consequently, unemployed workers may not be able to bid down the wage—even if they want to. Employers may refuse to lower the wage scale when they hire new workers, because they fear their existing workers will react negatively and destabilize production. Once wage patterns are in place, they tend to be perpetuated as workers strive to maintain their positions relative to one another. This helps to explain why wages (unlike other prices) rise easily but fall with great difficulty, why relative wage patterns tend to be maintained through time, why (as we will see shortly) involuntary unemployment rises in recessions, and why (as we shall see in the next chapter) inequality may be difficult to eradicate even when it cannot be justified by productivity differentials.

Wage levels will depend on what other workers are receiving. For example, when the United Automobile Workers receive a 5% wage increase, the United Steelworkers will be well aware of this increase and typically ask for the same. After all, it's only "fair." What is so visible in the presence of labor unions often occurs in nonunion settings as well. When considering wage increases, a bank, for example, might survey other banks in the area to see what they are paying. Indeed, some will go so far as to "peg" their wage at 80%, 100%, or 120% of whatever the average bank in the area pays. (Check with your bank teller, and see how it is done there.) It also works the other way, too. When workers in one industry agree to wage concessions or forgo cost-of-living increases, it becomes harder for other workers to argue for higher wages.

Wage levels often are based on *job evaluation*. The institution of job evaluation is widespread in the United States. Some research suggests that over two-thirds of all employees have their pay affected by job evaluation, while over 80% of large organizations use the system.[5] A firm or governmental agency using a job evaluation system will hire a consultant to examine each job and assign points to various as-

---

[4]*Ibid.,* pp. 251–252.

[5]Figures from Ronnie Steinberg, "The Debate on Comparable Worth," *New Politics* 1 (Spring 1986), p. 114.

pects of it, ranging from complexity to skill requirements to human relations to managerial responsibilities. The points for each job are then added and wages set accordingly. So, for example, if a job that is "worth" 150 points pays $300 per week, then a job "worth" 200 points will pay $400 per week.

Job evaluation: Systems that assign points to job characteristics to set relative wages within an organization

---

Job evaluation makes wage-setting appear to be objective, but it is not. Instead, it is rooted in cultural and historical notions of what certain kinds of work and workers are worth. Economist Marlene Kim (1989) has shown how gender bias was built into the California Civil Service pay system in 1930, when it was decided to pay "somewhat higher for those occupations filled predominantly by men" (1989; 42). This allowed the state to pay a higher wage to men without explicitly paying women less than men for the same job. Partly as a result, women in the Service were paid 73.9% as much as men in 1937. Once these differences were locked in place, they proved difficult to remove. As recently as 1975, the wage-setting body for the California Civil Service admitted that maintenance of existing relative wages (*ie,* men's jobs paying more than women's) was "more important than responding to short-term changes in prevailing rates" (1989; 47). The term *prevailing rates,* of course, means supply and demand as measured by wage surveys of other organizations, so it is not surprising that by 1986, women earned only 74.9% as much as men in the Service.

This case demonstrates that historical context matters. It also demonstrates conflict between groups or collective behavior, because the only reason we know these facts is Kim's involvement in a comparable worth lawsuit that was filed by women against the California Civil Service. The suit was ultimately lost, but this does not mean that conflict or change was contained. Similar lawsuits in Minnesota and Washington state have been successfully pursued.

Looking more closely, sociologist Ronnie Steinberg (1990) has undertaken detailed studies of job evaluation systems. Steinberg finds that gender bias often is hidden in seemingly objective evaluation criteria. For example, in the Massachusetts state job evaluation system, potential employees for four male jobs (*ie,* labor, skilled labor, carpenter, painter) were each required to have the "ability" to lift heavy objects, stand for a long time, climb, and so on, and they were given separate points for their "willingness" to do the exact same tasks. In female jobs, points were given for "ability" to deal tactfully with others, establish and maintain harmonious relations, exercise discretion, and so on, but their "willingness" was not mentioned and, thus, presumably did not count![6]

That firms use biased criteria for setting wages rather than simply letting the market do it fits the political economy emphasis on the importance of context. The forces of supply and demand may still be there, but they have moved far into the

---

[6]This example is from Ronnie Steinberg and Lois Haignere, "Equitable Compensation: Methodological Criteria for Comparable Worth," in *Ingredients in Women's Employment Policies.* Christine Bose and Glenna Spitze, eds. Albany, NY: SUNY Press, 1986; 167.

background. Instead, we see an emphasis on traditions, collective action, social custom, and notions of fairness.

Home Production and the Family Wage

Wages are paid to the individuals that work in a firm, but any individual's wage may have to support more than one person. For example, suppose there is only one parent in a family that earns a wage. He or she has to bring home enough money to support all family members. If this worker can't find a job that pays enough to make his or her monthly housing expenses, buy enough food, provide child care when kids are not at school and he or she is at work, pay for health insurance and clothing, then this worker and family are in trouble. He or she may have to rely on family members or friends to help out—or even on public assistance to help assure they have the basic necessities. If many families are supported by one parent and there are not enough jobs that pay living wages for many of those adults, then society as a whole is in trouble. Jobs and wages just do not match family needs.

Now, imagine if our single working parent lives with another adult (perhaps a husband) and he stays home and takes care of the kids, cooks, shops, sews, and cleans house. Because there is another adult in house, the woman's paycheck will need to buy more food, clothing, and health care. But, because there is another adult, he also can take care of the children, do chores around the house, and cook meals. If he is "cost-effective" (*ie,* the new needs he brings to the household cost less than the money saved by having him work at home), then her family's standard of living has significantly improved. If he also goes to work for part of the day when the children are at school, she now can actually "afford" to take a job that pays less or requires fewer hours.

As this situation illustrates, wages are the outcome of how workers and capitalists meet in the labor market, but they also are an important distribution mechanism for family members who don't have access to wages. This means that the customary standard of living depends not only on the wage but also on work at the site of the home, the typical family structure, and as will be argued shortly, government supports.

More formally, the value of labor time includes the time and energy that it takes to get wage workers to work, which includes important—although often unpaid—work done by family members and communities, such as raising children and providing volunteer time to neighborhoods, schools, churches, and temples not only to improve the quality of our lives but to make sure family members are taken care of and get the moral, ethical, and spiritual support to grow up and become workers themselves.

An implication of this argument is that if all workers are to experience similar customary standards of living, then a worker with no dependents should receive lower wages than a worker who is financially supporting children. The lone worker is not helping to "produce" future workers, so he or she is worth less (although not worthless). If you accept this logic as fair, you might, for example, support a subminimum wage for teenagers, because they need less money to achieve a given standard of living. As a firm, you might provide health benefits that cover workers' dependents so that workers with dependents actually receive more health benefits.

Historically, this logic was tied to the domination of women by men through the notion of the *family wage*. The idea of the family wage is itself gender-neutral: an individual worker should be able to earn enough money at a full-time job to support an average-sized family. The idea was used concretely, however, as the basis for explaining why women should earn less than men. Women worked for "pin" money, while men had to earn enough to support entire families. As historian Alice Kessler-Harris (1982) documents, this notion has been prevalent since the inception of wage labor in the United States in the early 1800s. For example, in 1912, a New York State Factory Investigating Commission set out to make a case for increasing the minimum wage applying to women, so it surveyed several thousand employers on the wage that was "required to support in health and efficiency" people in the following categories: women who are teenagers, men who are teenagers, adult women living alone, adult men living alone, and one man supporting a wife and three children (Kessler-Harris, 1982; 42). The ideal of the family wage—and its restriction to male heads of households and breadwinners—was clear. Kessler-Harris goes on to show that much of the debate around this time over minimum wages for women centered on whether higher or lower wages were more likely to drive single women into prostitution; the issue of women raising children without a working husband was not even on the agenda (Box 7.2).

Family wage: The amount that a single wage earner requires to financially support an entire family

---

This notion that good jobs with good wages should be reserved for men supporting families was linked to the historical exclusion of women, and particularly white married women, from the labor force. As noted in Chapter 5, the most stark evidence of this phenomenon is found in the marriage bars holding in professions like teaching and nursing from the 1900s through the 1960s in the United States. By cutting off opportunities for women in the labor market, many women may have escaped direct exploitation. The general domination of women by men was reinforced, however, and opportunities for indirect exploitation, like those outlined earlier, were enhanced.

While the family wage was intended to "free" wives from the burden of paid employment, many capitalists took it as a signal to intensify the demands on workers receiving a family wage. To see why, consider a simple story. A husband goes to work in a firm while his wife stays at home and takes care of their children. Suppose the husband buys a sandwich at lunchtime for $2.00. One day, the boss says, "Look, your wife could make those same sandwiches at home for $1.00, so I'll cut your pay by $1.00 a day, your wife can make sandwiches, and your customary standard of living won't change." The wife now has more work to do at home for her husband, and her husband is receiving a lower wage. In this case, the family is getting less income but the husband's standard of living has not fallen, because the lost income is being made up by more of the wife's time being spent serving her husband. The wife now is being "exploited" partially by the firm and partially by her husband!

BOX 7.2

THE STRUCTURE OF FAMILIES IN THE UNITED STATES: A HISTORICAL PERSPECTIVE

Before wide-scale industrial capitalism in the United States, many people lived in extended families on farms. Surviving grandparents, parents, and children often shared the same quarters, and all were typically engaged in production. While there was a fairly strict division of labor by age and gender, all members worked. Older family members, women, and young children typically produced goods for home production (eg, clothes, candles, child care, soap), while men and older male children primarily were responsible for goods produced for market (eg, livestock, wool, food). Taking care of children was women's and older members' responsibility, but this care took place at the same place as all other economic activity: the household. Land ownership provided the primary source of income (Matthaei, 1982). Only white men were allowed to own land, which gave them considerable power over women and anyone who wasn't white.

With the advent of widespread wage labor in the mid-1800s, both the work done in households and family structure changed dramatically. Ability to earn wages—not land ownership—became the primary source of income for most families. Also, while custom dictated that women did most of the child care, capitalism reshaped women's inferior status. The development of the family wage came with the influx of immigrants and the movement of rural families into cities to seek employment at the newly developed factories. Men went to work; women stayed home with children. Young men who were not in line to inherit their livelihood through land transfer often left their families as soon as they were able to earn enough to support themselves. Young women usually left only on marriage and to set up their own household. By the 1900s, the typical family was no longer extended but nuclear: a married couple and their children. Further, married women tended not to work outside the home.

Certainly not all families were nuclear, nor did all men earn enough to support their families. In low-income families, especially those who faced racial and ethnic discrimination, wives and children often had to find some form of employment or income-producing ac-

tivity. Still, the emerging capitalist job structure developed with a particular type of family and a very set notion of who the main breadwinner in that family was. The sexual division of paid labor and the corresponding wages reflected this notion of family structure.

It is not only job structure that reflects a certain family structure. Many of the most important governmental wage support systems were created in the 1930s with the nuclear family with one male breadwinner in mind. The social security benefit system, unemployment insurance, and Aid to Families with Dependent Children (all originating in the 1935 Social Security Act) were established to replace the wages of male breadwinners.

Now, consider the radical change in family structure that has occurred over the last 40 years. In 1955, only 30% of married women worked for wages; now, 40 years later, almost 70% do. Indeed, the fastest-growing household type is that of a person who lives alone or with other unrelated people. Between 1970 and 1993, the numbers of women who live alone increased by 95% (from 7.3 million to 14.2 million), compared with the 167% increase of men living by themselves (from 3.5 million to 9.5 million). Currently, about 10% of all men and just under 14% of all women live alone. Fewer people (especially women) are getting and staying married. In 1970, about 72% of all people over 18 years of age were married; that percentage dropped to 61% in 1993.

Perhaps more important, however, more and more women—especially women with children—are working for pay. It no longer is an oddity to see women of child-bearing age at work, and women have entered the labor force for many reasons: some because they want to and, like men, get an important sense of themselves from work; and some because they must make ends meet. Therefore, it now is virtually expected that women will work (vividly echoed in welfare reform efforts) regardless of whether they have children.

Source: U.S. Department of Commerce, *Marital Status and Living Arrangements (March 1993)*, Washington, DC: Government Printing Office, 1994.

Economists Randy Albelda and Chris Tilly (1994) call the set of jobs that pay family wages but also assume the worker does not have to spend time taking care of others *jobs with wives*. These are jobs where the main breadwinner (usually the husband) is freed from obligations to deal with household duties, particularly child care. He often is expected to work long hours and not be interrupted during the day with family matters. To succeed in his job, he may even be expected to have his wife be a good entertainer for work colleagues. At the turn of the 20th century, the working class dream was to have a wife who didn't work. Until the 1950s, jobs with wives were mainly for white managerial male workers, but with large-scale unionization in many manufacturing industries during the 1950s, many blue-collar skilled and semiskilled jobs also became "jobs with wives."

Jobs with wives: When a family wage is paid and the job makes extensive demands on a nonwaged spouse

---

No one has calculated the number of men who received a family wage historically. What we do know is that the family wage has been eroding in the United States since the 1960s. As the numbers presented in Chapter 2 show, men's wages have been declining since that time, implying that fewer men receive a family wage. Related to this is that many of the blue-collar jobs that historically have paid a family wage have disappeared. Additionally, the exclusion of women from the family wage has been illegal since passage of the Equal Pay Act: women must receive the same wage for the same work. Finally, a key condition that made the family wage viable for male, married managers—jobs with wives—has evaporated as women have entered the professional ranks and the number of nonemployed wives has dwindled (Box 7.2).

The context for firms paying a family wage—the declining possibilities for jobs with wives—has changed, but firms may be behind the times in recognizing this shift. As Ellen Bravo (the Executive Director of 9 to 5, National Association of Working Women) notes, only 8% of households have a husband working for pay and a wife at home full-time, but the remaining 92% have precious little say over corporate policies. Of those who do set such policies (*ie,* managers), a full 91% are men with a wife who is home full-time (Bravo, 1995; 4–5).

Even if corporations are moving only slowly, the shifting context for the family wage has changed the implications of supporting this idea. The main reason for this change is that employers paying a family wage find it increasingly difficult to demand that the wives of male employees provide work with no remuneration from the firm. In other words, with some important exceptions (like president of the United States or a corporate manager), the link between "family wages" and "jobs with wives" is being broken. In turn, this means that family wages can be made available to anyone, whether male or female, married or single.

Economists Deborah Figart and June Lapidus (1995) argue that this changed context for the family wage implies it is an idea that women can use to their advantage. To see why, imagine the government increased the minimum wage or implemented comparable worth policies nationwide so that all jobs paid a family wage. Who would benefit? Figart and Lapidus conclude that single, working mothers would receive the lion's share of such benefits. Ironically, this idea, which historically was tied to the exclusion of women from the workforce, now may have become an idea that could foster equality, because the notion of "jobs with wives" is an idea whose time is rapidly passing.

Income Supports and the Social Wage

In 1935, sweeping wage-support legislation was passed by the Federal government—the Social Security Act. In this watershed law, the government established itself as supplementing families with income when the main breadwinner could not find work. The Old Age, Survivor, and Disability Insurance (OASDI) system—what we commonly refer to as Social Security—Unemployment Insurance, and Aid to Dependent Children (the precursor to Aid to Families with Dependent Children [AFDC]) all were established under this Act. The notion was that not everyone in a market-based system can, or is able to, find work; hence, they might not have a wage or live with someone who has a wage. Retired persons, the unemployed, and single mothers fell into this category. In each case, the idea was to supplement or replace a male breadwinner's wages.

This legislation suggests another important underlying component of the value of labor power and of the wage—the degree to which necessities are provided by communities or government rather than purchased with wages. If families must spend time and money to educate their children and provide health care to their families, then the value of labor power must rise as well, because the amount of time and money that it takes to care for children is higher. The larger the *social wage*—the value of necessary goods and services that are provided by pooling resources in communities and through government—the lower an individual's wage can be. Think about it this way. If the U.S. government provided low-cost or free child care to children aged 3 to 5 years (as they do in France), then one huge expense to workers with children would be reduced, and parents of young children might be willing to take jobs at a lower wage than if they had to pay for all child-care costs themselves. An even more immediate example is the cost of health insurance. If all people in the United States had health-care coverage, workers might be willing to work at jobs with lower wages if, in effect, they would have more take-home pay.

Social wage: That part of the customary standard of living that is provided by government

---

Of course, community-based and government-provided goods and services typically are paid for through fees, tithing, or taxes. If taxes on working people are higher than the benefits they receive, they indeed might require higher wages to make ends meet. The relationship of the social wage to the actual wage rate will depend on the structure of taxes. Since World War II, the United States traditionally has had a much lower social wage than other industrialized countries. Most countries offer health care, child care, K–12 education, and social security benefits for the elderly. The United States only offers the last two universally.

Various political economists have calculated the social wage, and their results vary. Samuel Bowles, David Gordon, and Thomas Weisskopf (1983) find that the social wage rose from the 1950s through the 1970s as workers struggled to improve their standard of living. This is the same period that large, state university systems were mainly built, the interstate highway system was put into place, and both Medicare and Medicaid were created. They argue that workers successfully increased their standard of living at the expense of profits.

More recently, economist John Miller (1992) found a negative social wage during this period—workers were paying more in taxes than they received in government services. Basically, Miller argues that the government was mainly taxing workers (not capitalists) to fund not only social benefits for workers but also the military. Miller goes on to show that the Reagan years made the social wage fall even further, as military expenditures rose and taxes on capitalists fell.

The important point here is not so much that political economists agree on the exact size of the social wage or the amount of unpaid work that is performed in the home. Rather, the point is that for political economists, "wages" need to be looked at in the social context, and work in the home as well as government taxing and spending policies are part of that context. Further, wages are more than just another market transaction. Wages are the primary source of income for families and, therefore, also an important component of income distribution and equity in capitalist economic systems (Acker, 1988).

MACROECONOMICS: BUSINESS CYCLES AND UNEMPLOYMENT

Another ingredient in the political economy view of wages concerns unemployment. In Chapter 4, we saw that neoclassical economists view unemployment as being subject to negative feedback so that if something bad happens (*eg,* unemployment), it will be stamped out (*eg,* wages will fall and labor markets will clear). Keynesian economists believe in positive feedback, so that some unemployment will create more, unless the government steps in.

Political economists are closer to the Keynesian view in believing that free markets will not stamp out unemployment. They go farther, however, by arguing that capitalism may require unemployment. Here, Keynes' optimism in government intervention takes a pessimistic turn.

Again, we look back to the work of Karl Marx, who believed that involuntary unemployment is both generated and required by capitalist economies. On the one hand, each individual capitalist has an incentive to improve productivity and individual work effort and, hence, to use fewer and fewer workers while producing more and more products using the cheapest labor available. A dramatic example occurred in agriculture, and is still occurring in manufacturing. Such cost reductions force more people into the labor market as families discover they cannot make it on a single income. Thus, capitalism creates unemployment as part of the normal processes of competition and growth. On the other hand, capitalism requires the government to permit and facilitate unemployment to keep the cost of losing a job high. If unemployment disappeared, then workers would slack off, demand higher wages, and be more likely to act collectively against capitalists. So, Marx interpreted unemployment as a necessary byproduct of market competition and the conflicting interests of capitalists and workers. Any government trying to eliminate unemployment does so at its own peril, because a stronger working class would undermine capitalist exploitation and control.

Nonetheless, Marx saw unemployment as contradictory. While capitalists profit from the high levels of work effort and low wages that extensive unemployment permits, unemployment also means there are fewer consumers with money to make purchases. Only workers form a large enough block of consumers to purchase the mass of products that capitalism creates, and if workers are unemployed or their wages fall, they do not buy very much. Therefore, capitalists are caught between their need to shed labor and reduce wages to compete and their collective need to sell products to those same workers.

Marx's understanding of unemployment is used by modern political economists in three ways. First, unemployment is central to the "cost of job loss" (discussed later), because without unemployment, profits are likely to fall. For the same reason, welfare spending and other measures that insulate workers from unemployment generally are opposed by the business sector (Cloward and Piven, 1982).

Second, political economists focus on the ideology of unemployment. If workers collectively understand unemployment as a strategy to reduce their wages and make them work harder, then workers are likely to support full-employment policies. In a democratic system such as ours, workers could always win through votes if the will was there, but of course, profits would then fall. So, capitalists have an incentive to peddle to workers the neoclassical belief that unemployment is an individual event and responsibility. To the extent capitalists can sell this idea successfully, workers will see unemployment as something they as individuals can avoid through hard work and initiative.

Evidence from a recent plant closing at RCA provides a glimpse at how successful capitalists have been in convincing workers that unemployment is an individual responsibility.[7] It is pertinent because clearly, no single worker can prevent a plant from closing. In a sample of comparable workers who were continuously employed as opposed to workers experiencing job loss through the shutdown of the RCA plant, it was found that the individual's sense of mastery over his or her environment was significantly higher for the continuously employed. The lack of any sense of mastery among those experiencing the plant closing was related to their also giving up on the ideology that capitalism rewards hard work, with around two-thirds disagreeing with the statement: "There is a good job waiting for me if I just look harder."

More generally, this "blame the victim" mentality regarding unemployment affects the unemployed themselves; it sets the context for their beliefs about themselves. Although the federal government has known how to control unemployment for over half a century, studies nonetheless find that a one-percentage-point increase in un-

---

[7]The evidence here is from Carolyn C. Perrucci, Robert Perrucci, Dena B. Targ, and Harry R. Targ, *Plant Closings, International Context and Social Costs,* New York: Aldine De Gruyter, 1988.

employment (*eg,* from 6 to 7%) increases the incidence of suicides by 4.1%, homicides by 5.7%, and admissions to mental hospitals by 4.3% for men and 2.3% for women.[8] Third, modern political economists draw from Marx the view that business cycles are inherent to the capitalist economy (Boddy and Crotty, 1975). In a business cycle of 4 to 6 years, we find unemployment first rising and then falling. Government policy makers have been unable to eliminate the business cycle (although Keynesian economists attempted to do so during the 1960s). The problem political economists see as driving the business cycle is that not merely high but *rising* unemployment is periodically required to reduce workers' wage demands and keep their efforts high. After all, if the same people were unemployed year after year, that would hardly act to motivate workers who hold jobs. Therefore, when times are "too good," in that unemployment is low and sales for firms are high, investors become fearful of workers working less hard and demanding higher wages. Investment slacks off, leading to higher unemployment. Unemployment alone would not bother investors, however, except that there also is a positive feedback effect as newly unemployed workers (or those fearing unemployment) decrease their purchases, thereby creating even more unemployment. When workers are sufficiently cowed, investors will slowly move back into the market, thereby reducing unemployment and improving sales.

The business cycle is important here because women and minorities often are the last hired when the economy improves and the first fired when it deteriorates, so when the white male unemployment rate increases a little, the rate for blacks and women increases a lot (Reich, 1981). Further, wage inequality between blacks and whites and between men and women increases as well. Both of these issues receive further discussion in Chapter 8.

LABOR MARKETS IN CAPITALISM: MOTIVATION AND THE LABOR PROCESS

As stated earlier, labor markets do not operate like other markets. When a firm purchases a worker's labor time (*ie,* labor power), it is the performance of actual work (*ie,* labor) that the firm really wants. The employer faces the problem of transforming labor power into actual labor; this also is known as the problem of capitalist management.[9]

Now, we ask how capitalists get workers to perform. As noted, part of the answer lies in the fact that capitalists have the money to buy capital equipment and to hire workers, while workers can afford to do neither. However, this is not the entire story, so we now consider two additional avenues for capitalists to extract surplus labor and keep wages down in the bargain: the cost of job loss, and the labor process.

---

[8]See D.W. Riegle, Jr., "The Psychological and Social Effects of Unemployment," *American Psychologist* 37, October 1982.

[9]"Manage" originally meant "to train (a horse) in his paces." Now, it means "to get (a person) to do what one wishes, especially by skill, tact, flattery, etc.; to make docile or submissive to control." *Source: Webster's New Twentieth Century Dictionary, Unabridged,* 2nd ed., New York: Simon & Schuster, 1979, p. 1093.

The Cost of Job Loss: Unemployment Is No Picnic

Think about what happens if you get up in the morning and say to yourself, "This job stinks. I'm doing all the work and the guy that owns the joint goes to the bank everyday. I think I'll just stay home." Go ahead, stay home—but you'll be out of a job. Then what? Unless you are independently wealthy or find someone (like a wife/husband or the government) who is willing to support you, you had better hit the pavement and start looking for work. And this may be a problem. With over 6 million people unemployed on any given day in the United States, it may not be so easy to find a new job. So, in the end, you get up and go to work. You may not like being exploited, but considering your options, you'll take it.

Surprisingly, this story implies that capitalists are actually paying workers "too much," or providing a positive *cost of job loss* to make people work hard.[10] As economists Herbert Gintis (1976) and Samuel Bowles (1985) tell the story, suppose that capitalists pay workers the market-clearing, competitive equilibrium wage where there is assumed to be little or no unemployment (see Chapter 4). Workers then have no reason to work beyond the absolute minimum level of work. If workers get tired of dealing with an irate customer on the phone, they'll hang up. If workers are worried about the quality or safety aspects of what they are producing, they may slow down and force the firm to miss an important deadline. If workers want to sing, dance, or listen to poetry, there is nothing the capitalist can do. Fire them, and they all walk across the street and get another job at the same wage. If capitalists raise workers' wages, then some people will be unemployed (by the law of demand), but those who are lucky enough to still have a job will work much harder as they worry about losing their jobs, homes, cars, and source of family support. They worry about the "cost of job loss."

Cost of job loss: The difference between income for holding onto or losing your job

---

The basic argument here is that as the cost of job loss rises, workers work harder, and conversely, when the cost of job loss falls, workers reduce their efforts. The capitalist can, of course, simply raise wages to increase the amount of labor being extracted from workers, but the cost-of-job-loss logic suggests several other devices to get more work out of workers: supervision, home production, and the social wage.

If the capitalist threatens workers with job loss but does not monitor them closely, they will commit acts of sabotage, steal from the firm, and generally goof off. After all, why help someone who has just threatened you? In response, capitalists hire supervisors to make sure these things don't happen. Supervisors don't produce anything, but they do help to extract work from workers.

The capitalist has to spend money to increase the cost of job loss by raising wages or hiring supervisors, so other ways of increasing the cost of job loss may be considered. Among them is the notion of "jobs with wives" (discussed earlier). Suppose

---

[10]There also are various neoclassical versions of this argument. See George Akerlof and Janet Yellen, eds., *Efficiency Wage Models of the Labor Market,* New York: Cambridge University Press, 1986.

that an employer is choosing between two job candidates, one of whom has an employed spouse and the other a spouse who works in the home without wages. Which should the employer pick? With the notion of the cost of job loss in hand, the answer is obvious: pick the applicant whose spouse does not receive any wage income, because this employee has more to lose—the entire family income—following job loss. Better yet is a worker with a financially dependent spouse and children; that person is even more likely to worry about the cost of job loss. Of course, it may be illegal for an employer to ask job candidates about their family status. In many cases, however, the legality won't much matter, because the employee is likely to volunteer the information anyway. This is just one more aspect of the employer's power over prospective and actual employees.

Finally, capitalists can generate a high cost of job loss by asking the government to limit—or cut off—unemployment benefits or other income supports that are received by potential employees who are out of work. As mentioned in the last section, Bowles, Gordon, and Weisskopf (1983) argued that the social wage rose during the 1950s and 1960s. Further, they argue that this increase in the social wage reduced the cost of job loss, led workers to reduce their efforts, and reduced profits as a result. The capitalist response was the Reagan years, which involved cut-backs in the social wage so that by the end of the 1980s, workers again were "properly" fearful of losing their jobs. The social safety net was pulled out from under them (Miller, 1992).

The Labor Process: Simplify and Control

Having people who are motivated to work is not enough for the capitalist to turn a profit. In addition, the capitalist must make investment decisions and hire managers to figure out how the work is to be performed. In a worker-owned firm, this is not a problem, because it is in the interests of workers to find the best ways to get the job done. In a capitalist firm, however, workers might work very hard, but in general, they have little or no interest in letting managers know how the work can best be performed. Therefore, an important component for understanding labor markets, and with it wage rates, is how capitalists deal with the *labor process* itself (Braverman, 1974; Edwards, 1979).

Labor process: Methods by which work and workers are controlled

---

Much of the history of the development of the capitalist firm—and with it, labor markets—deals with how the workplace is structured to assure that workers indeed work, and in a productive fashion. Management develops in part to face the task of controlling workers and choosing technology, with the explicit goal of eliciting the desired work behavior. Managers are also workers, but unlike nonsupervisory workers, they have authority and a vested interest in making other workers work hard. Control can be exercised by increasing the cost of job loss, as discussed earlier, but technology and managerial strategies will play a role as well.

Because capitalists (and their hired managers) have the right to design and run the labor process, they do so in a manner that facilitates the extraction of labor from labor time. As economist Harry Braverman (1974) argued, one way to improve the extraction process is to simplify jobs. Jobs can be divided into components that require little training or skill and are easy to supervise. For example, typing used to be a highly skilled task, because the result had to be perfect the first time or else unsightly "white-out" had to be applied. With word processors, however, mistakes are easy to correct. (Indeed, you do not even need to know how to spell, because the computer can correct mistakes for you.) Braverman argued that if you look over the long sweep of history—the switch from skilled individual mechanics to assembly line production of bicycles, the switch from grocery checkers being skilled with arithmetic to needing only to punch in the right numbers, the switch from architects needing a steady hand to using a computer "mouse"—the pattern is one of jobs being simplified, and the reason is that simplification makes sense in firms where workers do not share in the rewards for their efforts.[11]

In addition to labor processes being simplified, they may be systematized depending on the product the firm produces, the technology it employs, and the market situation it is in. There are three types of control systems used by different types of firms (or sometimes mixed within a single firm): simple, technical, and bureaucratic control (Box 7.3).

All firms rely on some system of control—and sometimes on more than one. For example, think of the last job that you held (or ask a friend who has worked for pay). Were you watched closely by a supervisor? If so, you probably were subject to simple control. Was there equipment that either checked how much work you did or kept the work moving? If so, we have technical control. Were you trusted to "do the right thing"? If so, then bureaucratic control may have been present.

What the capitalist would like—but cannot often get—is *loyalty*. Given the conflicting interests between capitalists and workers, this is difficult, expensive, and takes time. The one system discussed earlier that can generate loyalty—bureaucratic control—requires high wages, real promotion opportunities, and fair rules to function adequately. In this case, it looks like conflicting interests disappear, but they have not. As soon as the capitalist finds another way to make more money, the interests of workers will be sacrificed.

To make the point more strongly, certain combinations of control strategies and historical context have, at times, given groups of workers shared interests with capitalists. In fast-growing industries and those with powerful worker organizations (usually unions), workers and capitalists can see eye-to-eye on sharing the gains from growth, so when profits go up, so do workers' wages. Historically, there have been times in the United States when workers and capitalists have seen their interests as shared and agreed with statements like "What's good for GM is good for America." During the 20 years following World War II, industrial unions and corporations in

---

[11]For example, a superior technological alternative to numerical machine tools (which can, supposedly, be operated by unskilled workers) was abandoned for this reason. See David Noble, *Forces of Production*, Oxford: Oxford University Press, 1986.

BOX 7.3

THREE FORMS OF LABOR CONTROL

In his book *Contested Terrain* (1979), Richard Edwards traces the development of three distinct forms of control that capitalists use in the workplace to extract work from workers. The first type is *simple control,* and it most commonly is used at the small firms that most closely correspond to the competitive model of neoclassical economics. Such firms typically exist in wholesale and retail trade or the service sector. Wage and skill levels generally are low, and job ladders (*ie,* promotion opportunities) are nonexistent. Incentives therefore are minimal. Instead, the employer (or the manager) directly supervises workers and evaluates their work. Workers who please the boss may be given small incentives, such as better working hours, but the primary means of exercising control is the threat of unemployment. Workers in these firms are easy to replace, so management has no hesitation about firing those who it feels are not working hard enough. The personal exercise of authority is used to control the pace of work and to elicit the desired work behavior from workers. Try describing simple control to anyone who's worked at McDonald's or Kmart, and it should sound very familiar to them.

In contrast, *technical control* relies on machinery to set the pace of work. This system of control most often is found in large or very large firms in manufacturing and mining industries. These firms frequently are unionized, and the personal authority of managers is limited by grievance procedures and seniority rights. Nonetheless, supervisors still are needed to ensure that workers keep up with the assembly line. Workers tend to be more highly skilled and paid, and management has more of a stake in reducing turnover to stabilize production and minimize the costs of on-the-job training. The classic example of technical control is the assembly line, which regulates both the type and pace of work. However, technical control also can be associated with low wages, especially in nonunionized, light manufacturing and in some service industries. For example, computers now allow managers to know easily and quickly how many telephone calls an operator answers, or how many groceries a checker handles. Because the design and implementation of technology is in the hands of management, the labor process will be organized in a way that maximizes output and profits, not necessarily wages.

Bureaucratic control is the third method of eliciting desired work behavior from workers. This system relies on pay and promotional incentives and, frequently, also on internalization of the norms of the firm. The worker wants to succeed because she or he believes in doing the best job possible to scale the job ladder. There tend to be high returns to seniority and education, and credentials are important as a means to job placement and advancement. This is most common among professional, technical, and administrative workers in large corporations where work cannot be standardized by technology or supervised in a one-on-one fashion. If you ask yourself which of the three control strategies you would personally prefer for your own job, the answer is likely to be bureaucratic control.

---

automobiles, steel, rubber, and coal all struck agreements that tied wage increases to gains in productivity. Workers in those industries saw their wages rise with profits. However, as is all too painfully obvious to those who live in midwestern cities that housed these industries, this compact was short-lived. International competition facilitated a massive downsizing that decimated employment (and with it, union membership) in those industries and reduced wages.

There are three major qualifications to our discussion of the labor process. First, workers exert some control over the labor process through collective and individual behavior. Second, there is nothing "natural" about having capitalists control the labor process. Third, there is nothing "unnatural" about working hard (when it is in your interest to do so). Let's take these in order.

Are workers powerless in the face of capitalist control over the labor process? Hardly. Indeed, much of the historical evolution of the systems for control has been a response to worker resistance (Gordon, Edwards, and Reich, 1982; Jacoby, 1985). Seniority systems, wage ladders, grievance procedures, and other aspects of technical and bureaucratic control in many ways emerged as a concession to workers. Unions and the labor movement were influential in the attitude of class compromise, which was consolidated after World War II—only to see this compromise evaporate since the late 1970s as unions have grown weaker and weaker. The systems of control thus serve the interests of management, but they do so in a way that responds to the demands and struggles of working people. Conflicting interests do not disappear even with the most effective managerial control.

Employers have a legal right to design the labor process, but this does not have to be the case. We can imagine a system where workers make the decisions about work organization, work rules, pay and promotion, technological choice, and so on. This would require a very different type of economic system than ours is at present. In capitalism, the owner of capital is vested with control over all aspects of the labor process as a result of property rights—the legal rights that are imbued in capital ownership. Capitalists have the right to make these decisions, because the government has granted them the legal right to do so, not because there is some economic necessity in their being the decision makers. To us, it may seem inevitable simply because it is all that most of us have ever observed, but in fact, it is nothing more than a legal arrangement—albeit one with substantial consequences.

Finally, note that this conflict does not mean work is inherently disagreeable. Most of us gain more from work than our paycheck. Much of our identity and self-respect comes from work. This, however, does not mean that our primary objective at work is to maximize the firm's profits. Of course, the more stake that workers have, the harder they will work. Studies have shown that productivity rises when workers can exercise their judgment, express themselves, and/or directly benefit from the work process or product (Appelbaum and Batt, 1994). Unfortunately, few of these conditions apply to most work situations. Most workers have little or no say in what is produced, how it is produced, where investment should take place, or what the firm's priorities should be regarding its workers and community. Work is designed to benefit the capitalist; workers are only a means to an end.

EXPLAINING WAGE DIFFERENTIALS

We now turn to the ways in which political economists explain wage differences among workers. Political economists have two ways of explaining these differences. The first, labor segmentation, refers to a hierarchy of jobs that have developed in capitalism over time. We have already alluded to a hierarchy of workers by discussing the role of managers in shaping the work process. The second explanation of wage differences has to do with tradition (*ie,* customary levels of wages for different jobs), but more importantly for different workers. This second explanation largely relies on understanding how discrimination works in labor markets.

Labor Segmentation: Divide and Conquer Everywhere

So far, we have seen that managers try to motivate workers through threats of job loss and to govern them with various control strategies. However, there also are larger patterns in the economy that help the firm to extract labor at low cost. These patterns concern the fact that distinct types of workers are hired for particular types of jobs by certain types of firms, so firm, job, and worker types are connected. The theory that makes this connection and explains wage differences between workers is called *labor segmentation theory* (Gordon, Edwards, and Reich, 1982).[12]

Segmentation: A bundling of firm, job, and worker characteristics that limits worker opportunities and divides the work force

---

Segmentation means that the labor market is split into distinct portions, which diverge in terms of the organization of work, wage and employment setting processes, and labor market outcomes. Table 7.1 summarizes the characteristics of labor segments. There are two main labor segments (or sectors): the primary and the secondary.

Primary independent sector: High-wage, white-collar, professional jobs with career ladders

---

The primary sector contains jobs that pay living wages, have opportunities for promotion or regular wage increases, and in which education and experience pay off. The primary sector is divided into two subsectors: the primary independent and the primary subordinate. The primary independent sector contains white-collar, high-paying jobs in which entry largely is a function of educational credentials. The primary subordinate sector contains blue-collar, high-paying jobs. The jobs often are unionized, and pay increases come with seniority and experience. Primary subordinate jobs require specific skills, but these often are obtained on the job. Social networks and family connections are important factors in getting these jobs.

Primary subordinate sector: Medium-wage, blue-collar, semiskilled jobs with job security

---

The secondary sector contains jobs that pay poorly, offer little or nothing in the way of job benefits, and typically are dead-end. Many of us have held these jobs at

---

[12]The term *labor market segmentation* originally was used to capture the idea that one group of workers—inner-city black men—were locked out of labor markets for good jobs. In recent political economy discussions, the simpler term *labor segmentation* is used, because segmentation applies to jobs within firms and types of firms as well as in markets.

TABLE 7.1
CHARACTERISTICS OF LABOR SEGMENTS

Segments	Type of control	Job conditions	Wages	Examples
Primary independent	Bureaucratic or simple	Job security & job ladders	High	Managers, engineers
Primary subordinate	Technical bureaucratic	Job security	High to medium	Auto workers
Secondary	Simple	No job security	Low	Sales clerk

some point in our lives, but chances are that if you are reading this book, you are trying to get the necessary skills or credentials to never have to work at a job in this sector again.

Secondary sector: low-wage, blue- or pink-collar, unskilled jobs with no job security

---

Mobility between the segments is restricted, so the competitive assumptions of neoclassical economics have only limited applicability. In addition to the forces of supply and demand, labor markets depend on social and institutional factors, such as the control system in the labor process, the race and gender of the workforce, and the size and structure of the firm—but this is jumping ahead of the game. We return to the role of race and gender in labor segments in the next chapter.

According to the theory of labor segmentation, distinct types of labor control strategies will be linked to different types of labor markets (Edwards, 1979). Workers in simple control systems pass through the *secondary sector* of the labor market, workers in technical control systems the *primary subordinate sector* of the labor market, and workers in bureaucratic control systems the *primary independent sector* of the labor market. Each sector has distinct wage and employment setting processes and, consequently, distinct sets of labor market outcomes.

Wage- and employment-setting processes vary from one control system and segment to another. This assertion received confirmation in an influential study by economists William Dickens and Kevin Lang, who found that wages are set in the economy in different ways, with some people (primary subordinate and primary independent sector) receiving higher wage returns to education than others (secondary sector).[13] This means that supply and demand provide only a partial explanation for how wages are decided. Let's take a closer look at how wages are set in the three sectors.

The secondary sector is the low-wage portion of the labor market. Skill levels and on-the-job training are minimal, so wage growth is limited. Employment growth is sensitive to the business cycle, because these firms usually subsist on cash flow, making their employment highly responsive to current sales. With few returns on expe-

[13]See William T. Dickens and Kevin Lang, "A Test of Dual Labor Market Theory," *American Economic Review* 75(4), September 1985.

rience or education, turnover tends to be high. As a result, unionization is difficult. Jobs in this sector are more likely to be part-time and/or part-year jobs. This gives employers maximum flexibility. People with less than full-time labor market commitments (*eg,* full-time students, people with young or several children) often have to take these types of jobs—even when they have considerable experience or education—because they need jobs that require less than a 40-hour-per-week commitment.

With people regularly flowing in and out of secondary sector jobs, you might think that the laws of supply and demand would apply more strongly here than in either of the primary sectors. This is basically correct, but there are two important reasons why, even in the secondary sector, supply and demand do not rule alone. First, the government sets minimum wage levels, so even secondary sector jobs may be hard to get. For example, anthropologists Katherine Newman and Chauncy Lennon (1995) document the extreme difficulty that people have in getting even minimum wage jobs in Harlem. Second, because secondary sector jobs provide no job security or career ladders, the firm may have to pay enough so that the cost of job loss is positive; it's the only way to get workers to perform in such jobs.[14]

Firms that are characterized by technical control set wages and employment by different means. Wages and benefits are set by negotiations with unions and depend on bargaining strength as well as supply and demand. These firms are capital intensive, which means that disruptions to production (*eg,* strikes) are expensive. Therefore, they tend to pay higher wages, offer decent benefit packages, and limit managerial discretion with seniority rules and grievance procedures. Returns on education are low, but returns on experience are high. Employment traditionally is stable, because on-the-job training is costly, encouraging firms to "hoard" labor during economic downturns. However, unemployment can become severe during periods of economic turmoil, such as in the 1980s.

In firms or labor processes that are characterized by bureaucratic control, professional, technical, and administrative functions are dominant. These positions generally are nonunionized but highly paid, with high returns on both education and experience. Wages and benefits usually are determined by *internal labor markets* (Doeringer and Piore, 1971), where people are paid according to their job title and rewards take the form of promotions to job titles with higher pay. Internal labor markets are separated from the forces of supply and demand, because wages and promotion opportunities are set by administrative rules. Incentives are created by well-developed promotional ladders offering opportunities for mobility within the firm. On-the-job training is extensive and supplemented by high average levels of education among the workforce. Therefore, employment tends to be stable as the costs of turnover are high for both the employee and the firm. Further, employers expect workers to be fully committed to their jobs and available for overtime or to take work home if necessary. Here is where the firm requires loyalty and often creates "jobs with wives," leaving workers precious little flexibility or time for activities such as caring for children or older relatives.

---

[14]Economist James Rebitzer finds evidence that secondary sector employers set wages high enough so that a positive cost of job loss exists. See James Rebitzer, "Unemployment, Long-Term Employment Relations and Productivity Growth," *Review of Economics and Statistics* 69(4), November 1987.

Internal labor markets: Where a firm creates job ladders and promotes workers from within up the ladders

---

In sum, supply and demand play a strong role under simple control in determining wages, but this is tempered by government minimum wage requirements and the need to set wages high enough to produce a positive cost of job loss. Under technical control, the game of bargaining between organized workers and employers will work alongside supply and demand to determine wages. Under bureaucratic control, wages are attached to positions on job ladders and set internally by management, with only a minimal role for supply and demand.

Now, we need to bring *divide and conquer* into the picture. We introduced this notion in Chapter 6 when discussing ways for firms to profit by setting subcontractors or employees into competition with each other (see Box 6.2). Political economists such as David Gordon, Richard Edwards, and Michael Reich (1982) argue that labor segmentation exists because it divides workers and, in the process, conquers them, such that the firm can make money.

Divide and conquer: Capitalist attempts to profit by splitting workers into groups that compete against each other

---

Divide and conquer fits into labor segmentation in several ways. First, consider the problem of management. To produce, capitalist firms create a natural group that has an interest in *collective behavior*—the firm's employees. However, if the employees act collectively against the firm, profits will fall. Segmentation solves this problem partly by dividing workers into the employed and the unemployed. Employed workers may believe they are being exploited and so band together, but if the cost of job loss is positive, the firm can always threaten to replace every last worker who makes so much as a move to join a union or band together in other ways. The firm can simply leave for sunnier shores with lower wages.

Second, in the case of bureaucratic control, workers are divided by promotion opportunities. Workers are told to "keep your nose clean" and you'll get promoted; joining a union in such circumstances is a pretty sure way to damage your career.

Third, workers are divided by education and occupation, such that those with good jobs will believe they have little in common with those who do not. Limits on mobility between the segments are partly responsible for this division, but the lack of "good" jobs and their being given only to highly educated workers also contributes. This division has become even more severe in the last decade. Jobs in the primary subordinate sector have been severely cut by deindustrialization as manufacturing firms closed their doors in the United States and reopened them in Taiwan or Singapore. Jobs in the primary independent sector have grown, but much more slowly than jobs in the secondary sector have. Most job growth over the 1980s went to low-wage jobs, many of them part-time or contingent (Harrison and Bluestone, 1988). Thus, the ability of workers to transit between the secondary sector and the primary sector has become even more limited. This restriction also has led to "credential inflation," because employers increasingly can demand higher and higher levels of schooling from applicants seeking primary sector jobs. It also has meant that many workers, including many white males, have found that their probability of downward mobility has been much greater than their probability of upward mobility. In addition, by the logic of divide and conquer, capitalists will strive to convince white male workers who are threatened with losing their primary sector jobs that it is not the fault of the firm but instead of affirmative action, immigrants, or government interference that caused the problem.

Along with providing a theory of wage differentials, labor segmentation (like the cost of job loss and labor control strategies) represents another capitalist response to the problem of conflicting interests with workers. Workers have a material interest in collective behavior, but the context of labor segmentation inhibits them from acting in their interests. Labor segmentation implies that the link between productivity and wages is tenuous at best (Box 7.4).

Traditions: Faces Filling Places

As it turns out, workers are divided under labor segmentation by race and gender. Jobs in each sector are not shared proportionately. The primary independent sector is disproportionately white and the primary dependent sector disproportionately male. Women and people of color have the lion's share of secondary sector jobs. However, segmentation theory per se does not tell us why certain groups find themselves in the secondary or the primary independent sector, only that those divisions exist.[15] In short, certain faces end up filling certain places, and this is not an arbitrary process.

One way to understand why women and blacks fill the lower rungs of the job ladders in the primary sectors and predominate in the secondary sector is to argue that those are the jobs that women and blacks have always held. Traditional gender and race roles in the labor market get reproduced over time. Although this is true, scratching the surface and asking *why* the tradition exists requires thinking more seriously about labor market discrimination. Political economists have much to say on this topic, and it is the subject of the next chapter.

SUMMARY

The political economy view of wage-setting starts with the notion of conflicting interests: capitalists seek to exploit workers, and workers try to stop exploitation. The labor theory of value helps to explain why exploitation continues, because wages are set at the customary standard of living while workers produce more than is needed to maintain that standard. We then looked more closely at the role of tradition and institutions (as opposed to supply and demand) in influencing wages. Neoclassical economists who have been involved in actual wage-setting procedures admit that supply and demand play only a limited role, while political economists who delve more

---

[15]The segments define jobs, not the people who fill them. See Randy Albelda and Chris Tilly, "Towards a Broader Vision: Race, Gender, and Labor Market Segmentation in the Social Structure of Accumulation Framework," in *Social Structures of Accumulation,* David M. Kotz, Terrence McDonough, and Michael Reich eds., Cambridge: Cambridge University Press, 1994.

BOX 7.4

MARGINAL PRODUCTIVITY AND WAGES?

Productivity differentials may be more of a consequence than a cause of wage differentials. If they expect to receive different returns, women and minorities may make different investment decisions in their human capital than white men. High quit rates may result from low wages rather than the frequently asserted converse. Low-wage workers may not have the opportunity to exercise their intelligence and creativity, as opposed to earning low wages because they lack intelligence and creativity. Low wages may reduce incentives and, therefore, output. Although neoclassical economists believe that causality runs from productivity to wages, it is easy to think of likely ways in which causality runs from wages to productivity. The same association between wages and productivity exists in both cases, but the direction of causality—and hence the interpretation of inequality—is opposite.

The suspicion with which political economists view the wage–productivity relation is understandable in light of the extreme difficulties that are attached to measuring productivity. No one has ever measured marginal productivity for anything other than special groups, such as baseball players. For most workers, an increase in hiring corresponds to an increased use of capital, so it is impossible to isolate the pure effect of a change in labor input on output. It is equally difficult to prove that the productivity of capital determines profits, because there is no agreement on how to define or measure the contribution of the capitalist to production.

Further, the belief that pay rises with skill is more difficult to prove than you might think, because skills are multidimensional and cannot be summed into a single measurement. Some skills, such as child-rearing, go almost completely unrewarded despite being at least as complex as, and probably more important than, other types of highly rewarded skills, such as financial management. It also is worth noting that in some historical periods (eg, the 1950s and 1960s), wage and productivity growth both were closely tied together, while in other periods (eg, the early 1990s), wage growth has lagged behind productivity growth. The belief that productivity determines incomes frequently is used to justify the inequalities created by capitalism, but there simply is no clear-cut evidence that this linkage holds true.

If you ask around, you will find at least a few people who have taken a job and begun working *without even finding out how much they will be paid!* Usually, this can be traced to the job applicant's fear that "if I ask, I might not get the job." Political economy explains this phenomenon by the fact that many workers have few viable alternatives to working for capitalists, so they will take a job almost regardless of the wage. For political economists, wage determination is complicated, as the employer in this case would likely take the context into consideration (eg, how much other employees are earning, how much the employee expects to earn) as well as the revenues the job will generate.

deeply into wage-setting institutions find that historical gender bias tends to survive in apparently "objective" rules.

The standard of living depends on more than take-home pay, however, because work in the home and the social wage also influence the standard of living. Considerations of home and the government dictate that we broaden our context for understanding wages and provide additional avenues for conflict and change over such ideas as the "family wage" or "jobs with wives."

We also considered unemployment and business cycles, because they affect wage levels as well. In the political economy view, capitalist economies require unemployment and periodic increases in unemployment through business cycles to keep wages down and the cost of losing a job up. Unemployment is contradictory, however, because it reduces sales and may lead to collective action on the part of workers. One implication is that capitalists must constantly strive to convince workers that only individual hard work for low wages will "save" them from unemployment.

In their battle to extract work from workers, capitalists have various tools. Most important is lack of a viable alternative to employment for most people. Additionally, capitalists may create a positive cost of job loss so that workers worry about losing their jobs and work hard in response. Capitalists also may use various labor control strategies, such as simple, technical, or bureaucratic control, and the way that wages are set will depend on the control strategy that is applied to each group of workers.

Finally, we considered how political economists explain differences in wages among workers. Labor segmentation argues that different types of jobs carry different types of wages. Because there are several labor segments (some with job ladders), there will be different wages. The three sectors are the primary independent, primary subordinate, and secondary sectors, which correspond to the three strategies of control. The labor segments also help to explain wage differences and to create divisions between workers that are so effective that workers will be loyal to the firm and, possibly, even have shared interests with the firm's owners.

While labor segments describe why wages differ by *jobs,* it does not explain why women and blacks tend to get the worst jobs. Political economists turn to theories of discrimination for that, which are discussed in the next chapter.

DISCUSSION QUESTIONS

1 If you wanted to, could you start your own business and make as much money as you would with a career-type job?
2 Can you think of examples from your own experience where one person provided unpaid labor to the firm where a spouse was employed?
3 Is there some form of governmental support that, if removed, would reduce your standard of living? If there is, would you be willing to give up that support if your taxes were reduced accordingly?
4 Have you ever worked at a job you worried about losing because of lost wages? If so, could you calculate the approximate "cost of job loss" for that job?
5 Can you identify further examples of jobs with simple control, technical control, and bureaucratic control?
6 What has happened to someone you know who used to work in the "primary subordinate" sector and lost a job during the 1980s or 1990s? Did the person find another primary subordinate job or instead move into the "secondary" or "primary independent" sector?
7 Thinking of a job that you or someone you know has held, do you believe the wages were set by supply and demand, so that people performing similar jobs at different workplaces received the same wage? Do you think considerations of fairness entered in? Were job evaluations used? Did the wages set by the organization lead to women earning less than men or blacks less than whites?

8 If you know someone who recently lost his or her job, do you think it was that person's fault? Does the person who lost the job *believe* that it was his or her fault? What happened to that person's standard of living and lifestyle after losing the job?

SUGGESTED READINGS

Acker, Joan. 1988. "Class, Gender, and the Relations of Distribution." *Signs,* 13(31).

Albelda, Randy and Chris Tilly. 1994. *Glass Ceilings and Bottomless Pits: Women, Income and Poverty in Massachusetts.* Boston: Women's Statewide Legislative Network, 1994.

Appelbaum, Eileen and Rosemary Batt. 1994. *The New American Workplace.* Ithaca, NY: ILR Press.

Boddy, Radford and James Crotty. 1975. "Class Conflict and Macro-Policy: The Political Business Cycle." *Review of Radical Political Economics* 7, Spring.

Bowles, Samuel. 1985. "The Production Process in a Competitive Economy." *American Economic Review* 77(1), March.

Bowles, Samuel, David M. Gordon, and Thomas E. Weisskopf. 1983. *Beyond the Waste Land: A Democratic Alternative to Economic Decline.* New York: Anchor/Doubleday.

Braverman, Harry. 1974. *Labor and Monopoly Capital.* New York: Monthly Review Press.

Bravo, Ellen. 1995. *The Job/Family Challenge: Not for Women Only.* New York: John Wiley & Sons.

Cloward, Richard A. and Frances Fox Piven. 1982. *The New Class War: Reagan's Attack on the Welfare State and Its Consequences.* New York: Pantheon Books.

Doeringer, Peter and Michael Piore. 1971. *Internal Labor Markets and Manpower Analysis.* Lexington, MA: Lexington Books.

Dunlop, John T. 1979. "Wage Contours." In *Unemployment and Inflation.* Michael J. Piore, ed. White Plains, NY: M.E. Sharpe Inc.

Edwards, Richard. 1979. *Contested Terrain.* New York: Basic Books.

Figart, Deborah and June Lapidus. 1995. "A Gender Analysis of Labor Market Policies for the Working Poor." *Feminist Economics* 1(3).

Gintis, Herbert. 1976. "The Nature of Labor Exchange and the Theory of Capitalist Production." *Review of Radical Political Economics* 8, Summer.

Gordon, David M., Richard Edwards, and Michael Reich. 1982. *Segmented Work, Divided Workers.* Cambridge: Cambridge University Press.

Harrison, Bennett and Barry Bluestone. 1988. *The Great U-Turn: Corporate Restructuring and the Polarizing of America.* New York: Basic Books.

Jacoby, Sanford. 1985. *Employing Bureaucracy.* New York: Columbia University Press.

Kessler-Harris, Alice. 1982. *Out to Work: A History of Wage-Earning Women in the United States.* New York: Oxford University Press.

Keynes, John Maynard. 1936. *The General Theory of Employment, Interest, and Money.* New York: Harcourt, Brace and Co.

Kim, Marlene. 1989. "Gender Bias in Compensation Structures: A Case Study of Its Historical Basis and Persistence." *Journal of Social Issues* 45(4), Winter.

Matthaei, Julie. 1982. *An Economic History of Women in America: Women's Work, the Sexual Division of Labor, and the Development of Capitalism.* New York: Schocken Books.

Miller, John. 1992. "A Negative Social Wage and the Reproduction Crisis of the 1980's." In *International Perspectives on Profitability and Accumulation.* Fred Mosley and Edward N. Wolff, eds. Aldershot, England: Edward Elgar.

Newman, Katherine and Chauncy Lennon. 1995. "Finding Work in the Inner City: How Hard Is It Now? How Hard Will It Be for AFDC Recipients?" Mimeo. Department of Anthropology, Columbia University.

Reich, Michael. 1981. *Racial Inequality: A Political-Economic Analysis.* Princeton, NJ: Princeton University Press.

Solow, Robert. 1990. *The Labor Market as a Social Institution.* Cambridge, MA: Basil Blackwell.

Shulman, Steven. 1990. "Racial Inequality and White Employment: An Interpretation and Test of the Bargaining Power Hypothesis." *Review of Black Political Economy* 18(3), Winter.

Steinberg, Ronnie. 1990. "Social Construction of Skill: Gender, Power, and Comparable Worth." *Work and Occupations* 17(4), November.

8

THE POLITICAL ECONOMY MODEL OF DISCRIMINATION

INTRODUCTION: EXPLOITATION, DOMINATION, AND EXCLUSION AGAIN

In the last chapter, you learned how political economists view labor markets and the workplace. This chapter builds on that analysis to highlight race and gender inequality. In other words, we now put "faces" into the "places" outlined in Chapter 7. Those places are defined by inequality—between capitalists and workers, the employed and the unemployed, workers in the primary and in secondary sectors, and those who are expected to work for pay and those who are not. This chapter develops a theory of *discrimination* to understand who ends up in these respective positions.

For political economists, discrimination primarily is perceived to be "institutional" in that it is embedded in the customs and rules that govern the behaviors of institutions (*eg,* the family), organizations (*eg,* the firm), and markets (*eg,* the job market). The downside of this view is that institutional discrimination may persist even if the ideas and motives of individuals change. The upside is that institutions, organizations, and markets also can change, so discrimination need not last forever. Collective action can reduce race and gender inequality through its impact on social attitudes, market dynamics, organizational behavior, and government policies.

The emphasis on institutional discrimination does not mean that political economists are indifferent to racial and sexual prejudices and attitudes among individuals. Political economists are well aware that the conflicts between counterpart groups can encourage people to stereotype, objectify, and sometimes, even hate each other. Discrimination can provide "psychic benefits" if the damage inflicted on one group builds the self-esteem of another.[1] Indeed, it is exactly because discrimination creates social divisions that allow one group to gain economic, political, or social power by oppressing a clearly defined "other" that attitudes and beliefs can become so entrenched. In this sense, they can be viewed as the result of discrimination rather than the cause.

To give you a better idea of what's coming, we argue there are three keys to distinguishing the neoclassical and political economy views of discrimination. First, neoclassical economists believe that the *discriminator often pays* for discrimination, while political economists believe the *discriminator often benefits*. Second, neoclassical economists view discrimination as an *individual* phenomenon, while political economists view it as being related to oppression and counterpart *groups*. Third, and as a result, neoclassical economists believe that discrimination will have a *short shelf life* in a competitive economy, while political economists believe discrimination will *persist* in the absence of collective action to the contrary.

This chapter looks at the ways in which political economists understand discrimination: who are the winners and losers, why it persists, and how it changes over the business cycle—as well as over long periods of U.S. history. It explains why political economists view discrimination as being a function of group behavior and interests rather than individual tastes, which in turn is closely linked to exploitation, exclusion, and domination. In this view, discrimination is not simply inefficient; it helps one group to hold power over, or make money from, another.

DISCRIMINATION IN CONTEXT: WHAT YOU DON'T KNOW CAN HURT YOU

Political economists tackle the analysis of discrimination by applying the Four C's of political economy: *c*ontext, *c*ollective behavior, *c*onflicting interests, and *c*hange. Political economists think about discrimination in a way that connects our collective past with our collective present. Genocide, slavery, disenfranchisement, violence, poverty, segregation, and ghettoization are the backdrops for contemporary discrimination. At the same time, the Civil Rights Movement, women's movement, and other social and political changes have had an enormous impact on gender and race relations and fundamentally altered the way in which discrimination works. When political economists analyze discrimination, they seek to show how the present reflects the past, but also how it is different from it, and can be different still, in the future.

Because political economists see discrimination as part of a historical process, it is easy to see why they consider discrimination to be an important component of a system of racial and gender oppression. By paying women less than men or blacks

---

[1]For example, poor whites often have been described as more racist than wealthier whites because of their frustrated need for social status. A half-century ago, Gunnar Myrdal (1972:104) commented that "The white upper class person might feel a greater biological distance from the average Negro, but he has not the same need to emphasize the race dogma, since the social distance is so great and secure . . . The lower classes of whites seem to be much more careful to keep the race dogma straight . . ."

less than whites, capitalists not only exploit workers but also help to maintain systems of oppression that exist outside the firm and the labor market. If women or blacks are not paid enough to be self-supporting, their economic options are limited, and with limited economic options, it is difficult to escape other forms of oppression. Eliminating discrimination in labor markets is difficult, in part because it serves an important role in upholding long-standing and firmly held notions of the racial and gender pecking order.

Judging and harming people based on their skin color, country of origin, gender, or sexual orientation—*discrimination*—occurs today and has occurred for a long, long time. The political economist usually does not take it as his or her task to discover the original source of people's desires to discriminate, but rather seeks to understand how discrimination is translated into systemwide mechanisms that result in unequal outcomes. Why some people feel that women are best suited to stay at home to raise children is of less interest than understanding how that notion translates into a generally accepted assumption that women should earn less than men. The issue of individual productivity, which is so central to the neoclassical analysis of discrimination, drops into the background here, because productivity is associated with jobs rather than individuals and is only loosely connected to wages (see Chapter 7).

Discrimination cannot always be directly observed or measured. You might "know discrimination when you see it," but then again, you might not. Few people in this day and age admit to actively practicing discrimination, and even fewer will tell a member of a counterpart group, "Yes, I am discriminating against you by not hiring you, or not giving you a promotion, or not giving you a raise." Indeed, although numerous court cases have resulted in findings of discrimination, these cases frequently use statistical evidence that is unavailable when people apply for jobs. Similarly, studies in which equally qualified candidates—one black, one white—apply for jobs consistently indicate racial discrimination in labor markets (Box 8.1). What these studies demonstrate is that those who experience discrimination often will not know it unless a test is performed. On the other side of the fence, people who discriminate might not even know they are doing it.

The neoclassical understanding of discrimination presented in Chapter 5 presumes that workers can be unambiguously ranked in terms of their qualifications and that wages generally reflect productivity. More often than not, however, qualifications vary in subtle ways between job applicants, because the characteristics of actual people come in "bundles." Someone may have a slight edge on interpersonal skills, another may be a better word processor, another a better leader, and another better organized. This bundling of characteristics opens the door to subjective interpretations about who is more qualified than whom. Employers often must rely on hunches and first impressions when comparing job candidates who look objectively more or less comparable. Employers may honestly and truthfully deny that they have discriminated—even when their decision-making consistently leads them to prefer white men. Is it still discrimination if there is no conscious intent to discriminate?

Political economists answer "yes." Discrimination can, and often does, result from unconscious behaviors and attitudes in individuals. It can stem from a social context that is built into the rules and structures of organizations and markets. This view contrasts sharply with the neoclassical perspective, in which discrimination is

---

BOX 8.1

DIRECT TESTS FOR DISCRIMINATION

In 1961, John Griffin's book *Black Like Me* was released. Griffin, a white man, decided to see what it was like to be black in America. He convincingly transformed his appearance and experienced racial discrimination firsthand. His book describes how despite being exactly the same person, the white John Griffin was treated very differently than the black John Griffin. Griffin felt what few whites in our society have—the power of the color line in the United States. Griffin's "experiment" is not that different from the way in which some researchers have explored the degree of discrimination in the post–Civil Rights United States. One method used is to send letters inquiring about job openings where the only substantive difference in those letters and resumes are the gender or race of the applicant.

Another extension of this strategy is to have real people (called "testers" or "auditors") of different races and genders who have been trained to act similarly attempt to purchase automobiles, rent apartments, buy homes, or look for jobs. These studies provide some of the first truly direct evidence of discrimination, because the *ceteris paribus* (*ie*, all other things being equal) condition for neoclassical discrimination is met. Three researchers from the Urban Institute in Washington, DC—Marc Bendick, Jr., Charles W. Jackson, and Victor A. Reinoso—have analyzed some results from these efforts, particularly those of a study undertaken in the early 1990s by the Fair Employment Council of Greater Washington.

Comparing results for 149 pairs of black–white testers in job applications, they found that 48.3% of white testers received interviews, but only 39.6% of black testers did. This may not sound like much of a difference, but it means that a white applicant was about 25% more likely to get an interview than a comparable black applicant. Further, of those receiving interviews, 46.9% of white testers received job offers, but only 11.3% of black testers did. Matters continued to deteriorate even for the rare black testers who survived this far. In 16.7% of cases where both the black and white tester were offered the same job, the white was offered higher pay than the black tester—and the reverse never occurred. Black testers who made it this far also were more likely than white testers to be offered a job below the level they applied for and less likely to be offered a job better than that applied for.

Was statistical discrimination at work here? Recall from Chapter 5 that the way firms can profitably circumvent statistical discrimination is to develop tests to identify high-quality employees. If statistical discrimination is important, this argument suggests that firms have a particularly strong incentive to test minority job applicants.[2]

In fact, Bendick *et al.* report that of the testers who made it to the interview stage, 23.6% of whites but only 15.3% of blacks were offered formal tests by the firm. Moreover, professional employment agencies—who should carry particular expertise in identifying high-quality applicants—treated identically qualified whites more favorably than their black partners in 66.7% of cases. This evidence suggests that statistical discrimination cannot explain the adverse treatment received by black testers.

[2]This assumes that the cost of administering tests is less than the cost of failing to hire a qualified applicant. Because the former is cheap and the latter unknown, the assumption that firms should have an especially strong incentive to test minority applicants is a reasonable one.

Source: Marc Bendick, Jr., Charles W. Jackson, and Victor A. Reinoso, "Measuring Employment Discrimination Through Controlled Experiments," *Review of Black Political Economy,* Vol. 23, Summer 1994.

---

interpreted as a conscious choice made by individuals. The contrast is telling, and it is worth spending a moment to explore in some detail.

For political economists, discrimination involves more than individual choice. Of course, individuals can choose to discriminate, but discrimination also may occur even when individuals believe they are not discriminating. For example, if a firm recruits job applicants by using referrals from existing workers (the way that many job openings are filled), it may wind up with an all-white applicant pool because of residential and social segregation. Nobody at the firm is necessarily trying to discriminate, but the result is that nonwhites are systematically excluded from applying for job openings. It also may be the case that a male employer is more comfortable with, and sympathetic to, male applicants for a managerial position. He may not be trying to discriminate, but he will tend to prefer the male applicants and genuinely believe that they are "more qualified" or "less risky" hires than the female applicants. In addition, a seniority system may result in a last-hired/first-fired pattern among minorities, who can never accumulate enough seniority to avoid layoffs. In all these cases—and in others that we discuss in this chapter—rules of the game systematically disadvantage women and minorities.

These examples illustrate the notion of *institutional discrimination*, which contrasts with the neoclassical emphasis on individual discrimination. Individual discrimination is carried out as a conscious decision by individuals and results from their particular prejudices. For this reason, individual discrimination corresponds to Gary Becker's concept of a "taste for discrimination." Institutional discrimination, however, is created by the rules and incentives of organizations such as firms, markets, and the government. It can be overt (*eg,* segregation laws in the Jim Crow south) or covert (*eg,* irrelevant employment tests that systematically exclude minorities), conscious (*eg,* redlining minority neighborhoods by banks) or unconscious (*eg,* difficulties in socializing or communicating with people who are "different"), rational (*eg,* white unions minimize job competition by excluding blacks) or irrational (*eg,* unions refuse to organize female workers). In all cases, however, the issue has less to do with the decisions of individuals than with the rules and incentives that govern the behavior of economic institutions, alter people's preferences, and in so doing, disadvantage women and minorities.

Institutional discrimination: Adverse treatment of women and minorities because of the explicit and implicit rules that regulate society

---

For an example of how institutional and individual discrimination differ, consider the situation facing a woman on a university faculty. To hold the job for more than 7 years, she must be granted tenure, and to get tenure, she needs to work long hours (50, 60, or even 70 hours per week). If she has children, there is likely to be a serious time conflict, which ultimately may cost her the job. Few people would be surprised at this outcome given the sexual division of labor that is typical of most families. Yet, if we had been discussing a man going up for tenure, the issue of children would rarely even be mentioned, because the unwritten rules of family life work to benefit men—just as they work to disadvantage women. Nonetheless, it is doubtful that tenure rules were written with the purpose of discriminating. Nobody may bear any ill will toward female professors. The rules of the tenure game are applied equally, but their interactions with other rules make the game less fair.

A different face of institutional discrimination appears in the towns of Naperville and Aurora, Illinois, home of the Indian Prairie School District. These towns have turned down proposals for single-family houses in the $65,000 to $75,000 range in favor of houses on large lots in the $300,000 range along with townhouses and apartments with one or two bedrooms. The purpose was to increase the tax base while keeping the number of primary and secondary public school students down. The intent was clearly discriminatory in terms of families with children, but the effects were undoubtedly larger as single mothers and black families, both of whom tend to have lower incomes than two-adult and white families, also were effectively excluded (as well as many of the "Indians" for whom the school district is named). The "rules" were applied equally, but the inequality of results was virtually foreordained.[3]

Neoclassical economists focus on individual discrimination as it is consistent with their emphasis on individual choice and free markets. You know from Chapter 6, however, that political economists place more emphasis on collective behavior and conflicting interests. Political economists therefore are more interested in institutional discrimination. They disagree with the neoclassical belief that capitalism tends to erode racism and sexism, and they believe that the notion of institutional discrimination can help us to understand the economic problems faced by women and minorities.

GROUNDS FOR DISCRIMINATION: ECONOMIC INCENTIVES AND ORGANIZATIONAL ADAPTATION

Political economists have two main ways of explaining why discrimination exists in labor markets. The first is that some people directly benefit from discrimination. In other words, there are strong economic *incentives to discriminate,* and both capitalists and white males may have a direct financial stake in discrimination within the firm. The second reason has to do with mirroring inside the firm the relations of oppression that exist outside of the firm. We refer to this phenomenon as *organizational adaptation.* It speaks to the ways in which traditional social beliefs and practices are transported into the firm so that the firm does not "rock the boat," even if in the abstract it is not always the most profitable solution. We discuss each argument in turn.

Economic Incentives

The neoclassical possibility that individuals "pay" to discriminate (as they would to indulge any other taste or prejudice) is turned on its head in the political economy framework. Here, much discrimination is perceived to be in the interests of those who practice it, and it is exactly for this reason that the political economy theory of discrimination does not depend on personal prejudice. Instead, discrimination is held to be self-sustaining, because it generates rewards for those who are willing to dis-

[3]From Philip Langdon, *A Better Place to Live: Reshaping the American Suburb.* Amherst MA: University of Massachusetts Press, 1994.

criminate (or at least unwilling to act against discrimination). Indeed, the forces of competition in such circumstances actually can work to perpetuate discrimination, as we shall argue in the following section. For now, however, we need to understand how discrimination can confer benefits and how these benefits can influence behavior.

Economic incentives—the potential monetary gains from behaving in a certain way—provide an economic explanation for discriminating based on group identity and conflict. Of course, historical, emotional, and political reasons for group identity and conflict are important, but there also are powerful economic forces that encourage and reward individuals for identifying with groups and, as groups, for engaging in collective conflict with other groups.

Benefits can be classified in terms of who receives them. The two broad groups that interact in the workplace are employers (including management) and employees. The political economy analysis of discrimination focuses on the potential benefits received by members of each group.

As argued by economist Michael Reich in his work *Racial Inequality* (1981) and by economist Robert Cherry in *Discrimination* (1989), discrimination can benefit employers as a result of *class struggle effects*. Class struggle refers to the conflict between employers and employees over the distribution of income and the organization of work. Employers want to keep wages as low as possible and to maximize their control over the labor process. These goals are difficult to achieve when workers remain unified as a group. If workers recognize that they have common class interests and act together (*eg,* by organizing a union) to increase wages and establish their rights in the workplace, then management will face higher costs and lower profits. If workers fail to recognize their common interests, however, and therefore are unable to cooperate to achieve these goals, then management can retain the upper hand. Thus, management has a strong incentive to "divide-and-conquer" its workforce (see Chapters 6 and 7).

Class struggle effects: The impact of discrimination on the solidarity and bargaining power of workers

---

Given that class struggle is an inherent feature of all firms (except those that are employee owned), employers may systematically discriminate to physically and socially separate and stratify workers. In essence, this is an attempt to make it harder for workers to perceive and act on their common interests. The differences between white males, women, and minorities in society at large become mirrored in the workplace. Management may assign white male workers to the "best" jobs to reduce the chances that they will feel a need to cooperate with women and minority workers, who have the most to gain from a wage hike or improvement in conditions. Women and minorities may blame white male workers as much as management for their problems. If workers fight each other based on race or gender, they will find it much more difficult to unite as workers to achieve their common goals. As a result, wages for all workers (including white males) are kept down, and managerial control is enhanced.

In Reich's 1981 study, cities with greater income inequality between blacks and whites were found to be those in which profits were higher, and the majority of white workers suffered corresponding wage losses. Reich took this to mean that capitalists have an incentive to create racial inequality (*ie,* to discriminate) to weaken the bargaining power of workers. The conclusion of class struggle logic is that workers have the same fundamental interests, and that racism (and, by implication, sexism) results from "false consciousness."[4] The solution is for workers to "unite-and-fight" management for higher wages, better working conditions, and other demands. This is a simple and appealing strategy, and it often works.

Consider an example. As Reich documents (1981:257), the Congress of Industrial Organizations (CIO) was able to sweep by the old-line American Federation of Labor in the 1930s to win major gains for workers in terms of rights, job security, and wages, for many reasons. Among those was the CIO's explicit antiracism policy. Without such a policy of "unite-and-fight," it would have been impossible for the United Auto Workers (part of the CIO) to organize the massive Ford River Rouge plant, because 13% of the workers there were black.

Unfortunately, this is not the entire story. The historical examples of unity between white and black and between male and female workers are so rare that "false consciousness" is unlikely to be the entire explanation for racial and gender divisions. Other studies fail to confirm Reich's conclusion that class struggle effects account for continuing racial (or gender) divisions in the United States. For example, economist Steven Shulman (1987) finds that discrimination against black workers may improve the job prospects of whites. Therefore, the reason that whites and men have yet to unite with women and people of color may have less to do with their failure to see through capitalist attempts to divide-and-conquer than with the fact that they may benefit from discrimination.[5]

White male workers can benefit from discrimination as a result of *job competition effects.* The logic here is that if women and minorities are excluded from the "best" jobs, then white males will face less competition for them. This will improve their chances to earn higher wages, get promoted, and enjoy job security. Further, a reduction in job competition for white males means that they will be better positioned to find jobs for their (white male) relatives and friends. They also will be more likely to work among people like themselves, with whom they are comfortable and able to communicate. Job competition effects therefore benefit white males in five ways: higher wages, better promotional possibilities, enhanced job security, nepotism, and social comfort.

---

[4]The concept of "false consciousness" is rejected by many political economists who believe that it explains beliefs in terms of ideals rather than reality (Shulman, 1989). Nonetheless, it provides an interesting contrast to the neoclassical view that beliefs are always rational.

[5]More complicated distributional patterns exist as well. For example, white women may benefit from race discrimination, and black men may benefit from gender discrimination. Other groups as a whole may experience discrimination but still thrive economically (*eg,* Japanese-Americans and Jewish-Americans). For the sake of simplicity, we focus here solely on white men and capitalists as the potential beneficiaries of discrimination.

Job competition effects: The impact of the occupational exclusion of women and minorities on the wages and job security of white males

---

Job competition effects depend on the exclusion of women and minorities from consideration for certain jobs. Exclusion can result from direct or indirect intervention. Direct intervention (*eg,* a strike in protest of the hiring of black workers) was more common in the early part of the century: today, indirect intervention by white male employees is the common method of exclusion. Instead of boldly presenting their demands, white males exert pressure in a more covert fashion. Women coworkers may be sexually harassed. Black coworkers may be ostracized, ignored, or subtly informed that they got their new job through quotas rather than qualifications.

Management in general therefore is understandably hesitant to introduce women and minorities into previously all-white-male workgroups. Even if conflict does not arise, the fear of it is always present. Of course, management is not necessarily loathe to discriminate. Aside from benefitting by class struggle effects, management also may feel that it can maintain a positive relationship with its white male workers by encouraging them to feel that they have exclusive rights to certain jobs. This set of shared values and interests between management and workers (in this case, white male workers) is called *hegemony*. It is one means by which management maintains control over the labor process.

Although women and minorities are always hurt by discrimination, class struggle and job competition effects have contradictory effects on employers and white male employees. Class struggle effects benefit employers and hurt white male employees. Job competition effects benefit white male employees. The consequences of job competition effects for employers are more complicated. On the one hand, employers may benefit from the hegemonic control over white male workers that discrimination facilitates; on the other, job competition effects may reduce the ability of employers to make the best use of their human resources or to minimize their wage costs. It also may strengthen labor solidarity among white male workers, which can inhibit managerial control over those workers (see Chapter 7).[6]

In reality, both class struggle and job competition effects can simultaneously occur. This complicates the distributional effects of discrimination. White workers may gain from job competition effects and lose from class struggle effects, while the opposite may be the case for capitalists (Box 8.2). The net results may not be apparent to either workers or capitalists. For this reason, it is unlikely that discriminatory behavior is based solely on incentives in any simple or direct fashion.

Organizational Adaptation: Don't Rock the Boat

Just as exploitation is only one form of oppression, monetary incentives are only part of the political economy explanation for discrimination. Therefore, we now turn to

---

[6]In other words, job competition effects can offset class struggle effects if the solidarity that is lost between black and white and between male and female workers is offset by solidarity that is gained among white male workers.

BOX 8.2

BIG MONEY FROM DISCRIMINATING IN MILWAUKEE

While no one knows for certain how much capitalists or white males gain from discrimination, econometricians (*ie,* economists specializing in statistical techniques) have devised methods that allow us to calculate the approximate gains under the extreme assumption that either job competition or class struggle effects, but not both, exist.

In both cases, we control for differences in experience, education, and other factors that could influence individual productivity (although for political economists, many of these differences may themselves be traced to discrimination).[7]

Given these assumptions, we can estimate the wages that white males would receive if they were rewarded for their productive characteristics at the same rate as everyone else. The difference between what white male workers do make and what they would make if they were treated like women and minorities (holding the total wage bill constant) can be interpreted as an outer-bound estimate of their gains from job competition effects. Making this calculation using 1990 U.S. Census data for the metropolitan area of Milwaukee, Wisconsin, it is estimated that white males receive a wage premium of $1.15 per hour. This doesn't sound like much, particularly given that white women in Milwaukee earn an average of around $4 less per hour than men, with most of this differential being attributed to productivity differences. Nonetheless, for the average white male worker in 1990, the discriminatory differential added a solid $183.52 per month to his paycheck. For all employed white males in the area, this figure adds up to a total of $15.2 million per week—*or almost $1 billion per year!*

If instead it is capitalists who benefit from discrimination through class struggle effects, then the issue is not the gain of white male workers but rather the loss of female and minority workers. This loss can be estimated by comparing the earnings that women and minorities do make with the amount that they would make if they were rewarded for their productive characteristics at the same rate as white males. White women then would earn an additional $2.99 per hour, or $337.20 per month. Including women and men from minority groups (all of whom also would experience a wage increase if they were treated like white males), the total amount they lose—and that their employers gain—is over *$1.5 billion per year.* That wouldn't look too shabby on any corporation's annual report, but then again, no one will admit to making money from discrimination.

In reality, discrimination can involve both class struggle effects and job competition effects, so the amount that white male workers and capitalists each gain is likely to be below these estimates. Nonetheless, it is clear that substantial incentives for discrimination can exist for both white male workers and employers.

---

[7]Figures here control for years of schooling, high school or college diploma, years of experience, part-time employment, number of dependents, marital status, citizenship, language skills, school enrollment, public sector employment, military veteran status, location of job and housing, as well as occupation and industry.

Source: Robert Drago, "The Effects of Job and Housing Location on Race/Gender Wage Differentials in Milwaukee," mimeo, University of Wisconsin-Milwaukee, March 1994.

---

a second component of institutional discrimination: how practices inside of firms mirror practices external to the firm. In other words, we need to look at how discrimination gets "integrated" into the firm.

The basic logic here is that, if you want to "get along, you go along." Firms do this by adapting to whatever divisions—by race, gender, sexual orientation, or age—exist in a given society. *Organizational adaptation* refers to the tendency of firms to adopt social customs and practices from outside of the firm or to transport practices from other sites into the firm.

Organizational adaptation: The tendency of firms to adopt the social conventions that are prevalent in society

---

The transportation of practices may sound abstract, but the logic is simple: people do not leave the rest of their lives at the factory gate or the office door when they go to work, so the attitudes and customs that reign outside the firm are brought inside regardless of the firm's wishes. Somewhat differently, the firm has good reasons to avoid offending the government, their suppliers, their neighbors, and their customers. If these groups expect to see certain social relations in the firms, the firm will tend to adapt to their expectations.

To understand organizational adaptation in a practical sense, we have to look at oppressive relations outside of the firm and how these are brought inside. This process may have to do with economic interests outside of the firm. For example, if a husband benefits from the sexual division of labor in the home but the family needs a dual income, the husband will have an interest in the wife obtaining a job that pays less than his. If she earns as much as he or more, then her dependence—and his control—will be reduced. The husband then may generalize his need for his wife to earn less than he into a belief that all women *should* earn less than men and then act on that belief in his role as an employer or employee.

The process of organizational adaptation also may express domination pure and simple, as when a male manager expects his female secretary to get coffee and wait on him in other ways—because this is how he expects women to act. Similarly, having blacks and Latinos do all the clean-up work at the firm—as porters, orderlies, janitors, cafeteria workers, or dishwashers—serves to demonstrate and reinforce the subordinate stereotypes of people of color.

In addition, organizational adaptation may show signs of exclusionary practices outside the firm. As Rosabeth Moss Kanter (1977) shows, the division of labor in the home, which typically excludes women from authority and decision-making power concerning major issues (*eg,* where the family lives, where they vacation, the cars and homes they purchase, where children attend school), is mimicked inside the firm. This process will result in occupational segregation where the jobs with power and authority are defined as "male." Similarly, occupational segregation may reduce the opportunities for blacks as their exclusion from white communities is mirrored inside white-majority firms.

Organizational adaptation implies that firms who attempt to buck social trends will find such actions costly. If a major corporation finds that the most qualified candidate for Chief Executive Officer is a black woman, it may avoid appointing her because of potential repercussions. Perhaps the business press would make a big deal of this and accuse the firm of engaging in "affirmative action" at the expense of shareholders. How will she fare in a big meeting with bankers trying to arrange corporate financing? Will she be taken seriously? How will other senior managers respond to her when they are used to giving orders to, rather than taking them from, a black woman? And how will she do if she winds up in a smoke-filled room with a bunch of male union leaders? Organizational adaptation means that the firm probably won't take such a chance, and qualifications are *not* the issue.

Psychologist Jan Yoder (1991) has documented the effects of organizational adaptation in her research on "tokens," which are women (or men) who are introduced into a job and work setting where women (or men) were historically rare. Yoder argues that if men dominate women throughout society, then those relations of oppression will be mirrored inside the firm, regardless of whether there are many or few women in a particular type of job. Supporting this argument, Yoder finds that while token women in male-dominated professions such as firefighting and the military typically are isolated, receive little support, and often are harassed, these adverse effects stem mainly from *women entering men's jobs.* The proof in the pudding here is the finding that when men enter a female occupation or workplace as tokens, they experience few of the adverse effects that women experience when entering a male occupation. The domination of men over women in the home is transported into the workplace *even when men are in the minority.*

Ultimately, organizational adaptation implies that jobs and wages are socially determined. It is not just the productivity of an individual or a job that matters, and it is not just any immediate economic gains from discrimination that matter. What goes on outside the firm is just as important to understanding both wages and discrimination. For example, in a comparable worth case during the mid-1970s, the judges agreed that according to objective standards, it was difficult to justify paying tree trimmers more than registered nurses. Nonetheless, the judges ruled against pay equity in this case, because they saw it as "pregnant with the possibility of disrupting the entire economic system of the United States" (Steinberg, 1990; 468). While it is conceivable that the judges simply were trying to protect male wages, the fear expressed here reflects the logic of organizational adaptation: don't rock the boat.

Gender and race division of labor used to be almost universal. Over time, however, change has occurred. Social conventions have weakened, and it has become somewhat more likely to see female administrators or managers as well as male nurses and clerical workers. Minorities also are more likely to be managers, administrators, and professionals of various types, although many believe that they are treated as tokens and excluded from positions of real power (Pettigrew and Martin, 1987). The process of organizational adaptation can respond to changes in the external environment, as the occupational mobility of women and minorities after the Civil Rights Act of 1964 attests.

Nonetheless, once a firm establishes a division of labor, it tends to becomes entrenched and difficult to change. According to sociologist James Baron (1991;115), "The evidence suggests that social forces and discriminatory cultural beliefs prevalent when a job or organization is founded condition the way that positions are defined, priced and staffed, becoming institutionalized within the formal structure and informal traditions of the enterprise." Jobs become socially identified as male or female, white or black, and although change is possible, it usually is slow, costly, and difficult. New forms of segregation may emerge. For example, new job titles may be created for white men to shield them from integration with women and minorities who hold similar qualifications. Women and minorities may be less likely to wield supervisory authority than white men despite being qualified to do so (Lewis,

1986). Organizational structure thus maintains the race–gender hierarchy even as it responds to external political pressures for change.

Obviously, it is possible for organizational adaptation to operate in reverse, with changes inside the firm causing changes in the home and community. For example, economists William Darity and Samuel Myers (1994) argue that for a variety of reasons, corporations no longer need the labor of black men—and particularly young black men. The availability of low-wage women, whether black or white, as well as of low-wage production in other countries, has meant that black men largely are "unwanted" by the firm. Darity and Myers believe that society at large is adapting to this shift by further excluding black men, building prisons, reintroducing capital punishment in numerous states, and permitting—and even facilitating—often deadly violence among young black men.

THE DYNAMICS OF DISCRIMINATION

If people with power have an interest in discrimination and firms adapt to oppressive relations elsewhere in society, we would expect the capitalist firm to continue discriminating in the face of changing conditions and challenges to discrimination. The firm may integrate its managerial structure if necessary but, in the process, shuffle female and minority managers off to personnel and public relations—areas with small budgets and little real decision-making power. Workgroups may be integrated on the shopfloor, but a new division of labor may emerge that maintains the subordination of women and minorities. And, one way or the other, firms will strive to keep the wages, benefits, and promotional opportunities of *all* their workers—especially their female and minority workers—as minimal as possible.

This means that discrimination tends to be *dynamic:* it can change in response to political and economic pressures, yet does so in a way that is self-perpetuating. Any theory of discrimination must be able to explain its variations in intensity and form. Political economists believe that in contrast to the alternatives, their theory is able to do exactly that.

The dynamics of discrimination are both short-run and long-run. The short-run refers to fluctuations in discrimination over the business cycle; the long-run refers to the response of discrimination to changes in its broad social and political context. In both cases, we use the political economy approach such that within any historical context, conflicts and collective actions that are taken in response to those conflicts bring about change, which those in power will attempt to shape in their favor.

Discrimination and the Business Cycle

Political economists acknowledge that firms face costs from discrimination that can arise from either market pressures or the government. A refusal to hire qualified blacks and women can result in higher search costs and/or higher wage costs in the effort to find qualified white males. It can create inefficiencies in the use of human resources. It also can result in government sanctions if the firm is subject to antidiscrimination and affirmative action laws. This part of the argument is similar to that made by neoclassical economists; however, the political economy model goes one step further by noting that it also may be costly to eliminate discrimination. If it is costly to both continue or cease discriminating, then the firm's behavior cannot be predicted in an *a priori* fashion. Instead, it will depend on the concrete circumstances that make one alternative less costly (or, equivalently, more beneficial) than the other.

From the discussion in the preceding sections, we can identify five reasons why ceasing discrimination can be costly[8]:

1 A decline in discrimination can disrupt traditional patterns of association and authority; in other words, it can undermine organizational adaptation. Realigning social patterns is a risky and time-consuming proposition that may threaten the firm's internal and external stability. Placing minorities and women on a par with white males can raise costs, because it undermines the notions of fairness on which white male morale and productivity depend.

2 Ceasing discrimination can raise wage costs and reduce managerial control because of class struggle effects and the reduction of hegemony.

3 A drop in discrimination can change the rules of internal labor markets (*eg,* job ladders [see Chapter 7]) and reduce wage benefits for whites from job competition effects. Disrupting the established channels of recruitment, screening, allocation, training, wage setting, and promotion can "raise the inefficiency of the labor force adjustment process, at least in the short run, thereby imposing costs on both the employer and society. Only where the effect of discrimination has been to create a grossly inefficient internal labor market will there be any offsetting benefits . . ." (Doeringer and Piore, 1971;136). Increasing competition for a limited set of rewards and changing tried-and-true procedures inevitably create more conflict and risk.

4 A reduction in discrimination can increase training costs—a crucial component of labor costs and productivity—if white male workers refuse to train or work cooperatively with their female and minority coworkers.

5 Finally, a decline in discrimination can reduce team efficiency by reducing social homogeneity. Much work in this day and age takes place in groups whose output depends on the ability of members to work in a cooperative fashion. Trust, communication, and work-sharing are easier to attain within groups that are composed of socially similar people. It may be irrational for the cost-minimizing firm to introduce women and minorities into previously all-white-male working environments if the result is to impair the group process and reduce team productivity.

Discriminatory practices therefore can be costly and risky to change because of their impact on employers, white male employees, and organizational structure. If it also is the case that discrimination increases costs, then the firm faces a set of contradictory pressures. The direction that it is prone to take in the face of this contradiction is determined, in the short run, by the strength of the economy (*ie,* the business cycle).

For example, assume that the economy is moving into a recession. As unemployment rises, more white male workers become available to fill vacancies. Consequently, it is easier to find qualified white male applicants at the going wage if the

[8]An early version of this argument can be found in Shulman (1984).

firm chooses to discriminate against female and minority applicants. The costs of discrimination thereby fall.

At the same time, the costs of ceasing discrimination rise. In weak labor markets, workers place a premium on job security. The ability to protect one's job and to maintain some influence over the hiring process becomes increasingly important to white male workers as their occupational alternatives diminish. The significance of informal job distribution channels (*ie*, inside information) grows as the availability of jobs declines. White male workers thus face increasing incentives to discriminate as unemployment rises. Management is willing to accommodate them, because the costs of continuing discrimination have declined. Management has an incentive to do so, because wage growth will be dampened as a result of class struggle effects.[9] Management is able to meet short-term goals (*eg*, stability during a downturn) as well as long-term goals (*eg*, hegemonic control) by allowing the interests of white male workers to supersede those of other workers.

In short, during a recession, the costs of continuing discrimination will fall while the costs of ceasing discrimination will rise. This means that the incentives for discrimination will increase in a recession and, conversely, decrease in an expansion. *High levels of unemployment are bad for all workers—but far worse for women and blacks.*[10] The opposite process kicks in during an upturn (see Figure 2.8). The political economy model of discrimination therefore predicts that the intensity of employment discrimination against minorities and women should rise during recessions and fall during expansions.

The Long-Run Dynamics of Discrimination

The ups and downs of the economy in general and the labor market in particular help to shape patterns of institutional discrimination, but discrimination also is influenced by other contextual factors. Laws, customs, and traditions all change, particularly as people struggle collectively to reduce various forms of oppression in the firm, home, and community. These struggles can raise the costs of discrimination and alter the process of organizational adaptation such that discrimination enters a long-run period of decline. Many scholars—including some political economists[11]—have argued that economic and political forces have worked against discrimination in the post–civil rights period. Other factors, such as deindustrialization and the fiscal crisis of the cities, then would be responsible for the perpetuation of racial inequality.

Many political economists, however, believe the forces that can cause discrimi-

---

[9]This means that discrimination causes white male workers to trade-off job security against wage growth. In a recession, they will tend to increase the weight they place on job security, because the difficulty of finding a new job increases.

[10]This model accurately predicts that black unemployment will rise more than white unemployment in recessions (and fall more in expansions). However, unlike blacks, women do not face higher unemployment rates or unemployment changes than their counterpart group. Instead, the male–female wage gap appears to rise in recessions, suggesting that wage discrimination against women (like employment discrimination against blacks) rises when the costs of discrimination fall (Weinberger, 1993). More research on the relation between wage and employment discrimination—and between race and gender discrimination—is needed to clarify these contrasts.

[11]Perhaps the best-known scholar in this tradition is Wilson (1980).

nation to decline can be offset by other forces that can perpetuate it over long periods of time. These two sets of forces each result in what is known as *positive feedback,* which occurs when an adverse event leads to further adverse events or, conversely, a positive event leads to more positive events.[12] Positive feedback means that both virtuous cycles and vicious cycles can operate in a complicated pattern. It gives us hope that the forces working against discrimination will cumulatively and progressively force it to decline over time, but it also means that the forces working to perpetuate discrimination can set in motion a train of events that is very difficult to stop.

The focus of this section is on the latter. We look at positive feedback mechanisms that can sustain discrimination even in the face of pressures to eradicate it. These mechanisms can be divided into four types: perception, socialization, choice, and market interactions.

In his famous study of race relations, *An American Dilemma,* Gunnar Myrdal (1972) argued that white perceptions of blacks are reinforced by black life conditions.[13] Black poverty, and the problems that both follow from and surround it, reinforces negative white *perceptions,* which in turn reinforce discrimination by whites against blacks and, hence, perpetuates black poverty. In other words, perceptions make discrimination self-reinforcing, then prejudice becomes a self-fulfilling prophecy. For example, white employers may believe that blacks are more likely to be criminals, hence they are less likely to hire blacks, hence blacks become more likely to commit crimes as they have no other means of supporting themselves.

Perceptual feedback can be compared to the neoclassical model of statistical discrimination. In that model, individuals get treated based on their group's characteristics (see Chapter 5). That type of discrimination is not self-sustaining, however, because competition should push employers to use tests and other means of learning about individuals to make the best use of their human resources. In other words, the statistical discrimination model predicts that discrimination should not persist because of the convergence of expectations with reality (Darity, 1989). Feedback from perceptions, in contrast, leads to a convergence of reality with expectations. Discrimination creates conditions that reinforce bigotry and, hence, create more discrimination.

As an example of the feedback created by perceptions, consider the problem that is faced by women on welfare when they try to find a job. Many of them have spent time out of the labor force, and many employers will know (even if they are not told in so many words) that they have been supported by taxpayer dollars. While most welfare recipients are not black, many people think that they are, and the all-too-common racial and gender stereotypes of laziness, promiscuity, and unintelligence feed into the popular perceptions of welfare recipients—especially those who are

---

[12]We already have encountered this concept in the discussion of Keynes' theory of unemployment in Chapter 4.

[13]Gunnar Myrdal was the founder of the political economy view of discrimination. Both he and Gary Becker, the founder of the neoclassical view of discrimination, were winners of the Nobel Prize (see Chapter 1).

black. The result is that employers are reluctant to hire them, and so they are forced to stay on welfare no matter how motivated and intelligent they may be. Reality responds to stereotype in a manner that reinforces it.

Socialization is another source of feedback. Discrimination may change the conditions in which children develop into adults, and in so doing perpetuate itself. For example, residential segregation isolates many blacks in the inner cities, where they can grow up with few or no interactions with whites or people from outside the inner city (Massey and Denton, 1993). As a result, their cultural milieu is different from the mainstream: their speech patterns, appearance, and daily habits may make them stand out and appear to be inappropriate for mainstream work settings. Consequently, they have problems both finding and holding jobs and therefore are more likely to stay trapped in the inner city.

Mary Corcoran and Paul Courant (1986) argue that labor market discrimination against women discourages parents from raising girls to specialize in wage work. When girls grow into women, their standard of living will depend more on their husband's job than on their own, in part because discrimination lowers female wages relative to male wages. Consequently, parents will raise girls to specialize more in finding a suitable husband than in finding a suitable job. As a result, women will exhibit different work behaviors than men (*eg,* higher turnover rates), and employers will be encouraged to maintain occupational segregation.

The third avenue by which feedback occurs is through *choice.* Political economists are especially interested in the ways in which people respond to the availability—or unavailability—of opportunities. Consider the argument made earlier that capitalists, whites, and males may have economic incentives to discriminate. Those who are victimized by discrimination in turn experience incentives to behave differently than those who do not. For example, if job discrimination reduces the payoff from acquiring education, then blacks and women may choose to get less education (or a different type of education) than white men choose. Are their lower incomes then a result of their educational choices or of job discrimination?

In a related vein, economist Elaine McCrate (1991) argues that black teenagers are more likely than white teenagers to get pregnant, because future job opportunities (before pregnancy) are more limited. Consequently, the monetary losses from bearing and raising children during the teenage years is lower for blacks than for whites. Black teenage girls therefore may make the "rational" decision that getting pregnant is not such a disaster after all—but in so doing, reinforce their lack of opportunity. These are examples of the way in which choices can respond to circumstances and, in so doing, reinforce the circumstances. Again, inequality becomes self-perpetuating.

Finally, feedback can occur as a result of *interactions* between the job market and other markets, especially the housing market. For example, residential segregation may reduce job prospects for blacks if they are physically or socially isolated from vacancies. If jobs move from the cities to the suburbs and blacks are locked into the inner cities as a result of housing discrimination, then they will be in an unequal position compared with whites in the competition for jobs. Or, they may lack access to information about job vacancies, or job vacancies may be traditionally filled by the recommendations of existing employees. In situations such as these, blacks and whites may find themselves on an unequal footing in the labor market because of discrimination elsewhere in society.

Two recent studies provide telling evidence about the impact of segregation on racial gaps in education and employment. Douglas Massey and Nancy Denton's *American Apartheid: Segregation and the Making of the Underclass* (1993) analyzes the extent, causes, and consequences of ghettoization and housing discrimination. They show that segregation largely results from discrimination by banks, realtors, the government, and the white population as a whole. Residential location largely determines access to jobs and public resources such as schooling. Therefore, if residential choices are restricted by discrimination, inequality will be reinforced in other arenas. Here is one example:

> For blacks . . . high incomes do not buy entree to residential circumstances that can serve as springboards for future socioeconomic mobility; in particular, blacks are unable to achieve a school environment conducive to later academic success. In Philadelphia, children from an affluent black family are likely to attend a public school where the percentage of low-achieving students is three times greater than the percentage in schools attended by affluent white children. Small wonder, then, that controlling for income in no way erases the large racial gap in SAT scores. Because of segregation, the same income buys black and white families educational environments that are of vastly different quality (1993:153).

A similar argument is made by Gary Orfield and Carole Ashkinaze in *The Closing Door: Conservative Policy and Black Opportunity* (1991). They show that strong economic growth and local black political leadership were unable to reduce racial inequality or black poverty over the 1980s in Atlanta. Job growth primarily occurred in white suburbs. As a result of housing segregation, economic opportunity bypassed blacks who were locked into the inner city. The high schools were unable to provide equal educational opportunity in the context of the stratification of their student populations, so black access to colleges declined. The result was a vicious circle that sustained racial inequality despite the presence of political and economic circumstances that many conservatives (and liberals) believe are sufficient to create equal opportunity.[14]

Perception, socialization, choice, and institutional interactions all help us to understand how difficult it may be to escape traditional biases and stereotypes (Box 8.3). Good intentions may not be enough to create equal opportunity. For this reason, when political economists advocate activist government policies such as affirmative action or comparable worth, they consider the ways in which such policies can improve conditions yet also sustain the existing power relations—and discrimination—in practice.

WHAT TO DO?

The political economy theory of discrimination is both pessimistic and optimistic. On the one hand, it predicts that discrimination can adapt to and survive in a chang-

---

[14]We have just explained why political economists believe that economic growth should reduce the incentives to discriminate. The experience of Atlanta, however, shows that other factors (*eg,* segregation) also must be taken into account before predictions can be made about the impact of growth on discrimination and inequality. In other words, context matters.

BOX 8.3

WANT TO BE A MANAGER?

In modern America, women (like minorities) are heavily stereotyped. Studies have shown that both men *and* women expect women to be "easily influenced, submissive, sneaky, tactful, very aware of others' feelings, passive, lacking in self-confidence, dependent, unlikely to act as a leader, unaggressive, and uncomfortable about being aggressive." These behaviors might be fine for baking cookies and raising children, but they won't help you to get ahead as, for example, a manager for a major corporation. The males in charge might rationally view such a person as having poor management skills.

What's a woman to do? You could try acting "more like men," who are stereotyped as "assertive, defends own beliefs, independent, strong personality, forceful, has leadership abilities, willing to take risks, self-sufficient, and willing to take a stand." With the help of willing consultants and management trainers, many women have tried to do exactly this through "assertiveness training."

There is, however, a problem with this approach. Discrimination against women is dynamic enough to generate a new stereotype: the "aggressive woman." Indeed, studies show that women who do act assertively are consistently evaluated less positively than men for the *same* behavior.

The core of the problem—patriarchy—remains untouched in either case. Is there reason to think that abandoning patriarchy would improve the workplace, that men should behave more like women? Yes, because studies also suggest that if we wish communication to exist in the firm that results in positive consequences for all parties, women are superior to men. Women also score higher on tests of verbal ability.

Maybe women aren't the problem at all.

Source: Amy Herstein Gervasio and Mary Crawford, "Social Evaluations of Assertiveness," *Psychology of Women Quarterly,* Vol. 13, March 1989, pp. 1–25.

---

ing environment. On the other hand, it predicts that the individual and collective struggles of women, minorities, and their white male allies can result in meaningful steps toward race and gender justice. The result depends on the strength and success of these struggles.

Capitalism tends to reproduce race and gender hierarchies unless the pressure for reform is great enough to create changes in the policies and behaviors of firms and government. So, as collective struggles wear on, they must result in institutional changes if they are to have long-lasting effects, but what is done can eventually be undone. Movements for progressive change come and go while capitalism remains. For this reason, some political economists believe that race and gender justice will never be fully achieved until capitalism is replaced by a different economic system, called *socialism* (eg, Cherry, 1989).

Socialism is a system in which workers rather than capitalists wield economic and political power. The versions of political economy that are rooted in the work of Karl Marx are sympathetic to this vision. They believe that capitalism is fundamentally based on domination and exploitation. If this is true, then the effort to reform capitalism will never succeed in more than a superficial and a transient fashion. The system itself must be replaced by one in which human needs are more important than profits.

Other political economists are not so sure. They point to the existence of race and gender hierarchies in socialist societies such as the former USSR, China, and Cuba. While it is debatable if these societies should be called "socialist," it is clear that the elimination of capitalism is no guarantee that race and gender justice will be automatically achieved. Further, it is not clear how capitalism can be transformed into socialism, or even what socialism would mean in practice. For these reasons, many political economists now focus more on achieving race and gender justice within capitalism rather than advocating the establishment of socialism.

How can capitalism be reformed to achieve race and gender justice? Justice is not a state that can be once and for all achieved; rather, it is a process that tends to go forward or backward depending on the balance of forces. These forces include the dominant ideology, which in America can be characterized in terms of democracy, individualism, and opportunity. As Gunnar Myrdal (1972) noted a half-century ago, this ideology is incompatible with race (and, by extension, gender) exclusion and discrimination. Ideology is not powerful enough to singlehandedly create a momentum for justice, however.[15] After all, Jim Crow was ended by a civil rights movement, not just a civil rights ideology.

The process of race and gender justice depends most fundamentally on the *balance of power*. In this view, race and gender oppression result from the concentration of resources and power among majority males, particularly capitalists. Equity and justice depend on the transfer of power—and the resources on which power depends—toward women and minorities. Political economists thus advocate policies with a view toward their ability to redistribute resources and power in a more equitable and democratic fashion.

Remember, however, that attempts to redistribute resources and power can always be contested. Those with power usually are loathe to give it up. A transfer of power may appear to be unfair or unjust to those whose worldview depends on the power they have traditionally held. A *backlash* (Faludi, 1991) frequently follows on efforts to transfer resources and power to women, minorities, or workers. In fact, we can even think of domination-resistance-reforms-backlash-domination as a typical cycle of the distribution and redistribution of power.

Because political economists do not believe that competition will automatically erode discrimination, or that a few well-intentioned corporate leaders can overcome the legacy of racism and sexism, they turn to government intervention to transfer resources and power.[16] The government can directly provide *services* for women and minorities (*eg,* day care, battered women's shelters, community renewal programs) that the private sector fails to provide equitably, if at all. Further, the government can provide *tax relief* for low-income workers (*eg,* the Earned Income Tax Credit) as well as *tax incentives* for corporate day-care and other programs that disproportionately benefit women and minorities. Here, however, we focus on the government's power to *regulate* the private sector to achieve race and gender justice. The

---

[15]Phrased more precisely, Myrdal's "American Creed" is neither a necessary nor a sufficient condition for race and gender justice.

[16]Unions are another source of institutional change, and many political economists have argued that a revitalized, progressive labor movement could fuse race, gender, and class issues to meet the needs of an increasingly female and nonwhite workforce.

two most well-known programs in this vein are affirmative action and comparable worth. We begin with affirmative action.

Affirmative Action Revisited

As discussed in Chapter 5, affirmative action policies provide a controversial mechanism for levelling the playing field between men and women and blacks and whites. On the one hand, affirmative action offers a direct and powerful remedy to the extent that discrimination is a problem. It may improve productivity if it gives firms incentives to expand their applicant pools and make better use of their human resources. On the other hand, affirmative action may be inefficient and unfair to the extent that groups diverge in terms of their productivity at work.

Political economists view affirmative action quite differently. They discount the productivity connection in the first place (see Chapter 7) and instead see affirmative action as a tool for collective struggle against oppression. In this view, affirmative action is a means of transferring power: it undermines old boys' networks while creating a leadership group of female and minority managers, administrators, and professionals. It uses legal sanctions to disrupt the process of organizational adaptation that has concentrated positions of authority in the hands of white males. The result should be that decision-making prerogatives are transferred out of exclusively white male hands. As with any policy, however, political economists do not view affirmative action uncritically.

Economist Jonathan Leonard (1991) has analyzed the effects of federal government affirmative action policies. These policies mainly affect contractors selling to the federal government. Under Executive Order 11246, issued in 1964, such contractors are required to make their workforces look more like the working population in their geographic area. Leonard shows that affirmative action has had moderate, positive effects on the employment of women and minorities among contractors. This has created a serious problem, however, for those employers and workers who traditionally have benefitted from continuing discrimination: taken in conjunction with the requirement of equal pay (which is relatively easy to enforce where jobs are similar, as in construction), it looked like discrimination, in terms of both hiring and pay, might be drastically reduced.

The resulting backlash against affirmative action was part of the reason why Ronald Reagan was elected president in 1980. He immediately proceeded to stop the enforcement of affirmative action through bureaucratic maneuvering and reduced funding for the agencies that were charged with enforcing the policies. The highly publicized attack on affirmative action signalled to employers that they had nothing to fear from the government. One of the major costs of discrimination had been drastically reduced—and employment discrimination rose as a result (Shulman, 1984).[17]

The context for the backlash against affirmative action involved more than the

---

[17]Not all employers responded in this fashion. Some large corporations defended affirmative action on the grounds that the programs worked well and provided them with legal protection against claims of discrimination. These reactions support the neoclassical, pro–affirmative action view that the policy can improve productivity and labor market efficiency.

battle for the presidency, however. First, the decay of inner-city schools (Kozol, 1991) made affirmative action look increasingly irrelevant. Affirmative action cannot benefit people who lack marketable skills. If blacks tend to be less well educated than whites, many of them will be bypassed by the affirmative action process.

Second, affirmative action in the 1980s was occurring in a context where white males were losing primary subordinate sector (or blue-collar) jobs in droves, so it became a tool for employers to divide-and-conquer. An employer with a large manufacturing plant could, for example, move 1000 jobs to Mexico while promoting one or two blacks or women into supervisory and management positions in the hope that the remaining white men would blame affirmative action rather than capital flight for the loss of jobs, thus deflecting any efforts among the workforce to unite-and-fight.

Third, the backlash against affirmative action sometimes is the ironic result of affirmative action itself. Women and blacks who are hostile to affirmative action may be placed in positions of power and visibility in part to satisfy affirmative action and in part to attack affirmative action. The most well-known example here is U.S. Supreme Court Justice Clarence Thomas. Thomas was appointed to the Supreme Court by then-President Bush in what looked to be an affirmative action appointment. By 1995, however, when the Supreme Court issued a decision effectively reigning in affirmative action, Justice Thomas wrote that there was a moral and constitutional equivalence "between laws designed to subjugate a race and those that distribute benefits on the basis of race in order to foster some current notion of equality."[18]

Affirmative action has become more limited as a general means of achieving race and gender justice through recent decisions by the Supreme Court. It came into being as an effort to institutionalize the gains of the Civil Rights Movement, but it provoked a backlash that has fed into race and gender stereotypes and conflicts. Many political economists also believe there are good reasons to be critical of affirmative action. Some think that affirmative action does not go far enough in the search for race and gender justice. Others believe that it is irrelevant to the problems of workers and the poor. A few believe that it is divisive and unfair; however, most political economists support the policy despite its limitations and contradictions. In the political economy view, the evolution of affirmative action reflects an ongoing struggle over resources and power.

Comparable Worth

In Chapter 5, we saw that some neoclassical economists believe comparable worth has been effective (to a degree) in combatting the effects of discrimination. Men and women are concentrated in different jobs with different pay scales that may be very similar in terms of the skills and responsibilities they require. Sociologist Paula England (1992:2) cites the following examples:

---

[18]Quoted in *The United States Law Week*, Adarand Constructors, Inc., v. Secretary of Transportation, et al., No. 93-1841, June 13, 1995, p. 4534.

In the state of Washington, where female state employees sued over pay equity, the job of legal secretary, a female job, was found by an evaluation study to be comparable in worth to the job of heavy equipment operator, a job filled mostly by men. However, in 1972, heavy equipment operators made about $400 more per month. Stockroom attendants, mostly men, made much more than dental hygienists, who were mostly women . . . In 1975, nurses in Denver sued the city claiming that their jobs paid less than male jobs such as tree trimmer and sign painter . . . It would be hard to argue that the latter two jobs require as much skill or are as demanding as nursing. Women workers for the city of San Jose discovered in the mid-1970s that secretaries were generally earning less than workers in male jobs that required no more than an eighth grade education, including, for example, men who washed cars for the city . . . In 1985, the California School Employees Association complained that school librarians and teaching assistants (female jobs) were paid less than custodians and groundskeepers (male jobs) . . . To take yet another example, in recent years the city of Philadelphia was paying practical nurses (mostly women) less than gardeners (mostly men) . . . These are not atypical examples. In addition, one is hard-pressed to come up with a single example of a male job paying less than a female job that reasonable people would find comparable in skill, effort, or difficult working conditions.

The logic of comparable worth is that it forces discriminatory wage differences to disappear and links wages more closely to productivity. Admittedly, many neoclassical economists disapprove of such interference with the market, particularly given the possibility of hedonic wages (see Chapter 4). Nonetheless, some acknowledge that discrimination may be slow to disappear, so a policy such as comparable worth may be worthwhile.

When political economists analyze comparable worth, they are less concerned with the link between productivity and wages and more with the potential for comparable worth to reduce systematic wage inequalities among groups. In other words, political economists interpret the existing wage structure as reflecting the distribution of power rather than productivity. Comparable worth confronts this issue head-on. Because political economists view wages as being socially determined (see Chapter 7), comparable worth is viewed as a battleground where the values and biases that society carries can be exposed and contested.

Comparable worth often has provided women with a step forward in wages. Where it has been implemented by state governments, wage improvements for women have averaged between 10 and 20%.[19] This in itself makes comparable worth attractive from a political economy perspective. Economists June Lapidus and Deborah M. Figart (1994) found that comparable worth policies across the U.S. economy would improve the female:male wage ratio from 0.759 to 0.813. They also note that the major beneficiaries of comparable worth policies would be women who are poor, single mothers. Using the federal poverty line as a base, they find that the poverty rate among women could be reduced by as much as 40% through such policies. Finally, comparable worth initiatives have brought women together to act collectively against exploitation and discrimination at work.

A disadvantage of comparable worth is that it confines the terrain of conflict to the existing distribution of jobs. In other words, it takes occupational gender segre-

[19]From Heidi Hartmann, Stephanie Aaronson, and Elaine Sorenson, *Pay Equity Remedies in State Government: Assessing their Economic Effects,* Washington, DC: Institute for Women's Policy Research, 1993.

gation as a given and then attempts to reduce the resulting wage inequities. So, from the beginning, comparable worth is a strategy with limited potential that has inherently constrained gains for women in the workplace.

In the early days of comparable worth initiatives, as Ronnie Steinberg (1995) has documented, organizations such as various Chambers of Commerce, the Business Roundtable, and Personnel Management Associations came out with organized campaigns to discredit and halt the initiatives. This sort of explicit opposition, however, did not continue as comparable worth took off. Instead, quiet and subtle methods of thwarting comparable worth came into play.

First, comparable worth initiatives require some basis for judging how valuable a job is. As we know from Chapter 7, the job-evaluation people with expertise in this arena typically are those who created the biased wage systems in the first place.

Second, given fiscal constraints and the demands of male-dominated unions, governmental bodies involved in comparable worth initiatives have a strong incentive to contain any wage advances that are achieved while still being able to claim they have "done something." As Steinberg discovered in just such a study for the State of New York, when the outsiders (including herself) came up with comparable worth wage increases that were too high, the government simply appointed a managerially controlled committee of staff members to redo—and reduce—the numbers. The end result was an average 5% (or less) wage increase for female- and minority-dominated occupations.

Steinberg's work suggests that discrimination is institutional in that it often is written into the explicit rules (here concerning pay) of firms and other organizations. When attempts are made to change these rules, the powers-that-be will fight back in whatever fashion they believe will be most successful.[20] Once again, we see that reforms can provoke a backlash that, in the end, is capable of diluting, diverting, and even destroying previously made gains. In the political economy view, no governmental policy or economic pressure is ever finally enough. The process of race and gender justice is ongoing, contested, and constantly in need of renewal.

A FEW CONCLUSIONS

Political economists argue that because it may be profitable, labor market discrimination can be perpetuated by competition. Discrimination not only means lower wages for black and female workers, it also may mean lower wages for white male workers (*ie,* class struggle effects). It also is possible for discrimination to benefit white male workers by improving their job security and wages (*ie,* job competition effects). In addition, discrimination in the larger society may be transported into the firm as it attempts to stabilize its relations with its external environment (*ie,* organi-

---

[20]Institutional discrimination is not always intentional. During the early stages of one comparable worth initiative, personnel experts were brought in to evaluate several jobs. The comparable worth experts found that the personnel experts had consistently evaluated male managerial jobs above female positions that were ranked at the same level of complexity. The personnel experts were "surprised," suggesting they were discriminating and didn't even know it (Steinberg, 1990). For political economists, such unintended discrimination is to be expected.

zational adaptation). These incentives to discriminate offset the costs of discrimination that are emphasized by neoclassical economists. The balance between these opposing pressures is determined by the strength of the labor market so that discrimination will tend to increase in recessions and fall in expansions. The cyclical changes in discrimination occur in the context of feedback effects that can perpetuate discrimination over the long-run, such as perception, socialization, choice, and market interactions.

Connecting these reasons to discriminate back to the Four Cs of political economy—*c*ontext, *c*ollective behavior, *c*onflict, and *c*hange—leads to the conclusion that discrimination can adapt to changes in its environment. On the one hand, groups suffering from discrimination respond by engaging in collective conflict, which often results in change for the better. The Civil Rights Movement, women's movement, entry of women into the labor market, as well as political changes such as the Equal Pay Act, Affirmative Action, and Comparable Worth all have yielded positive results through such struggles. Such struggles are limited, however, by both backlash from those who directly benefit from discrimination and by a historical context in which our day-to-day ways of acting and understanding others tend to perpetuate discrimination.

In the political economy view, the end of discrimination will require collective action to expose unintended acts of discrimination, to make those who benefit from discrimination recognize the high political and ethical costs, to change practices in the home and community that favor discrimination, and to change the rules of the social game. This is a very tall order, but as we saw in the last section, change—and resistance to change—are ever-present possibilities.

DISCUSSION QUESTIONS

1 Identify one written or unwritten rule at your school or workplace that functions in a discriminatory fashion. Explain why the rule is discriminatory, and if possible, explain how it came into being and who benefits by it.

2 Discuss any instances of unintended discrimination where once the act was pointed out to whomever was involved (perhaps even to you), the behavior was changed.

3 How could passage of a balanced budget amendment to the U.S. Constitution be discriminatory? Discuss how this interpretation can help to explain who might support or oppose and benefit or lose from such an initiative.

4 In general, do you think that male or white workers benefit from the low wages paid to women and blacks? Explain why or why not, and use your own work experiences to illustrate your opinion.

5 In general, do you think employers often pit whites against blacks or men against women in the workplace? Again, explain why or why not, and use your own work experiences to illustrate your opinion.

6 Can you think of instances in a workplace setting (whether you worked there or not) where people "expected" women or minorities to perform certain tasks that were not expected of males or whites? If so, use the concept of organizational adaptation to explain the phenomenon. Do males or whites benefit in terms of money or power from the practice? Explain.

7 Discuss some ways in which the long-term decline of white male wages has affected their discriminatory attitudes. Do such attitudes benefit or harm employers? Do they influence the col-

lective behavior of white males? Use your own work experiences to provide examples that illustrate your answers.

8 If you had to choose between implementing an affirmative action program or a comparable worth program in a firm, which would you choose? Why?

SUGGESTED READINGS

Baron, James. 1991. "Organizational Evidence of Ascription in Labor Markets." In *New Approaches to Economic and Social Analyses of Discrimination.* Richard Cornwall and Phanindra Wunnava, eds. New York: Praeger.

Cherry, Robert D. 1989. *Discrimination: Its Economic Impact on Blacks, Women, and Jews.* Lexington, MA: Lexington Books.

Corcoran, Mary and Paul Courant. 1986. "Sex-Role Socialization, Screening by Sex, and Women's Work: A Reformulation of Neoclassical and Structural Models of Wage Discrimination and Job Segregation." Mimeo. Ann Arbor, MI: University of Michigan.

Darity, William A., Jr. 1989. "What's Left of the Economic Theory of Discrimination?" In *The Question of Discrimination: Racial Inequality in the U.S. Labor Market.* Steven Shulman and William A. Darity, Jr., eds. Middletown, CT: Wesleyan University Press.

Darity, William A., Jr. and Samuel L. Myers, Jr. 1994. *The Black Underclass.* New York: Garland.

Doeringer, Peter and Michael Piore. 1971. *Internal Labor Markets and Manpower Analysis.* Lexington, MA: Lexington Books.

England, Paula. 1992. *Comparable Worth: Theories and Evidence.* New York: Aldine de Gruyter.

Faludi, Susan. 1991. *Backlash: The Undeclared War against American Women.* New York: Crown.

Kanter, Rosabeth Moss. 1977. *Men and Women of the Corporation.* New York: Basic Books.

Kozol, Jonathan. 1991. *Savage Inequalities: Children in America's Schools.* New York: Crown Publishers.

Lapidus, June and Deborah M. Figart. 1994. "Comparable Worth as an Anti-Poverty Strategy." *Review of Radical Political Economics* 26(3).

Leonard, Jonathan. 1991. "The Federal Anti-Bias Effort." In *The Economics of Discrimination.* Emily P. Hoffman, ed. Kalamazoo, MI: WE Upjohn Institute.

Lewis, Gregory. 1986. "Race, Sex and Supervisory Authority in Federal White-Collar Employment." *Public Administration Review* 46(1).

Massey, Douglas and Nancy Denton. 1993. *American Apartheid: Segregation and the Making of the Underclass.* Cambridge, MA: Harvard University Press.

McCrate, Elaine. 1987. "Trade, Merger and Employment: Economic Theory on Marriage." *Review of Radical Political Economy* 19(1).

Myrdal, Gunnar. 1972 (first published in 1944). *An American Dilemma: The Negro Problem and Modern Democracy.* New York: Random House.

Orfield, Gary and Carole Ashkinaze. 1991. *The Closing Door: Conservative Policy and Black Opportunity.* Chicago: University of Chicago Press.

Pettigrew, Thomas and Joanne Martin. 1987. "Shaping the Organizational Context for Black American Inclusion." *Journal of Social Issues* 43(1).

Reich, Michael. 1981. *Racial Inequality: A Political-Economic Analysis.* Princeton, NJ: Princeton University Press.

Shulman, Steven. 1984. "Competition and Racial Discrimination: The Employment Effects of Reagan's Labor Market Policies." *Review of Radical Political Economics* 16(4).

Shulman, Steven. 1987. "Discrimination, Human Capital and Black-White Unemployment: Evidence from Cities." *Journal of Human Resources* 22(3).

Shulman, Steven. 1989. "Racism and the Making of the American Working Class." *International Journal of Politics, Culture and Society* 2(3).

Steinberg, Ronnie. 1990. "Social Construction of Skill: Gender, Power, and Comparable Worth." *Work and Occupations* 17(4).

Steinberg, Ronnie. 1995. "Advocacy Research for Feminist Policy Objectives: Experiences with Comparable Worth." In *Bridging Theory and Practice*. Heidi Gottfried, ed. Urbana, IL: University of Illinois Press.

Weinberger, Catherine. 1993. "College Major and the Gender Gap in Wages: Beyond Decomposition." In *Diverse Essays in Labor Economics*. Unpublished Ph.D. dissertation, University of California at Berkeley.

Wilson, William. 1980. *The Declining Significance of Race: Blacks and Changing American Institutions*. Chicago: University of Chicago Press.

Yoder, Jan. 1991. "Rethinking Tokenism: Looking Beyond Numbers." *Gender and Society* 5(2).

PART FOUR

FOUR

INEQUALITY TODAY

9

WHERE DO WE
GO FROM HERE?

DOES DISCRIMINATION STILL MATTER?

By now, you know that the question of discrimination is simple to pose but difficult to answer. The trends in inequality are complex and difficult to consistently interpret. This book has presented two alternative frameworks to explain race and gender differences in wages, but uncertainties about the causes and consequences of inequality have not been resolved by statistical tests or appeals to common sense. As a result, the debates between neoclassical and political economists continue to rage.

Discrimination is one possible source of race and gender inequality, but because it is difficult to measure, its importance cannot be directly assessed. Together, the neoclassical and political economy approaches suggest a variety of possible roles for discrimination. Inequality may result from discrimination outside the labor market but not inside it; it may be caused by discrimination in the labor market, either alone or in combination with other forms of discrimination; or it may result from the perception of discrimination (whether accurate or not) and its effect on socialization patterns and the family, schooling, and job choices of women and blacks.

To drive home this point, consider some interpretations of the data provided in Table 9.1 concerning median earnings by race, gender, and educational attainment for persons 25 years of age and older. You can see that blacks and women are proportionately less likely than white men to earn a college degree, and that the possession of a college degree substantially raises the incomes of all groups. Both neoclassical economists and political economists agree there is a relationship between education and wages. Their disagreement centers on the reasons for white men being more likely to get higher levels of education and higher wages. For example, educational attainment may be directly influenced by discrimination in schools or fam-

TABLE 9.1

MEDIAN INCOME BY RACE AND GENDER FOR ALL PERSONS OLDER THAN 25 YEARS
AND THE PERCENTAGE AND MEDIAN INCOME OF THOSE WITH A BACHELOR'S
DEGREE OR MORE

	Median income	% of white men's earnings	% with bachelor's degree or more	Median income of those with bachelor's degree or more	% of white men's earnings
White men	$27,342	—	25.7	$41,239	—
Black men	$18,506	67.7	11.9	$30,904	74.9
White women	$16,346	59.8	19.7	$26,289	63.7
Black women	$15,285	55.9	12.3	$27,745	67.3

Source: U.S. Department of Commerce, Census Bureau. 1993. *Money Income of Households, Families and Persons in the United States, 1992.* Series P60-184. Table 29.

ilies, so that women and blacks eventually find themselves in lower-paying jobs. Alternatively, women and blacks may choose to acquire less education based on the belief that job discrimination will prevent their schooling from paying off, or women and blacks simply may have different preferences than white men and therefore (absent discrimination) make different choices about whether to attend college and what to study. We can observe the correlation between education and pay, but by itself, that correlation cannot tell us which of these explanations is correct.

The third column of Table 9.1 raises even more perplexing questions about the relationship of education to income (not unlike the information presented in Table 2.12). The median income of women and blacks with college degrees still is quite a bit less than that of white men. While a college degree raises incomes for all groups, its dollar payoff is greater (although its percentage payoff is less) for white men than for women or blacks. Do these patterns reflect labor market discrimination? Some who study this question answer "yes," but others, with equally sophisticated models, suggest that the answer may be "no." Women and blacks may face discrimination in K–12 education; therefore, even with a college degree, they may be less productive workers. Or, they may specialize in different fields or just pick occupations that don't pay as well as the ones that white men pick.

If all of our large data sets, expensive computers, and complicated statistical models cannot answer our questions about the role of discrimination, why do we keep asking them? Race and gender discrimination have been such fundamental forces in U.S. history that we cannot claim to have progressed as a society without understanding their modern roles. Our society often seems to be hopelessly fractured, and to the extent this is caused by discrimination, we will need to understand and confront it if we are to progress further. We also will have gone some way toward understanding our economic system in general if we can understand the role of discrimination in particular.

There are many worthwhile reasons to care about discrimination, and every study on race and gender inequality somehow addresses this issue—even if only implicitly or indirectly. The values of individual researchers flavor the reasons why and the way in which the research is performed and, therefore, give studies of inequality a controversial subtext. Are you a supporter or an opponent of capitalism? Do you think that we really have an equal opportunity society? What, if anything, do you think should be done about race and gender inequality? Every study on inequality, no matter how technical or complex, takes a position on these questions. We will, too, but our purpose in this chapter is to move beyond debate and disagreement. The different schools of thought can reach a "common ground" that lays the basis for meaningful steps toward race and gender justice. These steps may not satisfy everyone, but they are capable of breaking the logjam that seems to have resulted from the never-ending debates over the causes of race and gender inequality. It is time to get beyond paralysis, and our hope is that this chapter will make a small contribution toward that end.

A COMMON GROUND ANSWER: LET'S LEVEL THE PLAYING FIELD

Politicians and political analysts tend to take extreme views relative to most economists. Conservative candidates for political office often "blame" inequality on differences in culture, work attitudes, education, and other factors on the supply side of the labor market. This focus is warranted in that the number and characteristics of workers do have an important effect on earnings and employment. Liberal candidates tend to focus on the demand side of the labor market, where institutional discrimination is alleged to reduce the opportunities of women and minorities and to have important effects on employment and earnings.

These two interpretations are not mutually exclusive. Many—and perhaps most—economists view *both* supply- and demand-side factors as being crucial for understanding discrimination. Inequality results from differences in the characteristics of workers *and* from differences in the treatment of workers. This perspective cuts across the divide between neoclassical and political economists. Potentially, it could do the same for conservatives and liberals in the population at large.

The Debate Is Frustrating

We hear about the conflict between conservatives and liberals every night on the news. Sometimes, it seems as though the body politic has become a corpse, killed by our never-ending failure to agree on social priorities and policies. Much of the cynicism that many feel today about politics can be traced back to this appearance of unresolvable and immobilizing conflict.

Disagreements about the goals and methods of public policy are inevitable and healthy. However, a democracy depends on our ability to learn from these conflicts and to resolve them in a productive fashion. Nowhere is this more true than in the issue of race and gender inequality.

Researchers have been unable to resolve the debate over whether supply-side factors are most important (as conservatives claim) or if instead demand-side factors are most critical (as liberals believe). Framed in this way, political debates around race and gender have a familiar—and slightly tired—ring. However, it is hard to believe that this is the end of the story. Can't we go any further than endless debate?

We believe that the answer is "yes." The emphasis on both the characteristics and treatment of workers that we discuss later in one sense creates a problem in that it is difficult to separate the two in the empirical analysis of discrimination. It also moves us forward, however, in terms of the hope it gives us that the two sides of this debate can be viewed as complementary rather than contradictory. Each has something to contribute to the explanation of inequality, and by the same token, each has something to contribute to the solution.

The Debate Is Unnecessary

Consider two adjacent essays in a recent volume edited by economist Susan Feiner that compare alternative views on race and gender inequality. June O'Neill (1994) takes the "pure" neoclassical position that discrimination is irrelevant to black–white wage differences. She argues that all of the gap can be explained by black–white differences in educational achievement. When blacks and whites with the same years of schooling are compared, blacks on average score lower on standardized achievement tests. O'Neill believes that this difference means blacks are less productive and, therefore, earn less than whites.

In contrast, William Darity, Jr. (1994), takes the "pure" political economy position. He argues that discrimination is to blame for the entire black–white wage gap remaining after controlling for education and other differences in productivity-linked characteristics. He believes that the lower achievement test scores of blacks are caused by reasons aside from ability and motivation, so the connection between low test scores and low black wages is irrelevant.

Both O'Neill and Darity are highly respected economists. Are their views really as irreconcilable as they appear? We believe not. Achievement test scores can reflect productivity *and* discrimination. O'Neill and Darity may be looking at two different sides of the same coin.

O'Neill's argument that differences in achievement account for differences in wages rests on evidence confined to males. This is understandable given that there is only a small racial gap in wages among women. The racial gap in achievement test scores, however, exists for females as well as for males. Why is it not the case that black women earn less than white women, just as black men earn less than white men? This type of inconsistency undermines our faith that standardized achievement tests are adequate proxies for productivity and that wages are determined by productivity.

On the other hand, Darity displays too little faith in achievement test scores. While he may well be right that they are not functions of ability or motivation, they do reflect verbal and quantitative skills. The cause of racial differences in standardized test scores has long been a source of acrimonious debate, but the consequence cannot be doubted. If blacks on average cannot read or compute as well as whites, their training costs will be higher and their productivity lower. This is a legitimate factor to consider in the analysis of wage and employment differences.

Achievement test scores are an example of *intermingling of the characteristics and the treatment of workers.* It would be surprising if differences in skills did not translate into differences in labor market outcomes; at the same time, skill differences to some degree result from the legacy, and current practice, of discrimination in all of its various forms. The result is that discrimination is contained within the other factors that cause inequality.[1] The debate over the importance of discrimination therefore is impossible to resolve by "separating out" discrimination from other factors.

It would be astonishing if centuries of racism and sexism did not affect the values and behaviors of its victims, yet this is exactly what is presumed by the artificial dichotomy between the characteristics of workers and the treatment of workers. On the one hand, sexism and racism have damaged the self-confidence, ambition, and productive skills of women and minorities who are trying to survive in a world controlled by others. On the other hand, women and minorities also have responded positively in the face of sexism and racism. They have developed skills and character traits that, as a rule, are particularly likely to be found among the oppressed, such as empathy, cooperation, altruism, a keen sense of justice, and other nonpecuniary values. In fact, it is exactly because the positive responses of women and minorities largely express nonpecuniary values that they do not get rewarded in the marketplace. Unfortunately, the negative responses do generate penalties. The result is that women and minorities suffer economic losses *because they are not white men.* Their characteristics result from their treatment[2]; human capital and institutional discrimination are intermingled.

This is not to say that all differences in characteristics result from discrimination, just that some of them undoubtedly are. The debate between O'Neill and Darity over the importance of discrimination is a legitimate one, about which reasonable people can disagree. However, the intermingling of characteristics and treatment means that this debate is unlikely to be resolved in any definitive fashion. The impact of discrimination on inequality cannot be determined, in part because discrimination is difficult to measure and in part because discrimination cannot be separated out from characteristics. This point has important implications for public policy.

Our interest in understanding the causes of inequality is not merely academic. To the extent that inequality results from discrimination, it is illegal and immoral, yet we have just said that this extent cannot be determined. It may be large, or it may be small. What then should policy makers do? How should they strive to create a just society in light of their inevitable uncertainty about the importance of discrimination?

Searching for the Common Ground

We have pointed out a significant area of overlap between many neoclassical and political economists. Most neoclassical economists agree with political economists that discrimination still matters, and that public policy should be combined with mar-

---

[1]This is one reason why the statistical models of discrimination are so difficult to construct and interpret.

[2]This is the flip side to the argument made in Chapter 8 that characteristics influence treatment (i.e., positive feedback).

ket mechanisms to get rid of it. Both groups see markets as an imperfect mechanism for distributing income within firms, families, and communities. They share the belief that market mechanisms should be relied on wherever possible, but that government action is needed in those instances where market outcomes contravene the social good.

Of course, many neoclassical and political economists would disagree with this assessment. One group would say that government should not be allowed to interfere with markets, while the other group would say that markets should not be allowed to interfere with democratic control over economic decisions (by now, you should know which group is which). These are the "purists" in both camps: their views defy reconciliation. However, many—and perhaps most—economists are pragmatists. They are willing to accept whatever works. Although the neoclassical pragmatists are prone to be skeptical of government and the political economy pragmatists of markets, they tend to meet in the middle in their desire to work with whatever tools we have to solve social and economic problems. This is the group from which we draw our inspiration—and to which we appeal.

It is possible to locate neoclassical and political economists in terms of beliefs in markets versus government. Neoclassical economists run the policy gamut from laissez-faire to interventionist, while political economists range from interventionist to socialist. They overlap as *interventionists*, although there is quite a bit of debate within this broad group over how much and what type of government intervention is needed to work with markets to achieve efficiency and equity.

This pragmatic approach to government intervention is the basis of what we are calling the "common ground." Government intervention is needed, because market mechanisms do not necessarily erode discrimination, reward productivity, or enable women and blacks to perceive and take advantage of opportunities. However, we have just pointed out that it is impossible to know the extent to which inequality is caused by discrimination. In light of this inevitable uncertainty, how can policy makers decide what steps they should take to achieve race and gender justice?

We believe the answer lies in shifting the focus of discussion away from race and gender issues *per se* and toward the problems that are faced by the vast majority of the population. By addressing problems that generally are found at the home, community, and workplace, we can develop policies with a potentially wide base of support because they are *universal*. Such policies do not single out particular groups for benefits; instead, they strive to improve the circumstances of all people who work. At the same time, such policies will largely benefit the predominantly black and female "faces" that fill the "places" on the bottom of the economic ladder. Universal policies thus solve three problems at once: (1) they avoid the political problem of singling out particular groups for benefits, (2) they avoid the economic problem of specifying the precise importance of discrimination, and (3) they can legitimately lay claim to the goal of "the greatest good for the greatest number."

We view universal policies in terms of two primary components. The first is *equal opportunity*. Policies cannot lay claim to universality unless the opportunities they create are open to all. Equal opportunity policies such as antidiscrimination enforcement, applicant outreach, and hiring oversight are overwhelmingly popular, even among white men. They are widely perceived to be equitable and efficient, because they break up old boys' networks and emphasize personal accomplishment over social background. The contrast of their popularity to that of a targeted program such as affirmative action illustrates the broad base of genuine support that universal policies can potentially generate.

The second component of universal policies is what we have termed *sufficient opportunity*. It is not enough to guarantee formal equality of opportunity. Opportunities must be sufficiently available for them to make a real difference in peoples' lives. Structural obstacles that make opportunities inaccessible, such as the lack of adequate schooling or affordable day care, make a mockery of the notion of an "equal opportunity society." The elimination of these structural obstacles is needed to *level the playing field* and to make the system live up to its own promises. We will spend most of the remainder of this chapter elaborating on this theme, because sufficient opportunity is much less familiar—and more contentious—than equal opportunity.

Equal opportunity means that the race is fair. Sufficient opportunity means that everyone who makes a good faith effort can "win" a reasonable chance for decent life. Equal and sufficient opportunity would involve vigorous enforcement of antidiscrimination, antiharassment, and equal opportunity laws; fairer funding of public schools; full employment; and family-friendly policies in the workplace and community. We believe that these policies will help to level the playing field so that all individuals, regardless of their race, class, or gender, will have the chance to achieve the American Dream. Of course, not all will make it—but that is not our intent. Outcomes can never be guaranteed, but as long as opportunities are equal and sufficient, society will have done its best.

The phrase "American Dream" is not meant to suggest that all of us should have two cars and a suburban home. Each of us has our own dreams. For some, it may involve owning lots of expensive things, for others time with family, and for still others artistic or spiritual journeys. We envision a society that is flexible and supportive enough to allow for a great diversity of paths. This is the American Dream, or at least our interpretation of it.

The American Dream bears a contradictory relationship to the ideal of race and gender justice. On the one hand, its ethos of individualism, opportunity, and democracy is inherently incompatible with the "group-think" of racism and sexism. For this reason, many believe that American society has and will continue to shed its traditions of white male privilege. On the other hand, the American Dream promotes a "blame-the-victim" interpretation of poverty and inequality that reinforces race and gender stereotypes. If each of us controls our own destinies, then the blacks and women who are doing so poorly in today's labor market must be responsible for their own ill fortunes. These two sides of the American Dream express the historical contradiction of capitalism: it has both oppressed *and* liberated women and minorities. Both in theory and in practice, capitalism has exhibited a *contradictory relationship* to racism and sexism.

As you now know, most neoclassical economists believe that capitalism erodes discrimination, while most political economists believe that capitalism reproduces discrimination. The common ground program that follows has the virtue of responding to the strengths of both positions by recognizing that capitalism can *both* erode and reproduce discrimination.[3]

This program is not meant to paper over the many legitimate areas of disagreement between neoclassical and political economists and, on a more practical level, between the political left and right. There is much to be learned from these debates, and not only about inequality and discrimination. They speak to our conflicts over the interpretation of the American experience in general and our economic system in particular. Interpretations will always be contested and rarely can be resolved by empirical tests or common sense. Both the positive and negative interpretations of American history are factual and sensible. That economists continue to disagree only reflects the complexity of the subject and the limitations of social science. Deeper insights come not from dogmatic adherence to either side but from an open ear to their dialogue.

Common ground solutions, such as those proposed by Nancy Folbre (1994), Michael Lind (1995), or William Julius Wilson (1987), accept and reject aspects of both sides of the debate. They accept the framework of an individualistic market system but also that markets frequently produce undesirable outcomes. Common ground solutions will necessarily reject laissez-faire policies, because they accept that existing levels of inequality are inequitable and inefficient. At the same time, common ground solutions reject targeted programs, because they create group conflicts and stereotypes. The common ground alternatives that we propose instead are designed to benefit the population at large.

Because the programs we propose are not based on singling out specific groups for special treatment, they could garner a broad base of public support. This does not mean that they will not arouse controversy. One of our proposals includes fairer funding of public schools, which has been a political hot potato for decades. However, because it is based on the universal principle that every child in this country has a right to a good education, it is capable of appealing to popular sentiments. Because of their potential popular support, common ground solutions can deal with racial and sexual inequality in a manner that brings people together around mutual goals.

Because we are promoting a variety of government programs that presume markets cannot automatically solve social problems, we are likely to be accused of siding with the liberals. To some extent, we must plead "guilty" to this charge, because all of us (*ie,* the authors) are sympathetic to the political left. However, we see important areas of commonality between conservatives and liberals that too often are ignored. Many conservatives believe in government programs to assist in human capital acquisition and to promote incentives for self-sufficiency. Consider, for example, the following quote by conservative economist Glenn Loury (1995;21–22): "It is obvious that in the areas of education, employment training, enforcement of antidiscrimination laws, and provision of minimal subsistence to the impoverished, the government must be involved. Some programs—preschool education for one—cost money, but seem to pay even greater dividends . . . [I do not believe in] benign ne-

---

[3]For an example of a similar statement by a political economist, see Eric Olin Wright, *Class Structure and Income Determination,* New York: Academic Press, 1979:201. On the neoclassical side, see Ronald Ehrenberg and Robert Smith, *Modern Labor Economics: Theory and Public Policy,* New York: HarperCollins, 1994:427.

glect." Another well-known conservative, Nathan Glazer, titled one of his articles "Reform Work, Not Welfare," and in this vein commented elsewhere (1988:13–14) that we should "increase the incentive to work by increasing the attractiveness of work . . . [We should] attach to low-income jobs the same kind of fringe benefits—health insurance, social security, vacations with pay—that now make higher paying jobs attractive, and that paradoxically are also available in some form to those on welfare." Nor are liberals necessarily hostile to the cultural critique of conservatives, as can be seen from the work of William Julius Wilson and the feminist demand for family-friendly policies. This gives us hope that at least some aspects of the program we propose can generate a "common ground."

EQUAL AND SUFFICIENT OPPORTUNITY POLICIES

We see three interrelated but distinct areas of policy reform that would reduce race and gender inequalities by providing more equal and sufficient opportunity than currently exists: (1) education policies, (2) full-employment policies, and (3) family-friendly policies. We have purposely picked areas that address the wage inequalities associated with the three particular sites—community, firm, and home—that were introduced and discussed in Chapter 6. Still, each set of policies attempts to draw on the insights of both neoclassical and political economists.

Education Policies

For the vast majority of us, education is the key to economic opportunity. This has been true for many decades, but the impact of education on earnings has increased over the last 20 years for a variety of reasons, including deindustrialization, deunionization, and technological change. Schooling reforms are one means of addressing the problem of equal and sufficient opportunity at the site of the community. These reforms consist of greater access to public higher education, effective schooling at the primary and secondary levels, fairer funding of public schools, and ongoing training opportunities for noncollege graduates.

The earnings gap between college graduates and those with less than a college education has widened dramatically over the past two decades. The payoff to education has increased for both men and women. Wages for men with only a high-school diploma have fallen, while earnings for women with college degrees have improved significantly. At the same time, the cost of a college education takes a bigger chunk of family incomes, especially at private universities. In 1970, a single year of college tuition, room, and board at a private university cost about 30% of the median family income in that year; in 1993, it was over 50%.[4] Thus, a first step in creating sufficient opportunity is to make higher education more affordable.

The United States does have a world-class system of public universities. However, federal financial aid has been cut back, and many states have taken the budget axe to higher education as well. Massachusetts, for example, cut funding and dou-

---

[4]From U.S. Department of Commerce, Bureau of the Census, *Statistical Abstract,* Washington, DC: Government Printing Office, 1994 and 1980.

bled tuition and fees in its state universities between 1988 and 1992. In a relatively short period of time, the cost of public education has increased dramatically. In 1980, the average tuition and mandatory fees for a semester at a public college or university was $1475; by 1993, it had nearly doubled (after adjusting for inflation) to $2610.[5] It is not surprising that many students find it difficult to pay for college.

There is a long-term payoff for government assistance to needy college students in the form of scholarships, low-cost loans, work-study programs, and community service/tuition forgiveness programs. We advocate expansion of these programs, all of which currently exist and most of which face cutbacks in the name of deficit reduction and tax cuts. Nonetheless, state public higher education is already a bargain. Some of the other programs discussed later (*eg,* subsidized day care) may do more to increase college attendance than additional financial assistance. If dollars were all that mattered, then sufficient opportunity in higher education already is a reality for many students who have the ability and the desire to attend.[6]

Preparing primary and secondary students to take advantage of public higher education is a more complicated story. Only about one-quarter of the adult population has a college degree. Many secondary students lack the incentive to earn decent grades as few employers will ever ask to see their transcripts, and even among those with decent grades, many lack basic skills. All those years in school do not always add up to much accomplishment. U.S. students have lagged behind their foreign counterparts for years with respect to their mathematical, scientific, and literary skills.

Because primary and secondary education are universal, every child in the United States is entitled—in fact, is required—to attend school.[7] It would appear, then, that this country already offers sufficient opportunity here as well, but the inability of the schools to teach necessary skills or to prepare more students for college makes it clear that educational reforms are needed. For too many students, schools are just holding tanks. Too many young people are alienated from education or drop through the cracks in the system. Too much schooling is irrelevant, boring, and bureaucratic. Schools must be organized in a fashion that responds to student needs and makes it possible for students to discover and realize their particular abilities.

This problem is particularly acute in the inner cities. Many inner-city schools face severe resource shortages as well as the organizational inefficiencies experienced by suburban schools (Kozol, 1991). Their students must deal with family and community problems that can make effective schooling much more difficult to achieve. Violence, drug abuse, teen pregnancy, as well as emotional and learning problems are much more prevalent in inner-city than in suburban schools. Drop-out rates ap-

---

[5]From U.S. Department of Commerce, 1994, *op cit.,* Table 280. Figures in 1993 dollars.

[6]Michael Lind (1995:330) proposes "turning higher education from a largely private luxury into a universal entitlement and a regulated public utility" by equalizing the costs of attending any university, private as well as public, perhaps through use of a single-payer system. His goal is to eliminate elitism in the form of legacy admissions, which benefit the "white overclass"; preferential admissions, which benefit women and minorities; the rationing of access based on parental income and wealth; and the very existence of elite educational institutions as such.

[7]Proposition 187, which is a referendum approved by the voters in California in November 1994, seeks to bar children who are illegal immigrants from attending public schools. A court case on the constitutionality of barring children from public schools is pending as of this writing.

proach 50% in many cities, and achievement test scores are distressingly low. What does sufficient opportunity mean in this context?

The contrast between inner-city and suburban schools makes it clear that sufficient opportunity cannot be separated from equal opportunity. One reason for the disparities is that funding for public schools primarily is based on local property taxes. Property-rich communities can raise money more easily than poorer ones. Inner-city schools should have access to the same resources—books, computers, physical plant, and especially, teachers—that suburban schools have. The problem of equal education is so seriously compromised by the funding mechanisms in place that state courts have ruled them to be unconstitutional in 13 states, and another one-third of all states face court cases challenging school-funding mechanisms.

Fairer funding of the public schools is no guarantee that inner-city students will improve their performance; more resources will not automatically be translated into higher achievement given the inefficiencies of most schools (Hanushek, 1994). Something else is at stake. Inner-city students are equal to suburban students as citizens. They have equal rights to public resources such as schooling. They are (or should be) equally innocent and important in the eyes of society as a whole. Therefore, their schools should be equalized with those of their suburban neighbors; otherwise, we cannot claim to live in a society that provides equal opportunity.

Equal opportunity will not necessarily produce equal results. Inner-city students may face disadvantages in their family and community circumstances that could still leave them behind in terms of educational and economic success. However, that is hardly an adequate reason to provide *fewer* educational resources to urban students than to their suburban counterparts. Equalizing schooling environments and resources is the least that society can do.[8]

Fairer funding of the public schools is a necessary, but partial, step toward creating racial equality of educational opportunity. It would be a worthwhile goal in any circumstance, but challenging current funding systems is especially pertinent in the context of persistent racial segregation. Segregation of the public schools has been increasing over time: an increasing fraction of black and Latino students attend schools that have few or no white students (Orfield, 1994). These are the schools most likely to have a deteriorating physical plant, obsolete texts, supply shortages, and overcrowded classrooms. Consequently, fair funding of the public schools is at heart a demand for civil rights. It is an issue of the citizenship of black Americans and their right of equal access to public resources.

The fundamental cause of schooling segregation is housing segregation, and residential segregation shows few signs of abating. Segregation largely is caused by discrimination, but white Americans have been unwilling to stop housing discrimination. In fact, their willingness to flee when blacks move into their neighborhoods

---

[8]The issue actually is more complicated than it may appear, because inner-city schools sometimes spend more per pupil than average as a result of compensatory and special programs (Hanushek, 1994;73). However, they still tend to lag behind in terms of capital and equipment expenditures, teacher salaries, and baseline per-pupil spending. A variety of methods have been proposed to achieve fair funding, including redrawing school district boundaries, centralization of school finance, tax capacity equalization, and others. See the essays in John Anderson, ed., *Fiscal Equalization for State and Local Finance*, Westport, CT: Praeger, 1994.

(so-called "white flight") makes it possible for banks and realtors to benefit from housing discrimination (Massey and Denton, 1993). Although residential discrimination has been well documented, little headway has been made in stopping it. As a result, black and white children live in vastly different communities and attend vastly different schools. It is difficult to take the claim of equal opportunity seriously in these circumstances.

There is still one more important area of education to consider. It is unlikely that more than one-half of our young people will ever have the desire, or the ability, to attend college. There is nothing wrong with this decision in a society as large and diverse as ours, but there is something wrong when that decision results in economic catastrophe. Noncollege graduates should be able to get the training they need to earn a decent living. Businesses should assist their workers in learning new skills, in attending apprenticeship and training programs, and in returning to school on a part-time basis. These programs are common and highly successful in Germany and Japan. In the United States, about 1 out of every 10 workers participated in employee-sponsored, work-related training in 1990.[9] This may be an idea whose time has come. Candidate Clinton discussed a payroll tax that would be used to fund workplace training and education efforts in his 1992 presidential bid; however, after the election, he dropped that proposal.

Workplace training and the other education reforms discussed here are especially important, because they have implications for equal and sufficient opportunity in the job market, to which we now turn.

Full-Employment Policies

Clearly, more and better education is not enough. Other policies also must be put in place for training programs to pay off. This section describes some needed labor market reforms that can increase the return to educational investments. Full-employment policies are designed to create equal and sufficient opportunity at the site of the firm. Full employment raises living standards and reduces inequality and discrimination. Further, as a society, we cannot expect every able-bodied adult to support him- or herself unless an adequate number of jobs pay living wages.

Some neoclassical economists have long argued that full employment is an impossible dream, because it drives up inflation. However, the fear of inflation must be balanced against the harm that is created by fighting inflation, especially the lost output and jobs resulting from recessions created by anti-inflationary policies. Further, the tendency of full-employment policies to raise wages and other costs of production can be offset by their ability to improve productivity and to lower unit labor costs and unit fixed costs. The obstacles to full employment are political, not technical.

The labor market has been functioning poorly for many, if not most, working people since the early 1970s. Between 1979 and 1993, 24 million new jobs were created. Virtually all of them were in the service sector. In fact, 3.2 million jobs were lost in the higher-paying manufacturing, mining, and construction sectors (Folbre,

---

[9]From U.S. Department of Commerce, 1994, *op cit.*, Table 659.

1995). While some service jobs are high skill and high pay, most are not. Productivity and real wage growth have stagnated. Many workers are stuck in part-time or temporary jobs with few benefits or prospects. Most U.S. families cannot count on rising living standards and must struggle to make ends meet despite sending more members into the labor market. The era of prosperity that followed World War II has come to an unhappy end, leaving insecurity and resentment in its wake.

At the same time the average quality of jobs has deteriorated, quantity has suffered as well. In the 1960s, economists considered an unemployment rate of about 3% to be equivalent to full employment.[10] Today, the Federal Reserve Bank (referred to as the "Fed") considers 6% to be the full-employment unemployment rate. This means that in the Fed's view, full employment exists when over 7 million unemployed workers are unable to find (or are unwilling to accept) jobs on any given day. The Fed argues that unemployment rates should not be reduced further, because lower unemployment rates drive up wages and thereby fan inflation. This fear of inflation has paralyzed full-employment policy and undermined our belief in America as the land of opportunity.

As Figure 2.7 showed, average unemployment rates have trended upward since the early 1970s. The general rise in unemployment has afflicted the entire industrialized world, and many countries have suffered from higher unemployment rates than that in the United States. Our problems are not solely caused by the unwillingness of the Fed to keep credit cheap—deindustrialization and deunionization also have contributed to the decline in employment and wage growth. However, the policy of labor market deregulation pushed by the Reagan and Bush Administrations throughout the 1980s did not provide solutions to these long-term problems. Instead, we must rebuild the institutions that guaranteed wage growth and high employment in the post–World War II period, although in a manner suited to current conditions.

The first step is to *renew our commitment to the goal of full-employment*—meaning a 3% unemployment rate. Many economists believe that the modern concern with inflation is excessive. Low unemployment will not necessarily translate into high inflation if it encourages a more efficient use of labor and capital resources.[11] In other words, productivity growth can offset the impact of wages on prices. The belief that 6% unemployment constitutes an inflation threshold ignores this effect by taking productivity growth as a given, but high employment and wages improve worker morale. High wages can work to build cooperative relationships between employers and workers, which can improve communication and innovation. Our strongest competitors, Japan and Germany, pay higher wages than the United States and, in return, receive higher productivity growth rates. Raising both wages and productivity is a feasible and desirable policy goal.

A commitment to full employment also is a commitment to an economy that is oriented to human needs rather than to corporate profits. Sometimes, these go hand in hand; sometimes, they come into conflict. The sacrifice of jobs to fight inflation

---

[10]There will always be some "frictional unemployment," even when the economy is at full employment, as a result of normal job search and mobility. Frictional unemployment is voluntary. As the estimates of frictional unemployment rose, the pressure on the government to reduce unemployment fell.

[11]Robert Eisner, "Our NAIRU Limit: The Governing Myth of Economic Policy," *The American Prospect* 21, Spring 1995.

may make sense to a banker, but it is unlikely to find much support among most U.S. workers. A commitment to full employment symbolizes that economic policy is not designed for the elite. This could be an important step in restoring the public faith in public policy.

Full employment has a variety of effects that can reduce race and gender inequality. Inequality generally tends to fall as the labor market tightens, and gender and, particularly, racial inequality tend to fall along with it. Because black unemployment is more cyclically sensitive than white unemployment, the black–white unemployment gap is unlikely to fall without a sustained drop in overall unemployment (Shulman, 1991). Low-wage workers tend to benefit from full employment more than high-wage workers, which means that black and female workers should see their wages rise relative to those of white male workers. Finally, a sustained drop in unemployment will pull discouraged workers back into the labor force. This means that some of the social problems that are associated with unemployment, such as crime and welfare recipiency, will become less severe. More employment opportunities alone cannot eliminate completely the black–white gap in unemployment, but coupled with better education and family-friendly employment policies, it should be substantially reduced.

In general, full employment raises the costs of continuing discrimination and reduces the costs of ceasing discrimination. For example, white workers are far less likely to resent black workers if the economy is strong and their own prospects look good. We may wish that they would not resent black workers even if it were otherwise, but the fact is that full employment makes it easier for people to get along. For these reasons, women and blacks have much to gain if the government were to pursue full employment consistently.

Full employment also tends to shift the balance of power toward labor, because workers are less afraid of losing their jobs. This is one reason the business community tends to oppose full employment (not necessarily because they fear inflation). A shift in the balance of power toward labor is good news for most of us. It means that the economy is responding more to the popular will and less to the demands of the corporate elite. Full employment in this sense increases democracy, and this can only work to the advantage of women and minorities.

Full employment can be pursued by several means. First, the mandate of the Fed could be changed so that full employment becomes its single greatest priority. Low interest rates are the easiest way to encourage economic growth. As noted earlier, the Fed has traditionally resisted this approach because of its fear of inflation, but low interest rates can actually reduce inflation as they mean lower financial costs of production. When the economy is slack, prices are unlikely to rise, because demand is weak. When the economy is strong, productivity growth can offset increases in labor and materials costs. The problem with the Fed is that it has always seen bankers as its constituency. It needs to broaden its vision to include the American people as a whole.

The second means to create full employment is a viable, pragmatic *public works program*. We do not mean a make-work program; there is an enormous amount of desperately needed work that the private sector is not providing (*eg,* rebuilding the inner cities, staffing schools, providing care for children and the elderly, park and library maintenance). If people cannot find jobs in the private sector, then the government should step in as the employer of last resort. Not only would needed work be performed, but work habits and skills would be learned. Programs also could include assistance for a worker's transition into the private sector. Instead of government hand-outs, the unemployed and indigent would be offered the opportunity to work. This is a strategy that rewards work, fosters self-sufficiency, and strengthens the public sphere on which citizenship depends (Kaus, 1992). As these jobs are needed precisely because the private sector is not doing them, a public works program should not undercut the private sector. In fact, if the work built vital social and physical infrastructure, it could even enhance growth and profitability in the private sector.

These two policies may not be enough, however. To make sure that productivity gains from full employment keep inflation in check, the government will need to pursue an *industrial policy*. This means that the government would work cooperatively with the business sector to improve competitiveness. If the government can reduce labor/management conflict and stimulate technological development and experiments in work organization, it can add to productivity growth. As the example of Japan shows, the government can play a positive role in industrial development. For example, it can enforce fair "rules of the game" to improve worker morale and labor/management cooperation, provide tax incentives for investments in human and physical capital, and reward firms that reduce inequality between workers and managers and encourage participatory decision-making.[12] These policies do not so much involve identifying winners in advance of the market (a common criticism) as facilitating productivity-enhancing processes and systems. As it stands, our existing industrial policy is primarily one of politically motivated tax breaks, excessive military spending, and tax incentives for financial speculation. The choice is not between having or not having an industrial policy; it is between having a rational or an irrational industrial policy. The former could go a long way toward restoring the rapid productivity growth that we enjoyed in the post–World War II period.

Even so, as other industrialized countries are now finding, new technologies and globalization are double-edged swords. Expanding production around the world and developing ever-more-efficient technologies help to increase productivity, but they also reduce employment. For full employment to be a reality, more work is going to have to be shared more evenly. The United States is plagued by both overwork and underwork. Some people work too much—they confront mandatory overtime, sacrifice their families for their jobs, and face enormous stress to complete the work expected of them. At the same time, millions of people go without work or are forced to work part-time. Wouldn't it make much more sense for all of us to share the work that was available? Moving to a *shorter work week* accomplishes just that. Workers have long struggled to reduce the work week, and until the 1930s, a key battleground for workers was the fight to reduce mandatory hours before overtime pay was required. A 35- or 30-hour workweek would have the potential to increase productiv-

---

[12]For the last decade, the "big three" U.S. auto makers have mandated that their suppliers involve employees in decision-making, and recent evidence suggests these mandates largely are successful. See Robert Lapota and Robert Drago, "Should Employee Involvement Be Mandatory for Firms? Evidence from the U.S. Automobile Supplier Industry," mimeo, Department of Economics, University of Wisconsin, 1995.

ity while spreading the work around. France is seriously considering this measure. The Kellogg Corporation of Battle Creek, Michigan, moved to a 4-day work week during the 1930s and kept it in place until the 1970s. Wages rose over that period (along with productivity), and workers liked the free time. The owner, W. K. Kellogg liked it too. He boasted that "the efficiency and morale of our employees is [*sic*] so increased, the accident and insurance rates are so improved, and the unit cost of production is so lowered that we can afford to pay as much for six hours as we formally paid for eight."[13]

The creation of more jobs—and more high-paying jobs—is a crucial step toward raising living standards, reducing inequality and discrimination, and achieving equal and sufficient opportunity. However, as with the education policies we have proposed, it also is not enough. Many women will not be able to take advantage of the opportunities created if they are limited by household responsibilities, especially child-rearing. In the absence of policies that support adults in their capacity as parents, it is unlikely that gender equity—and race equity, given that many black women also are single mothers—can be achieved.

Family-Friendly Policies

Family-friendly policies are designed to create equal and sufficient opportunity at the site of the family.[14] They attempt to resolve the contradiction that more and more women (and men) face in their roles as breadwinners and caregivers. We have become a society in which we expect women to work for wages; indeed, many women's income is vital for meeting the basic needs of their families. However, many women face a no-win situation: if a woman works for pay, she is neglecting her family, but if she takes care of her family, she is not able to compete in the labor market. For many single mothers, who are the sole breadwinners in their families, this situation has dire consequences in terms of poverty and related ills.

Family-friendly policies are designed to support workers who also are responsible for families. These policies include changes in jobs that would reduce the conflicts between work responsibilities and family responsibilities, such as flextime, family leave, and on-site child care. Family-friendly policies also include "de-spousing" and "de-firming" benefits like health care and pensions—in other words, making these benefits independent of marital or work status. In addition, family-friendly policies include programs that socialize the costs of raising children, such as early education, child care, afterschool programs, and child allowances, so that families with children can afford to go to work without sacrificing quality care for their children.

The economic and social activities that occur inside families and communities are vital for any society, but the work involved usually is unpaid. We already have discussed how this work becomes invisible in capitalism as it is absorbed in a "family wage" (see Chapter 7); however, the rising numbers of women now working for pay have put family responsibilities back on the social agenda as fewer and fewer fam-

---

[13]Quoted in Juliet Schor, *The Overworked American: The Unexpected Decline of Leisure,* New York: Basic Books, 1992;155.

[14]Many of these policies as well as strategies for implementing them are discussed in Ellen Bravo, *The Job/Family Challenge: Not for Women Only,* New York: John Wiley & Sons, 1995.

ilies have enough time for it. Families work harder just to stay in place, more and more kids come home to an empty house after school, single parents cannot make enough to support a family and also take time for their children, and adult children are unable to find time to care for their elderly relatives. We solve one set of problems by working for a wage—but only by creating another. However, this trade-off is not written in stone. Jobs that pay sufficient wages without absorbing so much of our time would give back some of that time we currently are missing in our families. In other words, we need to create *jobs without wives.*

As noted, one way to make more time is to establish a shorter work week without a large reduction in pay. Moving to a 35-hour (or 4-day) work week would give men and women more time to take care of their family and for community activities. In connection with full employment, it would allow people—men as well as women—to choose to stay home and raise children safe in the knowledge that they are not sacrificing economic security in the process.

In addition to reduced hours, other workplace safeguards would help to make jobs more family friendly. Flexible hours, work sharing, on-site day care, and paid family leave would enable workers with particularly significant care-giving obligations to keep their jobs and to provide the needed time for that care. Some firms have instituted some of these policies, but usually, it is in large firms—and usually, only highly paid employees are covered. For example, in firms with 100 or fewer employees, only 2% of employees had paid maternity leave as a benefit, and only 2% received any child-care benefits.[15] Only about 15% of all women are on flexible schedules.[16] Further, strict enforcement of regulations against discrimination and harassment are worthwhile components of any strategy to assure that women can compete with men on a level playing field. Many firms that have implemented these policies have enjoyed a rise in productivity, which offsets the cost of these programs, because turnover falls and morale rises (Hewlett, 1991).

A second crucial component of sufficient opportunity vis-à-vis the family is to detach health-care coverage and pensions from jobs and spouses, or to de-firm and de-spouse such benefits. Women typically bear the economic risks of having and raising children. They are the ones who usually leave the labor force and/or take reduced hours. Women are less likely to be covered by health-care insurance through their own job and less likely to have pensions. Women who are assured of these benefits through a spouse may not be so economically vulnerable. In this day and age, however, there are no assurances that people will stay married over the course of their adult lives. Universal health-care coverage only eludes the United States. Every other industrialized country has such coverage, and so do many developing countries. Pension benefits are tied to jobs, and the level of benefits are tied to wages received in those jobs. Therefore, women are penalized if they are not married—or don't stay married—to someone with those benefits.

A third aspect of family-friendly policies concerns spreading the costs of care and education of children over the entire society. Those who care enough to bear and raise

---

[15]From U.S. Department of Commerce, 1994, *op. cit.,* Table 673.

[16]Cynthia Costello and Anne Stone, eds., *The American Women, 1994–95,* New York: WW Norton Co., 1994:Table 4–6.

the next generation are doing the rest of us a favor, and they deserve some help. We all have an interest in the care and education of children, and we have already made that commitment to children through the financing of public education. There are huge gaps, however. Children under the age of 5 years need care and educational activities; kids typically don't go to school after 3:00 PM or in the summer. Working parents, and particularly mothers, are always juggling jobs and kids. Universal childcare subsidies (on a sliding scale), child allowances, and early childhood education would go a long way in allowing women to become equal participants in the labor market and men to become equal participants in raising children. The U.S. government provides little outside of tax credits for child care, and Head Start coverage for a limited proportion of qualified (*ie*, low-income) applicants. Child care is expensive and of uneven quality. Even for school-age children, school hours do not coincide with full-time work hours. There are not nearly enough affordable after-school programs, either. Many parents are left in an uncomfortable situation: take a part-time (or no) job, or let the kids come home unattended. There is no doubt that provision of these services would increase employment and productivity by reducing stress and sickness. In Sweden, where child care is available and affordable (close to 60% of all children aged 3–5 years participate in publicly funded child-care services) and there are generous child allowances, the labor force participation rate for women is 80% and that of men 85%, with close to 40% of all working women working part-time.

Socializing the cost of caring for children can be defended on the grounds of both equity and efficiency. If families were assured of quality day care when both adults chose to work, then both adults and children would benefit. If families with children are provided a child allowance (*ie*, a set amount of cash for each child), it would help to improve children's educational outcomes. Early childhood education (*ie*, ages 3–5 years) has a twofold benefit. It alleviates the need to find child care, and it helps to assure that all kids entering kindergarten have some basic, sound sets of skills and knowledge. Good early childhood programs are successful in stopping problems before they start and are cost-effective in the long run (Schorr, 1989). These policies reduce inequality in the present by shifting public resources toward poor children, and they reduce inequality in the future insofar as these children are able to improve their odds for escaping poverty as adults.

Other policies also may be needed to create gender equity in the broadest sense (*eg*, child support policies, sexual harassment policies). The policies that we propose are designed to create equal and sufficient opportunity in the labor market in particular. They would be a big step toward a truly just and efficient economy, but they are expensive. Can we afford them?

PAYING FOR EQUITY

Many (although not all) of the policies that we have proposed cost money in the form of hard-earned, taxpayer dollars. In this day and age, you may find these types of suggestions either crazy or "pie in the sky" dreaming. We do not, however, consider ourselves to be particularly idealistic. Each policy put forward in this chapter already exists on a small scale somewhere in the United States and on a much larger scale in other industrialized countries. Further, many countries have a large number of these policies in place and available to most of the population. What do these countries have that we lack?

One answer is taxes. The United States, believe it or not, taxes itself at a much lower rate overall than any other industrialized country. In 1991, taxes were 29.8% of gross domestic product in the United States, compared with 31% in Japan, 36% in the United Kingdom, 39% in Germany, 44% in France, and 53% in Sweden.[17] Not all taxes are alike, however, and there are a variety of ways in which this country could raise taxes without "stiffing" the poor or middle class.[18] For example, we suggest that tax loopholes be closed and the corporate tax rate increased back to its pre-Reagan level. There is no technical or economic reason why we, as a nation, cannot afford to pay for these programs—just as other industrialized countries do—if they are social priorities.

Further, spending can be reallocated if we take the goal of equity seriously enough. We do not propose that deficits be raised to finance this or any other proposal.[19] Instead, we believe that military spending can be cut[20] and corporate welfare abolished.[21] These steps can free up the funds that are needed to get these programs off the ground.

By not making equity a priority, we are incurring a substantial price. Poverty and discrimination create enormous psychic and financial costs for millions of individuals. Society as a whole suffers as well. We all pay for the lost productivity caused by overwork for some and underwork for others. We all bear the long-run costs of allowing nearly one-quarter of our children to live in poverty, such as increases in crime, low educational achievement, and ill health, and we all suffer the costs to society resulting from the hopelessness that seduces young men into gangs and young girls to have children. There also are the costs of living in a society that is fundamentally fractured along the lines of race, gender, and income. How can we afford not to question our priorities when they concern equity?

---

[17]From U.S. Department of Commerce, 1994, *op cit.*, Table 1376.

[18]For example, the following tax reforms would raise large amounts of money but not affect most low- and moderate-income families: cap the deduction on home mortgage interest (particularly on second homes and expensive homes), tax capital gains income at death, fully tax social security for persons with incomes over $30,000 from other sources, eliminate business write-offs such as lobbying, and restore progressivity to the income tax by raising rates on the top 5% of the population.

[19]There is a debate about the size and significance of the deficit. See Robert Eisner, *The Misunderstood Economy: What Counts and How to Count It,* Boston: Harvard Business School Press, 1994. Eisner provides an accessible presentation of the reasons why the fear of the deficit may be overblown. By accepting the deficit as a constraint on spending, we take a conservative stance on this question. The easy-money policy proposed here would reduce the deficit, because lower interest rates would reduce the government's payments on the debt (now the third largest category of government spending).

[20]Much of military spending represents "make-work" at its worst. Cuts in military spending would increase unemployment in the short run, but in conjunction with the full-employment policies outlined here, military personnel should be able to shift into civilian pursuits that add to economic growth rather than merely absorbing tax dollars.

[21]Corporate welfare consists of tax-and-spending subsidies to large corporations. Some estimates place the total amount at over $150 billion per year. See Robert Hershey, 1995, "A Hard Look At Corporate 'Welfare.' " *New York Times,* March 7, p. C1.

Inequality in the United States has risen for social and economic reasons, such as the rise in single-parent households and the shift in employment from manufacturing to services. Public policies also have increased inequality by reducing social spending that primarily benefits the poor while simultaneously reducing the taxes that primarily are borne by the wealthy. These policies have been justified by the claim that they will improve productivity and make the United States more competitive globally. However, several recent studies reveal otherwise. There appears to be a positive correlation between equity and productivity across nations—and even across U.S. cities. Countries like the United States, which have very high levels of inequality (measured as the ratio of the total income held by the richest 20% to the poorest 20%), also had the lowest rates of labor productivity growth.[22] Growing inequality is not only bad for those at the bottom, it also appears to be bad for business as well.

CONCLUSION: POSITIVE-SUM SOLUTIONS

The common ground program will not appeal to everyone. Objections will be heard from those who disagree with the goal of full employment, who think that the relevant programs will bust the Federal budget, or who believe that the government should discourage women from working outside the home. It also will be opposed by those who argue that it does not go far enough. Some inner-city blacks will still probably face high unemployment even if full-employment policies are adopted. Some single-mother families will still face high poverty rates even if child care is available when mothers are young, inexperienced, and lack education. We do not expect to avoid debate and disagreement. We do think, however, that the programs we describe have the potential to bring diverse groups together. There are enough neoclassical *and* political economists who would agree with enough aspects of the common ground program (even if they would disagree about others) to justify optimism about the ability of many of us to work together. The same could be said about conservatives and liberals. Their respective concerns with values and opportunities are not mutually exclusive. It is worth the effort to find a way to work together.

The common ground program is based on the notion of *positive-sum solutions*. A zero-sum solution is one in which my loss is your gain. A positive-sum solution is one in which we both gain. The common ground program is designed to benefit white males as well as women and minorities. Fairer funding of the schools and expanding postsecondary education and training opportunities, full-employment, and family-friendly policies are policies that would have many millions of supporters among all race and gender groups. The opposition primarily comes from an elite group who resent the loss of their social and economic privileges—and who are quite willing to sacrifice public good for private gain. This group is great in resources but few in

---

[22]Randy Albelda and Chris Tilly, 1995, "Unnecessary Evil: Why Inequality Is Bad for Business," *Dollars and Sense,* March/April.

number. In a democracy, we should be able to put people first. This is what the common ground program of equal opportunity and sufficient opportunity is designed to achieve.

DISCUSSION QUESTIONS

1 Would school-choice "voucher" programs that permit students and their parents to choose between various public and private schools, with partial or complete state funding, fit the "common ground" approach presented here? Explain.

2 If political economists are right that much discrimination is unintended but institutional, do you think the "common ground" policies would help to reduce that type of discrimination? Why, or why not?

3 If neoclassical economists are right that statistical discrimination is a serious problem for women and blacks, would the "common ground" approach help to reduce these problems? Explain.

4 Suppose you believed that full-employment policies would create such severe inflation that economic growth would ultimately decline. Are there other elements of the "common ground" approach that would still work, or does this instead mean that the approach is simply unworkable? Give some examples in your answer.

5 Are there elements of the "common ground" approach that favor women in particular? Are there others that tend to favor blacks? How can the common ground program be reconciled with the widespread opposition to preferential treatment?

6 Do you think that whites and males would benefit or suffer, on average, from "common ground" government policies? Justify your opinion.

SUGGESTED READINGS

Darity, William Jr. 1994. "Loaded Dice in the Labor Market: Racial Discrimination and Inequality." In *Race and Gender in the American Economy: Views from across the Spectrum*. Susan Feiner, ed. Englewood, NJ: Prentice-Hall.

Folbre, Nancy. 1994. *Who Pays for the Kids? Gender and the Structures of Constraint*. New York: Routledge.

Folbre, Nancy. 1995. *The New Field Guide to the U.S. Economy*. New York: The New Press.

Glazer, Nathan. 1988. *The Limits of Social Policy*. Cambridge, MA: Harvard University Press.

Hanushek, Eric. 1994. *Making Schools Work: Improving Performance and Controlling Costs*. Washington, DC: Brookings Institution.

Hewlett, Sylvia Ann. 1991. *When the Bough Breaks: The Cost of Neglecting Our Children*. New York: Basic Books.

Kaus, Mickey. 1992. *The End of Equality*. New York: Basic Books.

Kozol, Jonathan. 1991. *Savage Inequalities: Children in America's Schools*. New York: Crown Publishers.

Lind, Michael. 1995. *The Next American Nation: The New Nationalism and the Fourth American Revolution*. New York: The Free Press.

Loury, Glenn. 1995. *One By One from the Inside Out: Essays and Reviews on Race and Responsibility in America*. New York: The Free Press.

Massey, Douglas and Nancy Denton. 1993. *American Apartheid: Segregation and the Making of the Underclass*. Cambridge, MA: Harvard University Press.

O'Neill, June. 1994. "Discrimination and Income Differences." In Feiner, ed. *op cit.*

Orfield, Gary. 1994. "The Growth of Segregation in American Schools: Changing Patterns of Separation and Poverty since 1968." *Equity and Excellence in Education* 27(1).

Schorr, Lisbeth. 1989. *Within Our Reach: Breaking the Cycle of Disadvantage*. New York: Doubleday.

Shulman, Steven. 1991. "Why Is the Black Unemployment Rate Always Twice as High as the White Unemployment Rate?" In *New Approaches to Economic and Social Analyses of Discrimination*. Richard Cornwall and Phanindra Wunnava, eds. New York: Praeger.

Wilson, William Julius. 1987. *The Truly Disadvantaged: The Inner City, the Underclass, and Public Policy*. Chicago: University of Chicago Press.

INDEX